Faith and
Social Ministry
Ten Christian Perspectives

Values & Ethics Series, Volume 1

Faith and Social Ministry
Ten Christian Perspectives

James D. Davidson
C. Lincoln Johnson
Alan K. Mock

Loyola University Press
Chicago

Loyola University Press, Chicago 60657
Copyright ©1990 by Loyola University Press
All rights reserved. Published 1990
Printed in the United States of America

Library of Congress Cataloging-in-Publication Data
Faith and social ministry : ten Christian perspectives / [edited by]
    James D. Davidson, C. Lincoln Johnson, Alan K. Mock.
        p.   cm.
    Includes bibliographical references and index.
    ISBN 0-8294-0703-0 : $19.95
    1. Sociology, Christian—United States. 2. Church and social
problems—United States. I. Davidson, James D. II. Johnson, C.
Lincoln. III. Mock, Alan K.
BT738.F333 1990   90 - 38107
261.8'0973—dc20   CIP

*To our friend
and colleague*

Barbara Hargrove

*A woman of great
faith and
concern for others*

Table of Contents

Preface

In 1984, the three of us started working together on a research project on faith and social ministry. As we examined the literature and talked among ourselves, we realized how little we and others in our field knew about the approaches which various Christian churches take to faith and social outreach. We thought it would be exciting to bring leaders from several traditions together to describe their own churches and to talk about similarities and differences.

In the ensuing months, we contacted leaders from ten Christian churches. The leaders included Sister Marie Augusta Neal (Roman Catholic), Barbara Hargrove and Dana Wilbanks (United Presbyterian), Philip Amerson and Earl D. C. Brewer (United Methodist), Michael K. Roberts (Nazarene), Richard Jones (American Baptist), William Jere Allen (Southern Baptist), Cheryl Townsend Gilkes (National Baptist Convention), Edward Rodman (Episcopal), Ross Scherer (Lutheran), and Frederick Trost (United Church of Christ).

These people were asked for two reasons. First, they have the scholarly inclination to ask questions about the policies and practices of their churches. They are eager to understand their churches. They want to know what the patterns of faith and social ministry are in their churches, and why these patterns—rather than others—prevail. Second, they have played important roles in their respective churches. Thus, in addition to their scholarly interests, they have considerable firsthand experience with the issues of faith and social ministry. We felt their combination of scholarship and experience would maxi-

mize our opportunity to shed some new light on the twin components of Christian commitment: faith and social ministry.

We asked these leaders to prepare papers which would be
presented at back-to-back sessions at the 1986 annual joint meeting
of the Society for the Scientific Study of Religion and the Religious
Research Association. We also indicated that, if the sessions went
well, we might like to organize the papers into an edited volume. The
leaders agreed—expressing considerable interest in the subject. Nearly
every person said the topic was of considerable importance to leaders
in their respective traditions.

The ten leaders met at the SSSR-RRA meeting in October 1986.
We were ecstatic about the quality of the presentations and the
dialogue which took place. The leaders also were excited about the
quality of each others' papers, and the similarities and differences in
their traditions.

Because we had such a good experience together, we agreed to
go ahead with the idea of bringing the papers together in an edited
volume. The three of us prepared an introductory chapter which
summarizes the issues and specifies some of the principal concepts
and ideas we found in the original presentations. The church leaders
used the ideas in the introductory chapter as a framework for revising
and extending their papers. Finally, we added a conclusions chapter
in which we specify some of the major points of convergence and
divergence among the ten Christian traditions.

We have arranged the chapters according to the following
scheme. Chapter 1 is our introduction to the underlying issues we
asked all the authors to address. Chapters 2 through 11 are grouped
according to Roof and McKinney's (1987) categorization of Roman
Catholicism and Protestant denominations. Chapters 2, 3, and 4 deal
with three liberal Protestant denominations: the Episcopal Church,
the United Church of Christ, and the Presbyterian Church. Chapters
5, 6, and 7 include three moderate Protestant denominations: the
United Methodist Church, the Lutheran tradition, and the American
Baptist Church. Chapters 8 and 9 pertain to two conservative Protestant bodies: the Southern Baptist Convention and the Church of
the Nazarene. Chapter 10 has to do with the African American (black)
Baptist tradition. Chapter 11 is about Roman Catholics. Chapter 12
contains our overall conclusions based on the observations made in
the previous chapters.

We want to thank several people who made this experience possible. We are most grateful to Robert W. Lynn, former vice president for religion at Lilly Endowment Inc. Bob understood the importance of linking faith and social concern, and supported many efforts to integrate these two dimensions of church life. We hope Bob is pleased with the results of this project. Father Joseph Downey and the staff at Loyola University Press were very supportive and helpful throughout the process of producing this book. Dorothy East, who works with the Social Science Training and Research Laboratory at Notre Dame, helped us many times and in many ways, especially in the process of converting all the manuscripts to disks. We also thank our spouses and families for their support throughout this project. They have nurtured us and our interest in the issues addressed in this book. Special thanks also go to members of the Sorrento Seminar for their many contributions to this project.

Finally, we dedicate this book to our good friend and colleague, Barbara Hargrove, who died in October 1988. She was a very special person. Her faith fostered her concern for others and, in caring for others, she grew in faith.

James D. Davidson
Department of Sociology and Anthropology
Purdue University

C. Lincoln Johnson
Department of Sociology
University of Notre Dame

Alan K. Mock
Iliff School of Theology

Spring 1990

1

FAITH AND SOCIAL MINISTRY:
AN INTRODUCTION TO
ISSUES AND CONCEPTS

James D. Davidson,
C. Lincoln Johnson,
Alan K. Mock

The purpose of this book is to provide an overview of how ten Christian churches in the United States view faith, social ministry, and the relationship between these two dimensions of church life. The churches are: Roman Catholic, United Presbyterian, United Methodist, Nazarene, American Baptist, Southern Baptist, African American Baptist, Episcopal, Lutheran, and United Church of Christ. Our goal is to foster a greater understanding of each tradition, and a fuller appreciation of the similarities and differences between the groups.

In this chapter, we specify the issues and key concepts which the authors were asked to consider in the preparation of their chapters. Since these issues and concepts were included in the guidelines the authors used to formulate their ideas, they also should be useful to readers as you explore the similarities and differences between the various religious groups covered in this book.

Faith

In general, "faith" is an orientation toward the supernatural. Churches nurture faith to the extent that they cultivate an interest in, belief in, reliance on, and personal communication with the Lord.

But, churches have many different approaches to faith. They stress different sources of faith, emphasize different dimensions of faith, and conduct many different kinds of programs related to faith.

Sources of Faith

Religious groups tend to stress four sources of faith: scripture, tradition, reason, and experience. They are likely to combine elements from each of these sources, but also are likely to develop an emphasis which stresses one or two of these sources more than others. And, the patterns they develop have important consequences for church goals and mission.

Scripture Scripture-based approaches suggest that faith is grounded in the holy words, stories, events, and truths which are contained in sacred texts. These texts are seen as the most accurate accounts of what the supernatural is like and the message the Creator wants to share with humankind. The message includes God's conceptions of how we should relate to Him/Her and how we should conduct our lives in relationship with others. It also includes indications of the rewards for adhering to these expectations and the punishments associated with deviating from them.

Religious groups which stress the scriptural nature of faith tend to protect and make truth claims about their sacred texts. They create beliefs about the inerrancy of the scriptures. The contents of the holy texts are said to be absolutely true.

To be faithful, one must read and understand these texts. One must come to believe in the supernatural through the scriptures; rely on the scriptures to sustain one's faith; and use the scriptures to communicate with the supernatural.

Tradition Tradition-based approaches contend that "the Word" is constantly unfolding in the thoughts and actions of believers. The original message may be recorded in sacred scriptures, but the message is evolving in the more recent experiences of the faithful.

According to this approach, the supernatural revealed Him/Herself to ancient peoples in forms which were compatible with the lifestyles of their times, but revelations continue to take place as the people of God struggle with issues and conditions in the world today.

The faithful in churches stressing tradition understand that the truth is evolving over time. This orientation to faith assumes that what is true at one point in time may be understood differently, thus changed, at a later date. Thus, faith involves a willingness to put any one teaching into proper perspective, to question its appropriateness at some other time, and to look for the underlying message which the supernatural is trying to express through the ever-changing thoughts and actions of His/Her followers.

From this point of view, faith is grounded in the total experience of believers and recorded in many places. It is found in the oral and written accounts of gatherings of church leaders (e.g., councils, synods). It is found in special teachings which might eminate from such gatherings. It is found in extraordinary individuals, who come to be called "saints" because the community of believers feels their lives should be models for others who are faithful. Truth also is found in the words of church officials, who are given the right to speak on behalf of the supernatural. It is said that, under certain circumstances, these officials can even speak infallibly. Thus, infallibility is to tradition-based churches as biblical inerrancy is to scripture-based churches: a way of preserving the basis of faith.

Reason Other churches stress an intellectual approach to faith. These groups emphasize the individual's need to ask questions about fundamental issues such as the meaning and purpose of life. The faithful are expected to explore these issues in a rational manner. These explorations may eventuate in conclusions which individuals consider to be truths, but they also may not result in any firm conclusions. Whatever the outcome, individuals are expected to use these explorations as bases for their faith.

This approach to faith does not assume that all faith is entirely rational or logically consistent, but it does stress the goals of learning and intellectual growth. It cherishes the goal of testing the limits of what is known and probing the uncertain dimensions of the unknown. It appreciates the ability to tolerate uncertainty, while it celebrates certainty. It stresses "proper thinking" and "right belief."

Experience Finally, there are churches which stress the idea that faith is rooted in a very personal experience or encounter with the supernatural. According to this view, the individual must turn away from a life in which the supernatural plays no role, to one in which God or Christ is the center of one's life. The key to experience-based faith is personal conversion.

Groups which say that conversion is the source of faith place a great deal of emphasis on steps which make conversion possible. They reach out to "the unchurched" to increase their awareness of the sinful nature of life without God and to heighten their desire for a "life in Christ." They provide believers with numerous opportunities to renew their commitment. These opportunities for conversion and renewal are centerpieces of church life.

Issues Of course, we do not mean to suggest there are rigid boundaries between these four sources of faith. They are not mutually exclusive. Churches may stress one of them, but encourage the others as well. And, individuals may be more oriented toward one approach, but also engage in others.

We invite readers to think of these various bases of faith as you read the chapters which follow. If you belong to one of the ten groups discussed in this book, what orientation(s) does the author from your own religious group say your group has? Do you agree or disagree with the author's account of your church? Which other groups tend to share your group's orientation toward faith? Which one's seem most radically different from your church's approach?

Whether you belong to one of these groups or not, do you find these four concepts helpful in comparing and contrasting the faith orientations of the ten groups? Do the authors' accounts confirm or challenge your prior conceptions of these groups? If so, how? In what ways do they reinforce your perceptions or call them into question?

Dimensions of Faith

Groups which share a similar conception of where faith comes from may still develop quite different substantive orientations to faith. The contents of the faith they promote may be quite different.

We asked the authors to think in terms of four dimensions which sociologists and others have used to describe the content of faith. These include: individualistic and communal, vertical and horizontal, restricting and releasing, and comforting and challenging.

Individualistic and Communal This dimension relates to the character of faithfulness: is the focus on the individual, or on the community of the faithful? Is the church a collection of individual believers, or a community of people who share a common sense of ancestry and culture? Is faith personal, or collective? Is it private, or public? Is faith possible apart from the group, or not? Is the individual or the group the primary instrument of God's will in society?

Vertical and Horizontal This dimension suggests directionality. Where is God: up in heaven, or here on earth? Should the eyes of the faithful be looking upward, or outward? Is the faith experience focused on the relation of the "individual to God," or the relation of "person to person"? Are the faithful to be oriented toward the supernatural, or to other human beings? Are they to stress beliefs about the existence of God and the divinity of Christ, or beliefs about the need to love one's neighbor and do good for others?

Restricting and Releasing This is a boundary question. Does faith consist of a relatively well-defined set of truths which the faithful are expected to accept, or an idea which sets one free? Does faith emphasize the importance of "right living," or does it release the faithful to take risks? Does it stress the "thou shalt nots," or the concept of grace? Is the image of God punitive, or forgiving? Is the emphasis on law, or love? Does one's relationship with the supernatural resemble a contract, or a covenant?

Comfort and Challenge This dimension has to do with the consequences of faith. Is faith supposed to be a source of comfort, or is it supposed to challenge the faithful to improve themselves and the world around them? Do the faithful seek consolation, or visions of change? Do they want support, or reform? Is the message one of forgiveness, or prophecy? Does worship produce a sense of relief, or empowerment? Is the emphasis on turning to God in times of trial and tribulation, or on witnessing in the life of the community? Is the emphasis on the priestly or prophetic roles of the clergy?

Issues We asked each of the authors to think in terms of these dimensions, and any related concepts, in their efforts to describe the content of the faith which their churches espouse. Do their churches emphasize individualistic-vertical-restricting-comforting patterns of faith, or more communal-horizontal-releasing-challenging patterns? To what extent, and in what ways, do their faith groups combine elements from these various dimensions?

These sensitizing categories may help readers compare and contrast the faith orientations of the various churches the authors represent. What are the overall relationships among these various dimensions of faith? What emphases tend to go together most often? Which are the most individualistic-vertical-restricting-comforting groups, and which ones are most communal-horizontal-releasing-challenging?

Sources and Dimensions of Faith Combined

These sources and dimensions of faith can be combined to suggest additional lines of inquiry. For one thing, combining the two gives us ways of describing different patterns of faith. Let us give just three examples and invite readers to imagine all the other possibilities. One church might stress a tradition-based faith which is communal and horizontal in nature, and which releases people to challenge existing social structures and processes. This church would exhibit relatively prophetic patterns of faith, such as liberation theology. Another church might emphasize an experience-based faith which stresses the individual and vertical dimensions of faith, sets people free, and reassures them of God's presence and love. This church would express more evangelical patterns of faith. Still another church might accent a scripture-based faith which is individualistic and vertical in orientation, stresses adherence to a set of laws, and offers comfort and consolation in time of need. This church would have a more fundamentalist pattern of faith.

Which pattern of faith does the reader associate with the religious group you are affiliated with? Does the author agree? What is the reader's personal orientation to faith? How does that personal orientation compare with the group to which you belong?

Combining the sources and dimensions of faith also encourages the reader to consider a number of other analytic issues. For example, what dimensions of faith are emphasized most by the four bases of faith? Does a scriptural orientation tend to promote faith which is individualistic or communal, vertical or horizontal, releasing or restricting, comforting or challenging? How do the patterns emerging from scripture-based faith compare with those emerging from tradition-based, reason-based, and experience-based faith?

Readers are urged to look for answers to these questions as you read each of the chapters which follow, and as you compare and contrast the chapters. We will return to these issues in our concluding chapter.

Programs Related to Faith

We also asked the authors to describe the kinds of programs their churches have developed for the purpose of nurturing faith. This section of each chapter gives some concrete expression to the more abstract ideas in the previous sections.

We asked the writers to consider how the church as a whole cultivates faith. What kinds of faith-related programs do international and national church offices authorize? What sorts of sacraments, crusades, pilgrimages, workshops, educational materials, and other activities do their churches create in an effort to foster interest in, belief in, reliance on, and communication with the supernatural? We also asked the writers to tell us what goes on a the local level. What are local congregations and parishes doing to nurture faith? What are their principal approaches to faith?

These summaries of church programs related to faith not only give us some sense of what is going on within each group, but also a way to transport ideas across group lines. Readers can see to what extent other groups are using similar or different methods of fostering faith. You also can consider the extent to which programs found in other groups might be useful within your own tradition.

Social Ministry

All churches make at least some effort to influence society. We use the concept of "social ministry" to encompass all the deliberate attempts churches make to accomplish this goal. While all groups share an interest in social ministry, their outreach activities are quite varied. We asked the authors to consider variations along two lines: content and form.

Content

Churches place varying amounts of emphasis on different types of social ministry. We have conceptualized three dimensions of social ministry content: international-domestic, economic/political, personal/familial, and service-change.

International and/or Domestic   We asked the writers to indicate the extent to which their churches focus on issues of global concern and/or issues which are more peculiar to the United States. What is the focus of their churches' social concerns? Are they more likely to think in terms of foreign missions, or poverty in the United States? Are they more inclined to stress world peace and justice, or local hunger?

Economic/Political or Personal/Familial   Another issue concerns the institutional spheres which churches are likely to focus on. One approach to social issues is to assume that the economic and political spheres are the most important. This approach contains the belief that business and government are more directly responsible than other spheres are for the creation and distribution of scarce resources such as jobs and income. Churches and churchgoers emphasizing this approach are likely to put their energies into programs and activities which relate to issues such as unemployment, wages, job training, the actions of city governments, legislative proposals in Congress, and questions of peace and military expenditures.

Another approach assumes that the person and family, and to some extent education, are the most important sectors of concern. Those who espouse this approach emphasize the importance of the values a person learns at home and in school. Advocates of this approach want to make sure that families and schools stress sound values (e.g., love, respect for life, sharing, commitment). The asssumption is that if these values are learned at home and in the schools, they will be carried over into other spheres. The effect will be an orderly, just society.

Groups stressing this approach to social ministry are inclined to get involved in issues such as marriage counseling, school prayer, family life programs, abortion, pornography, drugs, and alcoholism.

Service and/or Change Finally, there are different ways of dealing with any issue at any level and in any sector. We asked the authors to think in terms of two approaches.

One approach to social ministry tries to increase the provision of social services to individuals within the context of existing social arrangements. This approach assumes that churches' main goal is to see that individuals have the food, clothes, and other essential services they need to live their lives within society as it is presently organized.

Another approach assumes that existing social arrangements are unjust and that churches ought to be trying to build a more just world. This approach questions the legitimacy of prevailing social arrangements, believing that they favor some groups more than others. It calls for social reforms which will produce more equal treatment of all groups.

Naturally, one can imagine all sorts of ways churches might be involved in social ministry. One group might take a prophetic approach to the problem of world peace. Another might become involved in a volunteer program to deliver food and clothes to low income families in one locality. A third group might lobby for federal legislation to increase the minimum wage. Another might organize against "adult bookstores" in their neighborhood. Another might participate in a program to feed the poor in Third World countries. Yet another might donate money to low income groups which are trying to organize around issues of unemployment in their communities.

Form

Churches also can use a number of methods to conduct their social ministry programs. We asked the authors to consider at least three methods: denominational and/or ecumenical, national and/or local, and corporate and/or individual.

Denominational and/or Ecumenical Churches can carry out their own programs through denominational channels. This approach is based on a denominationally-specific conception of the issue and, more often than not, a denominationally-specific view of costs and benefits. For example, a church might choose to sponsor self-help projects among low income groups in the hopes of improving social conditions and, in the process, winning converts to that particular religious group. An example would be the Catholic church's Campaign for Human Development

Or, groups might work with other religious groups, sharing all the necessary facilities, money, leadership, volunteers, or other means for achieving their common goals. When using this more ecumenical approach, groups tend to have a more universalistic conception of the issue and a willingness to share all the benefits. An example of this approach would be the social outreach efforts which mainline Protestant groups conduct through the World Council of Churches and the National Council of Churches.

National and/or Local Churches also can differ in the extent to which they want social ministry to take place at the national and/or local levels.

Groups can create, or take part in, national programs which use national church resources and are run by national church leaders. A program that has an office in national church headquarters, obtains its funding through a national church collection, and benefits people in all regions of the country would be an example.

But, groups also can assume that the local church is the proper focus of social outreach. When they use this approach, churches assume that programs should be created at the local level, should use local resources, and should be run by local people. Church-based soup kitchens in local neighborhoods would be one example.

Corporate and/or Individual There also is an issue concerning who the "actors" should be. Should "the church" as a corporate entity be responsible for the outreach program, or should it be individual church members? Should the congregation take the lead by officially sponsoring the activity, or should individuals in the church conduct the activity as a normal part of their civic responsibilities?

Of course, these three issues also can be joined. Some churches might take a corporate approach, stressing denominational sponsorship at the national level. Others might prefer a corporate, ecumenical approach at either the national level or the local level. Still others may prefer to see individual churchgoers conducting social ministry in their own communities

Programs Related to Social Ministry

We asked the authors to describe the kinds of social ministry programs their groups tend to emphasize. That way we could see the extent to which the groups covered in this book tend to emphasize similar or different methods in their efforts to express their concern for others.

Linking Faith and Social Ministry

The authors were asked to address two additional issues: what does your church say the relationship between faith and social ministry ought to be (the theological question)? and what, in fact, is the relationship between the two (the sociological question)?

Theological Perspectives

All Judeo-Christian groups communicate some sense of how faith and social ministry should be related. We conceived of four possibilities.

One approach churches might take is to assume that faith is the more essential of the two dimensions and that social ministry is a natural by-product of faith. This "conservative" orientation encourages churches and individual believers to emphasize faith-related programs and activities, assuming that the more faithful they are, the more they also will be concerned about the poor and others who are in need.

A second approach is to assume that social ministry is the more important of the two and that effective social ministry will enhance people's faith. According to this more "liberal" view, the more churches and individual churchgoers are involved in social and community issues relating to the needs of the poor and the powerless, the more they will realize their need to rely on the supernatural and the wonderous ways the Lord works in the world.

The third approach is to treat the two as equally important, but separate, goals. According to this "dualistic" view, both goals are indispensible components of Christian commitment: neither one is reducible to, or a function of, the other. Faith does not automatically lead to social outreach, and involvement in social issues does not necessarily foster belief in and reliance on the supernatural. If there is to be a relationship between the two, relationship will depend on efforts churches and their members make to forge one.

The fourth approach assumes the the two are equally important and inseparable. According to this "holistic" view, faith and social ministry need to be given equal emphasis, in part because they reinforce each other. Faith makes no sense if it is not expressed in concern for others; and social outreach makes no sense unless it is accompanied by faith.

We asked the authors to indicate which general orientation is most evident in the institutional policies and practices of their religious groups. We also asked them which orientation is most likely to be found among individual members of their tradition.

If they indicate there is supposed to be some relationship between the two, we asked them to show as best they can how the two are supposed to be linked. What mechanisms do churches and individual members use to link them? What church agencies and programs are responsible for linking the two (e.g., general assemblies, pastoral letters, sacraments, worship services)? And, how are individuals supposed to link them (e.g., private prayer, counseling)?

Sociological Perspectives

Next, regardless of how the two are supposed to be related, we also wanted to know what the relationship is in reality. It might be exactly what it is supposed to be, or the real situation might be quite different from what the churches believe it should be. To what extent does faith foster social compassion? Does social ministry enhance faith? Is it difficult to separate the two in real life?

If the theology of a church stresses the idea that faith leads to social ministry, does that pattern prevail in real life? Are there cases where the theology says the faith and social ministry are equal and inseparable, but the prevailing pattern is for faith and social ministry to be equal but separate? How often do churches stress the idea that social ministry enhances faith, but find that the two are equal but separate dimensions?

We asked the authors to bring whatever research evidence or

observations they could to bear on these questions. What have church-based researchers found out about the relationship between faith and social ministry on the global level (e.g., is it the same, or different, in First and Third World nations)? What about at the national and local levels? Are the two more highly correlated at one of these levels than at the other? Is the relationship the same for clergy and laity, or is it different for the two groups?

If the relationship is not as it is supposed to be, why isn't it? What conditions might account for the unexpected, or unwelcomed, gap between theology and reality? Several conditions might be considered. Societal forces might intervene. To what extent do secular values and interests affect individuals' religious beliefs and practices? Do these "outside" influences have more impact on the faith and social ministry orientations of lay people or clergy? Do they affect local clergy more than national or international churchleaders? Which secular values and interests are most influential? When, and under what conditions, do these external influences reinforce religious norms and values? When, and under what conditions, do they undercut them?

Religious factors also might intervene. For example, are national church leaders and local church leaders expected to carry out different functions regarding faith and social ministry? Do they receive different rewards for performing these functions? Are people who link faith and social ministry more, or less, likely than others to seek positions at the top of church bureaucracies? Do ambitious local pastors promote faith more than social ministry, believing that success in the faith area will lead to faster promotions?

We asked the authors to provide whatever statistical or qualitative data they might have related to these factors and their effects on the relationship between faith and social ministry. These data might be from national surveys, surveys of local churches, or case studies.

Conclusions

Our goal in this book is to foster understanding of how various Christian churches approach faith, social ministry, and the relationship between these two dimensions of church life. In this chapter, we have outlined the issues and concepts which we have found useful in organizing our thoughts related to these topics. The authors also

ship between these two dimensions of church life. In this chapter, we have outlined the issues and concepts which we have found useful in organizing our thoughts related to these topics. The authors were asked to take these issues and concepts into account as they prepared the chapters which follow. Because we and the authors have found them at least somewhat useful, we invite readers to use them to examine what is said about their own religious groups and to compare and contrast what is said about all ten groups.

2

FAITH AND SOCIAL MINISTRY:
A VIEW OF THE EPISCOPAL CHURCH

Edward Rodman

The Episcopal Church in the United States of America officially began with the consecration of Bishop Samuel Seabury following the American Revolution. It is the American expression of the Anglican tradition, a worldwide communion of national churches and/or provinces that look to the Archbishop of Canterbury as their symbolic head, and the Church of England as their spiritual home. Each national church or province is autonomous, having its own constitution and canons, and its own primate or archbishop. In the Episcopal Church in the United States, the archbishop's title is Presiding Bishop. The Most Reverend Edmond L. Browning was installed as the current presiding bishop in January 1986 at the National Cathedral in Washington D.C., commencing his twelve year term in this office.

The two million-plus-member Episcopal Church is a unique expression of Anglicanism, both in its history and its current practice. One notable historical fact about the Episcopal Church is that it was founded by those Anglicans who supported the revolution. Its most unique current feature is its leadership role within the Catholic

Church in the ordination of women to the priesthood, and its elec-
tion and consecration of the first Anglican woman bishop, the Right
Reverend Barbara C. Harris, Suffragan Bishop of the Diocese of
Massachusetts.

The Episcopal Church has historically been enriched by the
waves of immigrants to come from other parts of the world who
brought their own unique understanding of Anglicanism with them.
Apart from the English, the Episcopal Church also contains a rich
variety of West Indians, Haitians, Africans, Hispanics, Southern
Blacks, and Asians, who join Native Americans to comprise our
diverse membership. These, however, represent less than ten percent
of our membership, as reported by the Ethnic Desks of the Episcopal
Church.

Always known for its diversity in worship and social ministry,
the Anglican Church embodies within it rigid Anglo-Catholics and
charismatic, snobbish Anglophiles and social radicalist, thus always
making for interesting diocesan and national meetings. Indeed, any
church that can claim within its ranks George Bush and leaders of the
African National Congress, clearly runs the spectrum. Needless to
say, any attempt to generalize about the faith and order, and thus the
understanding of social ministry in such an institution, puts the
author at risk. And as one gains a fuller understanding of the polity
of the Episcopal Church, one will understand that this attempt could
never be comprehensive. Let me add that any comments contained
in this paper are mine, and any credit must go to good Episcopalians
who are laboring tirelessly in God's vineyard to make the gospel real
to a hurting world.

I also think it is important to state my biases. I am a black
Episcopal priest of some twenty-two years active ministry. I have
served in two inner city parishes, as well as on a diocesan staff. I have
served on the Executive Council of the Episcopal Church, its highest
elected body between conventions, as well as on numerous standing
commissions and committees of the church, dealing with diverse
matters such as specialized ministry, Black ministries, and church
structure. I have also been fortunate to be involved in the Union of
Black Episcopalians, the Black Caucus in the Episcopal Church, as a
staff member in the Urban Bishops Coalition, an unofficial progressive force of bishops within the church, and as a founder and
currently Coordinator of the Episcopal Urban Caucus, an unofficial
pressure group within the life of the church. I have taught in two

Episcopal seminaries, served on the board of directors of one, and had the opportunity to travel extensively throughout not only the church in America, but also in Africa and in Central America. Thus, one might assume that my perspective is left of center, supportive of liberation theology and an advocate of social ministries. Given this bias, I will now attempt to fill the requirements set forth by the originators of the study, following their suggested outline by analyzing the Episcopal Church as a community of faith, focusing on its doctrine and practice, and then an analysis of its social ministry. I will then conclude with a personal comment or two derived from the section in which I attempt to discern the relationship between faith and social ministry.

Episcopalians as a Community of Faith: Doctrine and Practice

There is no question that the Episcopal Church considers itself a community of faith. An historical catholic church, it supports, teaches, and reveres all of the historic creeds and doctrines of the Church, and has its own Articles of Religion promulgated during the Reformation in England. These outline some thirty-nine principles that put it firmly within the early stages of the Reformation. Given this history, the Episcopal Church can be seen as a bridge between Roman Catholicism and the reform tradition, revering in its polity and tradition the office of bishop and the importance of doctrine, while stressing the centrality of scripture, and affirming reason and experience as legitimate factors in discerning God's will.

It is instructive that even to this day, deacons and priests ordained into the ministry must subscribe to the doctrine, discipline and worship of the Episcopal Church (best expressed in our canons and Book of Common Prayer), but must also sign an Oath of Conformity which says that we believe that all things necessary for salvation are contained in the scriptures.

The Episcopal Church also prides itself in adding to the twin towers of a catholic faith, scripture and tradition, the third element of reason. This latter has inspired a high level of scholarship and academic inquiry that goes back to the Anglican divines of the 17th century. This tripartite understanding of the church is alive and well today in our seminaries where biblical criticism is taught, and a variety of theological expressions and understandings studied. The church has also been enriched by its Anglo-Catholic and evangelical traditions in its liturgy, and has recently found itself contending with a new wave of charismatic enthusiasm, as well as a rediscovery of our patristic roots.

Thus, if one is to characterize the understanding of faith that is most commonly taught in Episcopal seminaries and, therefore, indirectly in its church schools and other forms of education, for example the catechism, one could say that the Episcopal Church is clearly a trinitarian catholic church steeped in the creeds, but always seeking new ways to make these ancient beliefs relevant to the contemporary situation. Our confirmation service, once separate, is now contained in the baptism service and is a direct expression of the belief in individual salvation, the centrality of faith in Christ as a personal savior, and the commitment to resist evil in the world. The respect for this sacrament is equaled by the growing practice in worship which affirms the centrality of the eucharist.

The Anglican Church and, to a very large degree the Episcopal Church, also has viewed itself as a missionary church, having been very active in the last three centuries in propagating the faith throughout the world. Indeed, the Anglican communion has been so successful in this regard that it is probably the first major western denomination to have a majority of non-white members, a development that is hailed or viewed with alarm, depending on one's perspective. The visual expression of this phenomenon was evident at the Lambeth Conference in 1988, where the bishops of all the dioceses of the Anglican communion come together once every twenty years to discuss faith and order, and to view questions of social ministry in the womb of Canterbury.

Although the catechetical model is no longer in favor as the principle means of Christian education, a review of our catechism would reinforce the fairly traditional view of the faith as maintained by Episcopalians. It is important to note that the polity of the Episcopal Church, though based on the centrality of bishops as the symbolic expression of the unity of the Church, has by and large in the American expression of Anglicanism, stripped the bishops of most of their historic power. That is to say, Roman Catholic or Methodist bishops are clearly more powerful in practical terms than is an Episcopal bishop. Indeed, the Episcopal Church in many areas of the country could easily be described as a congregational church with a bishop. Yet, because of its diversity, it can also be described in other areas of the country as a catholic church that does not recognize a pope. Somewhere between these two poles is the reality of the everyday Episcopalian in America.

The Episcopal Church has several distinguishing features. Its belief in education is expressed by the significant number of private schools that are maintained by us. Its tendency to be identified with the social elite and prominent is a common myth, but statistics would indicate that the Episcopal Church is in fact in many areas of the country, primarily blue collar. And finally, its diversity of liturgical practices, all of which are somehow permitted within one Book of Common Prayer, may be the one unique contribution of Anglicanism to the broader Christian community.

In the area of social ministry, the Episcopal Church has distinguished itself in its early initiation of the social responsibility in investments movement some 20 years ago. Indeed, it was under Presiding Bishop John Hines that the first serious grant programs to militant Black power organizations were initiated, and where investments in minority businesses and banks were pioneered. These early efforts culminated in concert with others in the creation of the Interfaith Center for Corporate Responsibility, which has been in the forefront of this issue for the past ten years.

Needless to say, this section could not be concluded without alluding to what is one of the more controversial issues in the life of all catholic churches, and that is the question of women's ordination. The Episcopal Church clearly has taken a leadership role in this arena, not without some cost. Much has been written since the consecration of Bishop Harris on 11 February 1989, about the so-called traditionalists within the church who recently had a convocation in Fort Worth, Texas, in which they attempted to be a church within a church. However, the following quote from the recent House of Bishops meeting will, hopefully, put to rest once and for all how the Episcopal Church views this matter.

We have met in Philadelphia, two hundred years after the General Convention which gave us the first American Book of Common Prayer and the structures of our common life. Out of the confusion which prevailed among Anglicans during the separation of English rule emerged independent province in what we now know as the world-

wide Anglican Communion. At this meeting we welcomed, among other new members, the first woman
bishop in the Communion, The Right Reverend Barbara
Harris. With her consecration, the canonical process
begun in 1976 has been completed. The members of this
House recognize that reality. We joyfully affirm ordained
women—indeed all women—in the ministries which they
exercise in and through the Church.

Within the Anglican Communion and indeed even within our own church, there is not a common theological
mind or agreed practice on the matter of the ordination of
women. We acknowledge with gratitude the action of the
Lambeth Conference in calling for the appointment by the
Archbishop of Canterbury of a Commission to monitor
and encourage consultation throughout the Anglican
Communion and to ensure open dialogue. We acknowledge that within Anglicanism those who believe that
women should not be ordained hold a recognized theological position. In our deliberations, we have heard the
voice of those faithful lay people, bishops, priests and
deacons, members of the Episcopal Church who hold that
view, and we affirm them as loyal members of the family.[1]

To conclude on a personal note: many of us in the Episcopal
Church are appalled by the inordinate degree to which the attention
of Episcopalians can be riveted on such matters, and one of the
challenges for social ministry is to hold up the mission of the church
as the priority, with the questions of gender, language, and structure
kept in their appropriate secondary role.

The Episcopal Church and its Social Ministry

Because of the peculiar polity of the Episcopal Church, any
attempt to analyze the practical social ministry within its life must
take into account the several levels in which that expression can be
manifested. The Episcopal Church by definition is based on the
principle of dioceses, that is to say, the episcopate. Thus, for all

practical purposes, parishes exist as they are in union with the bishops and convention of a particular diocese. Most dioceses are related to state boundaries, and in large states, are related to a collection of counties along population lines that were agreed to when the original diocese was divided.

In addition, the Episcopal Church in America is organized into provinces. Currently there are nine such provinces: eight geographical divisions of the continental United States, including Alaska and Hawaii, and a ninth province that includes Central America, the Caribbean, and other overseas jurisdictions of the Episcopal Church. The function and roles of provinces are not as clear within the Episcopal Church in America as they are in other branches of the Anglican communion, but some provinces or synods provide a convenient focus for social ministry on particular issues. The Episcopal Church has a national headquarters at 815 Second Avenue in New York. The program of the national church is voted at the triennial gathering of deputies and bishops from the 120 dioceses currently within our jurisdiction. This General Convention is divided into two houses—the House of Bishops and the House of Deputies; the latter is divided equally between clergy and lay. These two houses must concur on all matters of faith and order, as well as any social policy position for it to be valid. Between conventions, the Executive Council is the governing body with the Presiding Bishop as its head.[2]

The similarity of structure of the Episcopal Church to the Articles of Confederation and, to some degree the Constitution of the United States is, of course, not an historic accident, but the direct result of some members of both conventions wearing two hats at about the same time. In addition, the Episcopal Church is a staunch member of the World Council of Churches and the National Council of Churches. Thus, it is possible in the Episcopal Church for a local parish to have a soup kitchen, support a diocesan hunger program, contribute to the Presiding Bishop's Fund for World Relief on the national level, and have, through the Anglican Communion, a partnership relationship to a missionary effort to refugees in other parts of the world. Members of that church also might be representatives of a Provincial Task Force on Hunger, which in turn might plan national events on that issue and work ecumenically on questions of refugee resettlement.

Thus it is fair to say that the Episcopal Church offers a wide range and variety of opportunities for social ministry from the street corner to the United Nations, or from ministry to persons with AIDS to those whose interpretation of social ministry would be a pilgrimage to Canterbury. Therefore, any attempt to articulate how and what social ministry is in the Episcopal Church would be difficult at best, and cursory at worse. But being a good Anglican, I will try to find a middle way.

First, I think it is fair to say that much of the social ministry for the Episcopal Church is issue-oriented, (i.e., directed toward a specific community concern). Probably the most common social ministries at present are feeding or shelter ministries in urban areas, and a commitment to the social welfare concerns of the rural poor.

In addition, given the church's historical commitment to healing ministries and education ministries, many clergy and lay persons function in some capacity that could be defined as "chaplain" to penal, medical, academic, and mental health institutions. These ministries are highly respected, and an ordained person can be canonically licensed to carry out these ministries in lieu of parochial responsibilities.

However, the principle focus of ministry within the Episcopal Church is parish-based, and certainly all forms of social ministry at whatever level of the church, are supported primarily by contributions from parishes. Needless to say, the church's issue orientation is not without controversy. A recent review of the history of the Episcopal Church would indicate a pendulum swing in the 1960s, which was highlighted by highly publicized commitments to social change ministries in our urban centers to, by the late 1970s, a retrenchment to spiritualism and much more traditional local ministries of a bandage variety. Within and through this history, there has always been tension between those who are concerned about systemic change in the form of advocacy for major social justice concerns, and those who believe that religion and politics should not mix, and that the task of the Christian is to feed the hungry, encourage the poor, and visit the sick and those in prison.

Though I have been unable to find verifiable statistics on the number and breadth of social ministries, I believe the average Episcopalian would be surprised at the vitality of social ministries at all levels. Concern for issues such as world hunger has elicited a surprising increase in giving to international relief efforts, either church-sponsored or private. Many Episcopalians have engaged in Volunteer for Mission programs, providing their own professional expertise in the Third World. Indeed, the Episcopal Church in the United States has developed a unique program of partnership relations with parishes and dioceses in America with their Third World Anglican counterparts, with surprising results on both ends. For example, the Episcopal Diocese of Massachusetts where I live and work, currently has a companion relationship with three dioceses in Zimbabwe, and thus has become deeply immersed in questions of front-line states, refugee resettlement, and understanding African socialism in the context of an emerging nation. Many other dioceses have similar experiences.

On the national church level, there are numerous specialized ministries with official status — that is to say, budgetary support and professional staff. One of the latest programs is the Jubilee Ministry, which is designed to support and identify Episcopal churches working among the poor. This program publishes a quarterly magazine, makes grants in the area of social ministry, and provides training and placement for interns to do volunteer work in urban and rural settings. In addition, through its Coalition for Human Needs, the church funds community organizations and church-related institutions that are involved in social change ministries. Beyond that, the national church also has four "ethnic desks" that have specialists in work with Black, Asian, Hispanic and Native Americans, each with a budget for program and grants. The Episcopal Church also maintains an office of Public Issues and an office of Social and Specialized Ministry focusing on issues of welfare, AIDS, and addiction. It is also reconfiguring its Washington office with an eye toward including Hunger and Peace Ministries. The church has also recently initiated an African Desk and a Caribbean Desk, attempting to bridge the World Mission department and the National Mission department with a focus on interrelated foreign and domestic ministries. Finally, the Presiding Bishop is fluent in Japanese, started his ministry in Okinawa, and has witnessed to a profound commitment to social ministries in all of their variety. This would bode well for the future.

One of the problems in analyzing social ministry at the diocesan level is that within the Episcopal Church, dioceses vary in size. Larger ones such as New York, Pennsylvania or Massachusetts maintain program units in the areas of social ministry that rival the work of the national church; smaller dioceses in the mid and far west, though unable to mount such ambitious programs, work ecumenically or on the provincial level to address social concerns. Most Episcopal bishops and priests identify to some degree with an area of social justice. Some, such as Bishop Burt from Ohio, recently retired, provide exemplary leadership regarding the issue of plant closings and economic revitalization.

Unofficially, the Episcopal Church also has within its ranks, organizations such as the Urban Bishops Coalition, the Episcopal Peace Fellowship, the Episcopal Church Persons for a Free South Africa, and Integrity; and thriving caucuses of ethnics, such as the Union of Black Episcopalians, not to mention a Women's Caucus and a regional ministry to Appalachian Whites. Needless to say then, the General Convention of the Episcopal Church is a very colorful and confusing event where all these varied issue-oriented groups come together and vie for church attention and resources in an atmosphere that can be generally described as receptive and supportive, though contentious.

On the local level, individual parishes are usually marked by an openness to community concerns. Many, through their ministers and lay people, are actively involved in civic organizations such as self-help community groups and/or specific ministries with youth, environmental protection, and police/community relations. A review of the recently recognized Jubilee Centers would be an eye opener for those skeptical of the degree to which social ministries exist and are supported officially within the life of the church. Because of their emphasis on education, many Episcopal churches pioneered tutorial programs, and may do the same with senior citizen day care centers. A review of the United Thank Offering grants that are made annually by the Episcopal Church Women, which is an adjunct to the National Church program, would show support to a variety of social ministries. Over $2 million is raised annually by the women and given away to support mission and ministry to the marginalized in our culture.

All of the above is not to suggest that everything is sweetness and light at every level in the Episcopal Church with regard to these issues. Much controversy has been, and continues to be, generated over many of these expressions of social concern. For example, the bishop of California and the bishop of Massachusetts may be actively advocating ministry to persons with AIDS, but they do this not without severe criticism from some quarters. Further, there is still theological confusion within the Episcopal Church over the difference between charity and social justice, and the role of private institutions versus that of the federal government in providing relief to persons in need. In many ways the proliferation of feeding ministries and other simplistic solutions to the problems of poverty, unemployment, and social dislocation could well be understood as a conservative response on the part of the church to social problems, rather than a radical critique of the contradictions in our society. In a similar vein, many dioceses within the Episcopal Church find themselves supported by industries that are based on defense contracts, and the constant concern for world peace and disarmament confronts directly the livelihood of many parishioners, not without some serious questioning of the church's authority to meddle in such affairs.

In addition, we must note a situation that seriously hampers the church's ability to be responsive in the area of social ministry. That is, in most of our urban centers, the Episcopal Church finds itself saddled with too many old and inefficient buildings. Thus, many dioceses are forced to decide whether to use their resources to maintain these, or carry out mission programs. Indeed, the question of what is the mission and ministry of the church becomes difficult when one has to choose between a ministry of presence or a social program. There is no question that from a cost effective point of view, more programs can be supported with fewer church buildings. But, is the continued presence of the church one of the principle witnesses a denomination can make about its commitment to an urban area, or for that matter, a rural community that is undergoing social dislocation? There is no national policy on this question and indeed, few dioceses have found a solution. The fact that many are struggling with it and trying to maintain both, is a tribute to the fundamental commitment of the church and its leadership to proclaiming the good news of the gospel even at a sacrifice.

One final note. In surveying the curriculum of Episcopal seminaries and in looking at the general ordination exams (which are a requirement now for all persons seeking ordination in the Episcopal Church), it is clear that the area of social ministries in terms of its teaching, its training and its deployment, has yet to become an authentic priority. It is fair to say that most people coming out of the seminary today do not aspire to be a neighborhood parish priest in any city in this country, or to be the friendly country parson in rural America. Problems of deployment and the so-called clergy glut exist in those areas that would be deemed most desirable to live and work, while clergy shortages still exist in other areas that clearly are not ideal. In addition, the Episcopal Church has failed in its recruitment, training and deployment of minority clergy to respond to the ethnic congregations within its midst. These realities speak volumes about the distance yet to go within the Episcopal Church in attempting to develop an authentic and comprehensive scheme of social ministry at the various levels of its existence and expression.

The Relationship Between Faith and Social Ministry

This is the section where, as a friend of mine would say, the rubber hits the road. At the risk of a generalization, I would suspect that many Episcopalians are self conscious about publicly expressing the relationship of their faith to their involvement in a given social ministry. Indeed, some Episcopalians who are involved in social concerns might view their involvement in spite of their faith (read in the context of the official doctrine) as opposed to their humanitarian concern, however derived or defined. As a matter of fact, one of the most difficult problems facing the Episcopal Church is the question of lay ministry and the authentication of the vocational involvement of lay Christians where they live and work as a full expression of ministry. Many dioceses currently are facing an incredible number of aspirants, that is to say, persons seeking ordination, who somehow feel that the only authentic ministry in the church is that which is ordained, rather than having come to terms with expressing their faith in their own professional or community lives. This same problem can be seen in a different way if one is to analyze the uncomfortableness that many Episcopalians feel in addressing issues such as the dislocation of traditional family models brought about by the sexual revolution, economic necessity, and the emergence of various sexual life styles within the church. (Recently one diocese had to abandon its Commission on Today's Families because the members of the commission could not come to a common definition of what a family in American society is today.)

The ordination of lesbian and gay persons ranks high on the list of controversial issues on both the local and national level of our church. Another sign of the time was the recent defeat at a General Convention of an attempt to write a so-called civil rights canon for the church that would extend Holy Orders in the church to all sorts and conditions of men and women regardless of their differences, including sexual orientation.

The cynic might observe that the Episcopal Church, like any other social institution, derives its ethical norms and standards from the culture, rather than visa versa. The optimist might suggest that the fact that the church openly debates and struggles with these questions indicates that the faith continues to inform and challenge contemporary prejudices of the faithful. However one reads it, the Episcopal Church is far from radical in its social analysis or social ministry, and can only be charitably described as being progressive, if one has to analyze the way in which the resources of the church are used to support social ministry.

One benchmark within the history of the Episcopal Church's struggle with the question of social ministry can be found in the book entitled *To Hear and To Heed*, a compendium of the hearings that the Urban Bishops Coalition sponsored in 1978 in several cities in the United States and Panama. Edited by the Reverend Joseph A. Pelham, currently Executive Director of the Episcopal City Mission in Boston, several choices were highlighted regarding the willingness of the church to respond seriously to the issues raised by the testifiers. Among them were:

> We must decide that we will be for the poor. We must decide to act in such a way that will dispel the widely held perception of the church as a chaplaincy service to the Establishment. This will mean "taking sides" and, in that sense, ceasing to attempt to be all things to all people....

We must make a commitment to a struggle which had no foreseeable end. This requires deciding in favor of staying power against faddism. It means a willingness on the part of the church to stay in the cities and to engage in what Gibson Winter referred to as a "pilgrimage" rather than a "crusade."

We must decide to move beyond discussion of the proper sphere of involvement of the church by recognizing that the church is already engaged in the secular realm through pension funds, endowments, properties and so forth, and admit that the only question is where and for what ends will the church be involved in the secular...

We must decide to shape the church's educational and liturgical life so that the urban crisis is held constantly before the People of God, and they are provided guidance and help in responding to the crisis. Leitourgia (liturgy) as the work of people in worship, and as the work of the people in service to the poor and anguished of the cities, must inform one another and be brought into continuing dialogue and interaction.[4]

The jury is still out in terms of the response in practical terms to these issues, but the fact that the Urban Bishops Coalition continues to exist, that it has spun off the Episcopal Urban Caucus, and that the social ministry of the church continues to struggle to address questions of advocacy, systemic change, and social justice would indicate that there is still hope.

The issues raised in *To Hear and To Heed* can be seen in a different way in a confrontation between conservatives and liberals on social policy matters when one is looking at them from a programmatic point of view. For example, the guidelines for the funding programs of the Episcopal Church expressly forbid resources going to any group that advocates violence as a means of obtaining its ends. Each local bishop still maintains veto power over any grant the national church might wish to give to an organization in his area. This is a carry over of the controversy that emerged in the 1960s when peace organizations and Black power groups sought church approval and funds.

At its most recent General Convention in Detroit, the Episcopal Church affirmed a new program on economic justice which calls for the church to focus on the four areas of worker owned businesses, credit unions, land banks and land trusts, as creative new ways to inspire the church to become involved in the concrete use of its resources, as a response to the deteriorating economic conditions in many of our urban areas. The church also reaffirmed its commitment to the Coalition for Human Need, which is the granting agency of the church which supports community-based organizations engaged in social change ministries. The effort is currently being made to coordinate the work of the Coalition for Human Need with the new Economic Justice program and the Jubilee Ministry program which supports churches who are engaged in social change ministries. The combination gives the Episcopal Church a significant theological and practical working unit engaging the current effects of the conservative trend in American society which is reducing government spending on social programs.

In a less dramatic but equally profound way, the collapse of public support for housing for low and moderate income persons has left many churches with a bitter taste when it comes to becoming involved in community revitalization and redevelopment. Many churches were hurt in the late 1970s and 1980s when the office of Housing and Urban Development withdrew direct support for housing, and began to foreclose on those projects that could not turn a profit because they refused to turn out the lower and moderate income persons who could not afford the rent or obtain a subsidy. Thus today, when one encourages church involvement on economic justice questions such as plant closings, there is skepticism and cynicism that belies a commitment based on faith to these enterprises. Indeed, there are many church treasurers and other lay people who will admonish their priest and fellow parishioners that Jesus did indeed urge us to be as wise as serpents, as well as to be as gentle as doves. To the degree that this reality effects all efforts of social change and social ministry, one has to be cautious when promulgating new causes. Or, as one candid observer of an Episcopal agency committed to urban ministry observed when characterizing the membership of his group, "We are what is left of the left."

Indeed, pollster George Gallup used his organization to document his belief that the social liberalism of the church, when combined with women's ordination and the revision of the Book of Common Prayer, had so divided the church that the majority who once considered themselves Episcopalians no longer actively participated. Whether one agrees with his figures or not, there are many bishops and pastors who can testify that positions taken on a number of issues have not been without significant cost, and the tolerance to bear that cost substantively is not easily increased, as the recent controversy over Episcopal clergy supporting the Piston Coal strike in Virginia, dramatically illustrates. The foot dragging of the Episcopal Church's own Pension Fund to divest from companies doing business in South Africa, even after the General Convention of the church voted in near unanimous fashion to do so in 1985, witnesses to that.

Thus, one can easily observe that the so-called liberal captivity of mainline Protestant denominations, as manifested in their church programs and positions, does not always play well in Peoria, and statistics are not always the most reliable guide in determining the degree to which there is full and complete support for what the Presiding Bishop or local bishop, pastor, or social action commission is doing in the name of the church. As more than one critical observer has suggested, it is easier within the Episcopal Church to raise money to support the ministry and work of Desmond Tutu in Johannesburg than it is to gain support to fight local zoning laws which restrict minority and low income persons from obtaining affordable and decent housing in our metropolitan areas. In fact, the main reason the national church and many dioceses "get away with what they do in the area of social ministry" has nothing to do with their understanding of the gospel, but with the fact that 75 percent of the money raised locally still remains in our own congregations, and goes to support things the local congregations deem appropriate, rather than to further the mission to the dispossessed through the other levels of the church. One, then, could question if these percentages were reversed, whether there would still be an Episcopal Church.

Personal Observations and Experiences

There is less interest in social issues and social ministries in 1986 than there was in 1976, and certainly far less than there was in 1966. The degree to which people engage in social ministries is a result either of the distance of the issue geographically, that is to say, the versus local zoning issue, or the degree to which personal involvement is required rather than social analysis, or the soup kitchen syndrome versus radical social critique and action. Parish social ministry increasingly involves people willing to give money to relief efforts, but not about to challenge governmental policy, which in many instances is responsible for the particular social concern to which the ministry is addressed. I also have observed what I call an 18 month cycle within the life of the church where an issue such as South Africa has some 18 months to two years to either become a permanent part of the structure and focus of the church, and thereby have some hope of being dealt with and resolved in the long run, or to be dismissed as a passing fad and easily forgotten. It will be interesting to observe whether interest in divestment and ending apartheid will be as great as it has been in the recent past.

I would further observe that the general conservative drift that has swept the country has very insidiously infected the church. Increasing numbers of Episcopalians are now comfortable voting for tax caps and/or have reconsidered their position on abortion away from pro choice toward pro life, as a direct result of what I consider the conservative malaise that has been spearheaded by former President Reagan so successfully. There is no question in my mind that ten years ago, many more Episcopalians would have been upset about the appointment of Bork to be a Supreme Court Justice, while today only a handful were willing to support Senator Kennedy and others in their efforts to defeat that nomination, even though many understand the historical significance of such events. In another vein, the increased emphasis on personal spirituality, prayer, and healing has had a deleterious effect on social ministry. This, when coupled with the economic necessity of more and more people working, has greatly diluted the reservoir of committed persons who historically could have been counted on to be involved in a tutorial or feeding program. Further, one only has to observe the amount of energy that can be expended in a discussion over homosexual ordination to understand that this issue demands more of the attention and interest of the average Episcopalian than the practical consequences of the moral majority's dispensationalist nuclear war theory.

The above does not suggest that social ministry is either more difficult or less popular than it was in the past, but merely that you need to be especially careful and sensitive as to what issue you champion, and the way you articulate your raison d'etre for church involvement. In the early 1970s, a person arrested for civil disobedience was considered a hero, and a person concerned about prison reform and abolishing the death penalty could command a wide audience for their views. Indeed, after Attica, a major emphasis of my own ministry was on issues of prison reform, being involved in a maximum security prison observer program, and helping to get hostages out of a prison in 1974. By definition, any argument against the death penalty must support life imprisonment without hope of parole as the alternative. Thus, suggestions of prison reform, clemency, or pardon for those convicted of capital crimes or the conditions in which they live, commands little or no audience. Yet at the same time, an increasing number of seminarians and lay Christians have approached my office with an interest in prison ministry in the traditional sense of the term, that is, bringing Christ to the prisoners and trying, in a very modest fashion, to keep prisoners happy and cared for. In no other arena has such a dramatic change occurred, except possibly in the area of concern for world peace, and even there, the opportunities for engagement and discussion are much greater than in dealing with the fear and hysteria over crime and drugs in our communities.

These, and many other examples that I could cite, merely point to the challenge of maintaining a consistency between proclamation and practice, and highlights the fertile field of burnout that so many of my colleagues have succumbed to in recent years. Yet, as my brothers and sisters in the Union of Black Episcopalians say, "Let there be peace among us, and let us not be instruments of our own oppression."

Conclusion

The Episcopal Church is not unique in its social ministry. One of the great benefits of the ecumenical movement has been the pressure that denominations put on one another to make an effort in this and other areas of ministry. Because the Episcopal Church always wishes to be appropriate if nothing else, it "continues to tolerate and, to some extent, support social ministry." As compared to what Bishop Tutu and other Anglicans and Christians are doing in Africa or elsewhere in the Third World, the response of American

Christians to the social crisis around us is minuscule. It would be my hope that this chapter will be one small step in encouraging each of us to redouble our efforts.

One final note. If one were to ask an Episcopalian what you have to believe to be one, the answer would vary from person to person, but each answer at some point should reflect a belief in Jesus Christ, an acceptance of the doctrine of the Trinity, and some recognition of the historic nature of the Christian faith. One would also hope that Episcopalians would have a relatively strong sense of world mission and of social ministry. And although Episcopalians may not be noted for getting their hands dirty, stewardship in the Episcopal Church has been steadily growing, and this expression of our solidarity with the suffering of the world through institutions such as the Presiding Bishops Fund for World Relief are, therefore, not inconsiderable.

May it also be pointed out in conclusion, that the Episcopal Church, from its beginning to the present time, has had some very colorful figures, both lay and ordained, who have had the courage to challenge the church's commitment to tradition, dogma and doctrine, and have been willing to risk heresy trials and public ostracism to challenge the faithful on such matters as the three-tiered view of the universe, the relevancy of the literal interpretation of the scriptures, and the consistency of capitalism with the will of God.

The one thing you can be sure of: Episcopalians take their doctrine and discipline seriously, and don't mind fighting about it. To that degree, the church is alive and well in its various expressions of faith, including social ministry, and only future events will determine the degree to which we are successful in making real in our lives and practice the proclamations that we preach.

Notes

[1] *Episcopal Chuch Annual.* "General Convention Issue, " Morehouse Barlow
Company, 1989, pages 324-326.

[2] Constitutions and Canons, Episcopal Diocese of Massachusetts, 1988, pages
19-21.This example of one diocesan structure, when coupled with the
National Canons which set up the general checks and balances between
bishop, convention, standing committee and proposers of programs,
budgets, and clergy placements, and the convention, council and bishop
parishes dispose these recommendations. The only real absolute authori-
zation an Episcopal bishop has apart from remarriage applications is over
diocesan missions and the clergy and real property thereof.

[3] Episcopal Church Annual, ibid, pages 14-19.   A careful analysis of the
statistics contained in this section clearly documents the disparity in financial and people resources between dioceses. Any particular diocean
analysis would have to be referred to that diocesan treasurer, who could
give specific data regarding the number of churches that have a full time
rector and budgets of $75,000 or more, and churches who have part time
rectors and budgets of less than $75,000.

[4] *To Hear and To Heed*, Forward Movement Publications, 1978, pages 51-53.

Bibliographical Note

The best general information about the Episcopal Church is available
from the Seabury Press in the Church's Teachings series.   The
principle unofficial publishing company is the Forward Movement
Press, whose catalog certainly runs the gait of topics relevant to the
Episcopal Church.

3

THE MEANING OF "FAITH" AND THE COMMITMENT TO "SOCIAL MINISTRY" IN THE UNITED CHURCH OF CHRIST

Frederick R. Trost

Introduction

"Faith" and "social ministry" are not synonymous. But they *are* companions. They belong together. They are woven of the same fabric. With the writer of the Epistle of James, members of the United Church of Christ would confess that "faith apart from works is dead." (James 2:26). And with Dietrich Bonhoeffer, many would affirm that our "true selfhood" is discovered in being present for others, that "the Church is the Church only when it is there for others."[1] As the signers of the "Kairos Document" have declared, there are moments in life filled with "grace and opportunity," moments in which "God issues a challenge to decisive action."[2]

The United Church of Christ, like other parts of the Body of Christ, has been called to live out the meaning of its beliefs. We are summoned to ministry despite the frailty of our faith and the doubt and temptation that mark our daily existence. As we do this, we acknowledge that "Jesus Christ, as he is witnessed to us in Holy Scripture, is the one Word of God which we must hear and which we ought to trust and obey in life and in death."[3]

In the pages that follow, I shall explore briefly the nature of "faith" and the meaning of "social ministry" in the United Church of Christ.[4] While I imagine that many members of the UCC would agree with my perspective, others (also devoted both to scripture and our traditions) may view the issues differently. This is not nearly as important, I believe, as the need among us for informed dialogue on the issues of "faith" and "life." It remains a challenge, given the theological diversity present in the UCC. Let us turn first to the meaning of faith, the promise it holds, the problems it presents.

Faith as Problem and Promise

Seventy-five years ago, the Swiss statesman Henry Fazy uttered a sentence that can be heard to this day in church and society. Speaking to a crowd gathered in Geneva to protest the prohibition of gambling by the Swiss Federal Council, Fazy exclaimed (to the delight and applause of thousands): "We respect religion, but people shouldn't bother us with it."[5] A thoughtful consideration of the nature of the church and its ministry, should take the distinguished Mr. Fazy into account.

In the world in which we are called to faith, there is an abundance of gods of every shape and texture. This presents us with a problem. The tumultuous theological battles that shook much of the church to its foundation in the early decades of this century were born out of a concern for the activity of "the gods." As we try to speak of "faith," we must ask ourselves: What do we mean? What are we talking about? Faith in what? Faith in whom?

Are we not always tempted to flirt (despite our good intentions) with that multitude of gods whose "existence" has accompanied the church since ancient times? Or do we truly seek to know God who, as the prophet Isaiah has said, calls us by name? Is God who summons the church to faith merely, as Fazy assumed, the creation of our own faint-hearted imagination? Or does God actually intercede on earth for justice, mercy, reconciliation, peace; for that day when "the lion" shall lie down with "the lamb?" Does God exist merely for our pleasure, for companionship in the hours of our loneliness, for succor amidst alienation,...our benefactor,...and the guarantor of success in the economic competition that exhausts body and soul? Or is it true that the God we worship, the God in whom we hope, meets us in Word and Sacrament, and in a million places of crucifixion and resurrection? Do we sense God addressing us now, calling the church from death to life, from indifference to discipleship, from idolatry to worship, from silence in the face of unspeakable horrors to "true selfhood?" When it comes to faith, these are questions with which we need to wrestle. In this sense, "faith" always remains something of a struggle!

The problem is an old one, faced not only by the UCC, but by every person of faith: "choose this day whom you will serve,...as for me and my house, we will serve the Lord." (Joshua 24:15). The Preamble to the *Constitution* of the United Church of Christ makes clear that our faith is rooted in Jesus Christ, who remains the center of our life together and the source of our ministry.

> The United Church of Christ acknowledges as its sole head, Jesus Christ, Son of God and Saviour.... It looks to the Word of God in the Scriptures, and to the presence and power of the Holy Spirit, to prosper its creative and redemptive work in the world. It claims as its own the faith of the historic Church expressed in the ancient creeds and reclaimed in the basic insights of the Protestant Reformers. It affirms the responsibility of the church in each generation to make this faith its own in reality of worship, in honesty of thought and expression, and in purity of heart before God.

In the United Church of Christ, faith is understood as anchored in the biblical story of God's redemptive acts in history, to which both the Old and the New Testament bear witness. The nature of the God we worship is revealed in the life, death and resurrection of Christ. We are asked to listen (and to listen carefully!) to the witness of scripture, to the traditions of the church, and to the ways through which God chooses to speak to us in the events of our time. The church "in each generation (is) to make...faith its own," through a way of life that is in touch with the biblical witness and the real presence of Christ among us by the power of the Holy Spirit.

Thus, in seeking to know God, we are not abandoned to "whim" or to "the devices and desires of our own hearts." The Preamble is not embarrassed by the Reformation insight into the importance of Word and Sacrament to the faith of the church. We celebrate the sacraments, like the Word, as a gift of God, given for the health, integrity and wholeness of the church, so we might live by faith. In baptism, we are embraced by God, summoned to die to ourselves that we might live to Christ. We are claimed for the grateful service of the gospel. In the Lord's Supper, we confess our hunger and need for a righteousness we are incapable of attaining by ourselves. We are nourished as pilgrims on a journey, for a life of discipleship.

As the *Statement of Faith* of the United Church of Christ declares: The One who "calls the worlds into being," who has created us in the divine image, sets before us even now "the ways of life and death." The UCC believes that "in Jesus Christ, the man of Nazareth, our crucified and risen Lord, (God) has come to us and shared our common lot...(bestowing) upon us (the) Holy Spirit, creating and renewing the church...binding in covenant faithful people of all ages, tongues, and races." So God calls the church "to accept the cost and joy of discipleship," and as a servant community "to proclaim the gospel to all the world," (resisting) the powers of evil, (sharing) in Christ's baptism and (eating) at his table, (joining) him in his passion and victory." According to the *Statement of Faith*, this gracious God promises to all who believe, "forgiveness of sins and fullness of grace, courage in the struggle for justice and peace, (God's) presence in trial and rejoicing, and eternal life in (God's) kingdom which has no end."[6]

The challenge, of course, is to make such faith "our own," to bring word and deed together, to live out our heritage and the noble vision of our covenants and creeds. The history of the UCC offers some evidence that this is possible. Thus, in the nineteenth century, when the Congregationalists in New England (see footnote 4 above) heard that a ship filled with mutineering Africans was about to be sent back to sea from the Long Island coast, they protested. When the government inquired what the church would do with the hungry and homeless aboard ship, they replied: "We'll feed them, clothe them, and educate them." Such attempts to be alongside the anguish of neighbor helped give birth among the Congregationalists to such black educational institutions in the United States as Tougaloo and Talledega Colleges and to Fisk University. It also engaged many congregations in the movement to abolish slavery.[7] Already in 1787, James O'Kelly, a founder of the Christian Church (which united in

1931 with the National Council of Congregational Churches), was denouncing the institution of slavery. This "social ministry" was rooted deeply in faith, in the promise and demands of the gospel, in Word, in Sacrament, and in a belief that discipleship is not merely an ideal, but an obligation, a joyous response to God's presence among us in Christ.

A contemporary commitment to the persecuted and hunted exile, is the "sanctuary movement" in which not only national UCC leadership but also members of congregations have responded out of faith to refugees from the horrendous violence in South Africa, Guatemala, El Salvador and other countries. Here we meet Christ too, literally knocking at the door of the church. The "sanctuary movement" underscores the crucial relationship between what we confess with our lips and what we do with our lives. This is not, of course, a new discovery for the United Church of Christ. It is present, for example, in the catechisms used by those members of the church who came to the United States in the 18th and 19th centuries from Germany and Switzerland. In response to the very first question of the *Heidelberg Catechism*, used in the German Reformed Church (one of the churches that became part of the UCC), it is stated that the believer's "only comfort in life and in death" is... "That I, with body and soul,...*am not my own*, but belong to my faithful Saviour Jesus Christ...." In William Bradford's historic account of the Pilgrims' voyage to the "New World," he mentions how they too understood themselves "not as their own but God's." It is essential, in attempting to understand the nature of the United Church of Christ, to grasp the significance of this. Word and deed *always* belong together. With all the "unfaith" that accompanies our life as a denomination, there is nevertheless an understanding of "faith" as that which sustains our life together and compels us to act in glad response to God and neighbor.

To believe,...to "have faith" according to the traditions that compose the UCC, is to confess that in the life, death, and resurrection of Jesus Christ, the truth about God and about ourselves is made known. It is to confess that God's love for justice, wholeness, and reconciliation (so deeply rooted in the message of the Old Testament prophets) is seen, heard, touched, and tasted in Jesus Christ, "the Word made flesh." Faith is more than a concept. It is to *hear* God's voice in the painful events of our time, to *see* God's love in the magnificence of creation, to *know* God's sorrow and to *behold* God's tears in all that demands human life. It is to acknowledge from deep within our own experience, how that which is holy, in a thousand different ways is rejected, nailed to a tree. It is to struggle with the fact *of* the rooster's crow in our lives, the shattering truth of the hammer and the nails tearing at the very flesh of God, and...nevertheless,...to believe! Faith, for members of the United Church of Christ, is accompanied by the prayer..."I believe, help Thou my unbelief."

What is Meant by Social Ministry?

John Calvin, who influenced much of UCC ecclesiology, enjoyed referring to the church as a "company of believers," borrowing a term used to denote the number of soldiers that can be fed at a single meal. A "company" is those who eat from a common loaf at a common table. They take bread and break it. So it is with the church of Jesus Christ. It is a community of those who "break bread" and share it. Thus, when we think of "social ministry" in the United Church of Christ, it is not something unusual, exceptional or particularly noble. It is "breaking bread." It is an attempt, in response to "the bread of life," to live our faith...to respond to our baptism, gratefully.

Once I visited an old monastery, now owned by Protestants, in a tiny village in the German Democratic Republic. We gathered that morning around the Lord's Table. A young pastor pointed to an ancient crucifix on the wall and said: "We live between here (the table where we are fed) and there (where Christ is crucified in the world). The life of the congregation is a pilgrimage between the place where faith is refreshed (at the table) and the place where the broken body of the Lord meets us (in the world of human need)." "Social ministry" is part of pilgrimage. It belongs to *each* member of the community of faith. It is not the exceptional work of a few, but the ordinary task of all. It is embracing (and being embraced by!) the crucified and risen Savior "in the world of human need."

"Social ministry" in the United Church of Christ is understood as any form of service offered in grateful response to "the Word made flesh," God with us in the world. It is, in a sense, conformity to Christ; being present to brothers and sisters in the name of Jesus. It is celebrated in our liturgies. It is sung in our hymns. It is attempting to live out the meaning of our creeds.

In the proposed budgets of the United Church of Christ for 1990 and 1991, voted by the Seventeenth General Synod of the denomination, the national priorities are reflected. We can gain some insight into the commitments of the UCC by looking at these figures. Nineteen point five (19.5) percent of the budget ($6,328,009) is devoted to "Church Development and Evangelism." This includes the development of Christian education curricula, the support of missionaries abroad, the formation of new congregations, church renewal and specialized ministries with children, youth, young adults, women and families. Eighteen point four (18.4) percent of the budget ($5,970,820) is for "General Education." Included here are literacy classes, vocational training, scholarships and career counseling for minority youth, support for schools and institutions of higher education overseas, financial grants to six colleges founded by the American Missionary Association (Dillard, Fisk, Huston-Tillotson, LeMoyne-Owen, Talladega, and Tougaloo), and partnership with all twenty-nine UCC related liberal arts schools in the United States.

Sixteen point seven (16.7) percent of UCC national funds ($5,415,577) is assigned to "The Church and Social Concerns." This includes a variety of projects focusing on peace, arms control, economic justice, racism, sexism, toxic waste disposal, advocacy for people in poverty, voting rights, human rights divestment and the social responsibility of corporations. Thirteen point eight (13.8) percent ($4,495,842) is budgeted for "Administrative Costs" and includes salaries, office costs, rent, insurance, and the expense of gearing boards and commissions of the church from all over the country. Five point zero (5.0) percent ($1,637,818) is designated for "Agricultural and Economic Development" abroad. This includes teaching of marketable skills, training in better farming methods, improved seeds and breeding stock, farm equipment, fertilizer, land management, reforestation, the drilling of wells, irrigation and water conservation.

Four point five (4.5) percent ($1,472,469) is devoted to pensions. Five point nine (5.9) percent ($1,898,435) is assigned to "Mission Interpretation," which includes efforts to tell the story of UCC mission to members of the church and to the public. "Health and Welfare Services" receive 3.3 percent of the budget ($1,075,733). This supports advocacy of adequate health care, especially for the poor, funding of clinics and hospitals overseas, community health, family planning, nutrition, work with the aged and persons with disabilities, issues of world hunger. (It does not include the millions of dollars that compose the budgets of the 11 children's homes, 13 hospitals, neighborhood and community centers, and more that 85 UCC related institutions caring for the elderly across the United States.[8]). Two point six (2.6) percent of the national budget ($851,718) is designated for UCC participation in "Ecumenical Organizations." Four point zero (4.0) percent ($1,296,795) is assigned to "Emergency Aid to Disaster Victims" which provides shelter, medicine, food, and clothing at times of natural disasters and funds for the care and resettlement of refugees. Three point seven (3.7) percent ($1,209,537) is for "Theological Education" among laity and clergy in the United States through residential, extension, and continuing education programs. (Financial support for the seven closely-related UCC seminaries is provided not from the national budget, but by UCC conferences, local congregations and individuals.) The remaining 2.6 percent of the budget ($834,971) is for "Fund Raising," including assistance given to the various regional Conferences and to individual congregations for this purpose.[9]

"Social Ministry" in the United Church of Christ also is advocacy and intercession on a wide variety of public issues. From 1957 to 1981, UCC "social policy" addressed (through the General Synod and/or the various national instrumentalities of the church) more than fifty separate social questions including abortion, aging, corporate responsibility, criminal justice, drug abuse, ecology and energy, economics, employment and poverty, gambling, the CIA, law, order and civil liberties, gun control, handicaps and, public health, housing, human rights, hunger, immigration and refugees, international relations (United States government policy towards South Africa, Central America, Indochina, Iran, the Middle East, Pakistan, the Philippines), amnesty, conscientious objection, the draft, Native Americans, Pacific and Asian Americans, population and family planning, racial justice, civil rights, violence in society, justice on behalf of the "Wilmington Ten," the "Right to Die," rural America, sexuality and sexual minorities, tax reform, the United Nations, and women's rights.[10]

In 1959 (two years after the founding of the United Church of Christ), the UCC Council for Christian Social Action issued a document "Call to Christian Action in Society" in which it addressed four specific areas of "social ministry": race, international relations, political life, and culture. In this statement, which guided the work of the council for many years, it declared segregation a sin and called for its removal from church life, housing, employment, education, public accommodations, and the exercise of political rights. The statement urged the peaceful relief of international tensions, the need to avoid the militarization of U.S. foreign policy, support for the United Nations, control and reduction of armaments, conservation of the earth's resources, an expansion of social services for people with special needs, the protection of migrant workers, sponsorship of refugees, reformation of the criminal justice system, and policies to safeguard the family farm.[11]

A look at one of the major issues of "faith and life," for example, "Peace and Arms Control," offers an insight into the ways in which the United Church of Christ has sought to address social concerns. The first UCC statement on this theme appeared in January 1958 (only a few months after the United Church of Christ was born). Issued by the Council for Christian Social Action, it endorsed negotiations for the reduction of armaments, advocated a United Nation's police force and the vigorous pursuit of international understanding through study, travel, and cultural exchange. It deplored racial segregation and called for a commitment to world economic development.[12] In January of 1960, the CCSA called for a comprehensive analysis of the arms race, endorsing negotiation of an arms limitation treaty, and urging increased efforts to alleviate poverty in the Third World. In June 1963, the CCSA issued a statement in support of the development of a nuclear test ban treaty. (The General Synod of 1963 adopted this statement as its own a few weeks later.) In 1965, the CCSA described war as irrelevant as an instrument of national policy and called again for disarmament by the major powers, urging long-term funding for the U.S. Arms Control and Disarmament Agency.

The Fifth General Synod of the UCC, meeting in July, 1965, declared (in receiving the report of the CCSA) that war is incompatible with Christian teaching. In January 1967, the CCSA spoke to the question of anti-ballistic missiles and the fueling of the arms race. It urged the United States to seek Soviet agreement for an indefinite moratorium on the deployment of major antiballistic missile systems. In 1969, the Seventh General Synod urged ratification of the 1925 Geneva Protocol against the use of chemical and biological weapons, the convening of talks on the limitation of strategic arms, the non-deployment of antiballistic missile systems and an end to the testing of Multiple Independently-Targeted Reentry Vehicles. The same synod called for the development of peace education and action ministries throughout the United Church of Christ so that persons might more effectively participate in the making of peace.

In 1970, the CCSA called upon the government to plan for conversion from a wartime to a peacetime economy. It encouraged a shift of focus from military to domestic spending. The Eighth General Synod, meeting in June, 1971, affirmed a statement on enabling U.S. power to serve humane ends. It again urged the ratification of the 1925 Geneva Protocol, and called for the abolition of the draft. It urged that the church develop educational resources regarding the Middle East, and called for support of relief efforts among Arab refugees. The delegates to the 1971 General Synod urged further the reshaping of government priorities "so that justice, development, liberation, health, education, and (a) life-giving environment will predominate."[13] In April 1977, the UCC Office for Church in Society (successor to the CCSA) called for a moratorium on nuclear-fission weapons and for a "no-first strike" policy in the use of nuclear arsenals. It voted education and action in the UCC regarding the issues of disarmament.

The Eleventh General Synod, in July 1977, called for a halt in the development and deployment of new strategic weapons systems, the completion of a test ban treaty, the renunciation of first strike weapons, and the prohibition of chemical weapons. The Twelfth General Synod, two years later, echoed that action and urged the deeper participation of the churches in the things that make for peace. The Thirteenth General Synod, on July 1, 1981, called for a public concensus before any attempts at the introduction of new weapons systems by the United States This synod voted as well that the United Church of Christ "become a peace church," working at this in depth in congregations. The synod also encouraged all governments in the world to settle disputes through peaceful diplomacy, seeking unilateral initiatives by the United States in the quest for disarmament.

"Social ministry" takes many other forms as well. UCC congregations faithfully support a broad number of social services both with funding and with the time and dedication of the laity. In 1987, diaconic ministry among the elderly in UCC institutions served more

than 16,000 persons. Charitable contributions for nursing and cus-
todial care in the church amounted to $9,460,313. Services to de-
pendent children and youth, including family counseling and assistance to victims of physical and other abuse, were offered by eleven
UCC facilities. Gifts from congregations and individual members of
the church for such ministries reached nearly $3,000,000 in 1987 and
enabled these institutions to serve more than 6000 young people.
Also in 1987, UCC related hospitals in the United States and Puerto
Rico cared for nearly 7000 persons (and an additional 48,778 out
patients). The budget for the delivery of health care was
$1,093,382,655.[14] The ministries among the aged, the young, and
the ill have received their inspiration from the scriptures and the
teachings of Jesus about healing the sick, welcoming the stranger,
and serving the neighbor in need.

"Social ministry," inspired by the gospel, comes to significant
expression in congregational life as well. "Diaconia" is lived out by
many church members. This includes visitation among the sick and
shut ins, prison ministries, the sponsorship of refugees from many
nations, food pantries, shelters for the homeless, day care centers,
counseling for people who suffer from drug or alcohol abuse, victims
of domestic violence, ministry to "street people," food pantries, and
the sharing of financial and other resources with persons in rural and
urban areas where the economy has collapsed. Congregational support for the state and national mission of the United Church of Christ
reached $30,046,193 in 1987, with additional gifts for special projects
of $18,033,389. Total support for the church, including the budgets
of congregations, amounted to $518,571,132.[15]

The diversity of "social ministry" in the United Church of Christ
and in the numerous diaconic institutions related to the denomination affirm an insight made by Dietrich Bonhoeffer years ago: "Our
relation to God," he said, "is not a 'religious' relationship to the
highest, most powerful, and best Being imaginable,... but our relation
to God is a new life in 'existence for others,' through participation in
the being of Jesus."[16] Whether it is a "pronouncement" by a General
Synod, a statement or ministry of one of the instrumentalities of the
church, or the decision of a local church to open a food pantry, the
willingness to act on behalf of neighbor is a fundamental dimension
of Christian discipleship; it is conformity to Christ without which the
church is impossible to properly understand.

Faith and Social Ministry

The great Old Testament scholar, Abraham Joshua Heschel, observed some years ago that the decline of religious institutions in the West is connected to an arrogant abandonment in modern times of the fundamental truths about God and the nature of human life. "When faith is completely replaced by creed," he wrote, and "worship by discipline, (and) love by habit; when the crisis of today is ignored because of the splendor of the past; when faith becomes an heirloom rather than a living fountain; when religion speaks only in the name of authority rather than with the voice of compassion, its message becomes meaningless."[17] Where the church is faithful to its calling, where in the United Church of Christ, national leadership, instrumentalities, regional conferences and members of local congregations are willing (as the Statement of Faith proclaims) "...to accept the cost and joy of discipleship," and "to proclaim the gospel to all the world," it is because the church is attempting to be truthful to the best of its traditions. I mean by this that "faith" and "social ministry" will always be inspired where the church is humble enough to gather around the Word and to listen to the biblical story. Where "faith" is real and "social ministry" has integrity, it is because the church is listening to the scriptures and is prepared...to pray! Only so will the church see Christ in society; in the sorrow, wonder, pain and miracle of life.

"The present form of the world passes away," Archbishop Oscar Romero said in a homily delivered about a year before his death, "and there remains the joy of having used this world to establish God's rule here. All pomp, all triumphs,...all the false successes of life...will pass... What does not pass away is love... In the evening of life you will be judged on love."[18] I am convinced that if "faith" and "social ministry" are to possess the integrity and impact God is intending, they will have to be sustained in every part of the church by disciplined study of the Bible and, by prayer. Where "faith" and "social ministry" break down, it is because our devotional life has collapsed.

The need to anchor the public witness of the church firmly, deeply, seriously and joyfully in dialogue with scripture, in Christian tradition, in the liturgy, in prayer and in careful theological work is absolutely crucial as the United Church of Christ looks to the future.

Where "faith" and "social ministry" are fractured, where "social issues" are neglected or despised as "engagement in politics," the reasons usually have to do with a neglect of our biblical and theological foundations, and a corresponding weakness in our teaching ministry. This is why the office of "pastor and teacher" in the church is so critical. If shallow, tenuous biblical work is being done (either in the national instrumentalities, the conferences, or local congregations of the UCC), "faith" and "social ministry" will have a very precarious relationship. A theological vacuum is created. Political ideologies will rush in to fill the void. The softening and distortion of the gospel follows. Subjective political viewpoints are accommodated. The cross and resurrection are removed from the center of church life. Nonsense and idolatry dominate. Where we fail to grapple either with the nature of the Body of Christ or with the Word addressed to us by God in Jesus, the church as witness collapses. Where the sacraments are brushed aside or treated sentimentally, the church comes to a dead end, despite "success" and applause.[19] Where scripture, prayer, and gratitude for Christian tradition are present, "faith" and "social ministry have a chance to breathe. Where there is enough humility to listen to the voices through which God seeks to address us from the world (most often from deep within the shadows of the cross), the church may come to experience transcendence, faith as "participation in the being of Jesus."[20] There, "social ministry" will have integrity.

I want to cite just three examples which offer hope as we look to the future of "faith" and "social ministry" in the United Church of Christ. 1) *There are deepening ecumenical contacts which could have great significance.* The UCC, as other North American churches, is learning much from sisters and brothers in distant places,... South Africa, the Philippines, El Salvador, the Republic of Korea, the German Democratic Republic, and other parts of the world where the church is lean, where the cross is part of the daily life of its members, and where congregations are paying a price for opening the Bible and daring to celebrate the sacraments. Very significant is the growing presence among us of missionaries, theologians, pastors and lay leaders from abroad. These friends are being invited to teach in our seminaries and to visit in various regional conferences where they are serving for various periods of time as "theologians in residence." Invariably, these ecumenical guests inspire members of the UCC to reflect on things crucial to faith, including a teaching ministry in which the cross is embedded in scripture and prayer. Partnerships are developing between some of our regional conferences (and local congregations) and Christian communities of faith in Central America, Asia, and Eastern Europe. Many of these partnerships have depth. They include not only exchange of information and occasional visits, but the sharing of liturgies, study documents, and common mission projects, particularly in relation to themes of justice and peace.

2) *There are increasing opportunities for focused theological reflection.* Recently, for example, the United Church Board for World Ministries published the initial draft of a major document entitled "Christian Faith and Economic Life" in preparation for the Seventeenth General Synod of the UCC in 1989. Since 1980, the Economics and Theology Covenant Group, composed of pastors, teachers, and lay leaders of the church, has been meeting to think through the teachings of scripture in relation to "the economic and material dimensions of human life." The document they have written has now been commended to the churches for study, critique, discussion and response. A process has been designed to assist members of UCC congregations dialogue with the sensitive issues raised in this document, and to share their ideas with national leaders of the church. The purpose of entrusting "Christian Faith and Economic Life" to the congregations is not to "sell" a point of view, but to encourage a thoughtful consideration of our national economy in relation to issues of faith and justice. The foundation for the dialogue is intended to be the Bible, and Christian tradition, rather than personal political political perspectives. The opportunity to struggle with critical issues of "faith" and "life" is being presented in terms of a covenant between national Instrumentalities of the Church and UCC congregations. This is an important step.

3) *There is an attempt to globalize our understanding of "faith" and "social ministry."* Numerous developments could be mentioned. One of these was the affirmation of "full communion" between the UCC and the Evangelical Church of the Union (EKU) in the Federal Republic of Germany and in the German Democratic Republic in 1981. Since then, a number of common projects have been undertaken by the churches in each of the countries, focusing primarily on the search for peace across "dividing walls of hostility." In 1988-1989, the UCC and the EKU explored together the meaning of "the

righteousness of God" as it is understood by laity and clergy in the three countries. Common biblical texts were used as a foundation for a "consultation" which sought to understand how God's righteousness (or justice) impacts particular social issues. In the UCC, the "consultation" took place in seven different locations. In North Carolina, for example, members of the church studied the meaning of "the righteousness of God" in terms of an ecological and social crisis in which dumping of toxic wastes is taking place in areas of the state which are heavily populated by blacks. In Minnesota, the dialogue brought together members of the UCC to examine the meaning of God's justice in the context of agriculture, the family farm, and the ownership of land. In Colorado, the theme explored the connection between wealth and poverty. Representatives from the church in Taiwan, South Korea, and the Philippines were invited to participate. Each of the seven regional "consultations" included the study of scripture, theological work and the creation of a "justice project" for the region in which the ideas and faith shared were linked with action. What is promising in this is the international dimension; common work at "faith" and "social ministry" despite the "dividing walls of hostility."

Conclusion

Not long before he died (March, 1984), the famous pastor, teacher and resistance leader, Martin Niemoeller told a moving story about the heart of his theological ethics. He spoke about the village tailor whom he remembered from childhood. He had gone with his father (an ordained minister) to the home of the tailor, who was dying of tuberculosis. While his father went upstairs to take the dying man Holy Communion, young Martin remained downstairs in the tailor's workshop. "I took in the bare room," he wrote, "with nothing but the loom and white-washed walls. In one corner I noticed something under glass, embroidered with pearls. It was a piece of cloth into which were woven the words: "What would Jesus say?" I've never forgotten it, never, for that is the sum of Christian ethics.[21]

What is necessary for us in the church in North America at this point in the 20th century is similar to that which, by the grace of God is happening among Christians in so many other parts of the world, namely,...a patient, prayerful, expectant "opening of the Word." Both at the "national level" and in the "local church," the need is for recovery of a disciplined and joyous study of scripture in which we come face to face with the question posed long ago by Pilate: "What is truth?" The "faith" and "social ministry" of the church cannot afford to hide from the truth about God or from the prayer of the publican: "Lord, be merciful unto me, a sinner." As we look to the future of the United Church of Christ, we shall want to "teach our minds to understand the true demand (of faith) and to teach our conscience to be present, (for) too often the call goes forth, and history records our conscience is absent."[22] The Bible, prayer, and a doctrine of the church in which the cross and the resurrection of Jesus Christ are at the very center of our thinking (and not at the edge or the periphery of our life) remain of crucial importance to the life of our denomination. Because this is true, it is good for us to remember a very old prayer heard often before in the life of the Christian community: "Veni Creatur spiritus!" "Come, Holy Spirit!"

Notes

[1] See Dietrich Bonhoeffer, "Outline for a Book" in *Letters and Papers from Prison,* p. 203 (revised and enlarged edition).

[2] "The Kairos Document" was published in 1986 by Christian leaders in Africa and is a powerful statement on the witness of the church in a time of crisis, under the cross.

[3] Article One, "Barmen Declaration," 1934.

[4] The United Church of Christ (USA) is a diverse body of Christians in which a plethora of theological traditions and perspectives is unified by a common confession that "Jesus Christ is Lord." The UCC came into being when representatives of the Congregational Christian Churches and the Evangelical and Reformed Church voted for union at a General Synod held at Cleveland, Ohio in June, 1957. The United Church of Christ currently has approximately 1,665,000 confirmed members, including persons who trace their roots to Africa, Central America, Cuba, Japan, Korea, the Philippines, Armenia, Lebanon, the USSR, Switzerland and other countries. The UCC consists of a number of Native American congregations as well. The Congregational Christian tradition can be traced through Josiah Strong, Horace Bushnell, Solomon Stoddard, Jonathan Edwards and others to John Cotton, William Brewster, the Separatist Puritan pastor John Robinson, Plymouth Rock, the Massachusetts Bay Colony and the English Reformation to 16th century Calvinism. The Evangelical and Reformed Church was composed of both Lutheran and German-Swiss Reformed elements, and was indebted in its teaching to Martin Luther, Philipp Melanchthon, and Martin Butzer on the one hand, and to John Calvin, Ulrich Zwingli, and Zacharias Ursinus on the other.

[5] Quoted by Eberhard Busch in his biography of Karl Barth entitled, *Karl Barth: His life from letters and autobiographical texts* (Philadelphia, Fortress Press, 1976) p. 58.

[6] "The Statement of Faith" of the United Church of Christ was adopted by the Second General Synod, June, 1959.

[7] See article by Irene Stock in *Borderlines*: A Publication of the UCC Refugee Resettlement/Asylum Office, Vol. 1, No. 4, September 8, 1986).

[8] According to the 1988 *Yearbook* of the United Church of Christ, the total operating income (from all sources) of Health and Welfare institutions related to the UCC was $1,424,858,377 in 1987.

[9] These figures are from a document called *Uniting in Mission,* published in 1989 by the UCC Stewardship Council.

[10] See *United Church of Christ Social Policy,* published by the Office for Church and Society, UCC, 105 Madison Avenue, New York, NY 10016. (September, 1981).

[11] Ibid., p. 2.

[12] Ibid., p. 37.

⁸ According to the 1988 *Yearbook* of the United Church of Christ, the total operating income (from all sources) of Health and Welfare institutions related to the UCC was $1,424,858,377 in 1987.

⁹ These figures are from a document called *Uniting in Mission,* published in 1989 by the UCC Stewardship Council.

¹⁰ See *United Church of Christ Social Policy*, published by the Office for Church and Society, UCC, 105 Madison Avenue, New York, NY 10016. (September, 1981).

¹¹ Ibid., p. 2.

¹² Ibid., p. 37.

¹³ For a complete description of this and all other action taken by theGeneral Synods and Instrumentalities of the UCC between 1957-1981 in relation to "Peace and Arms Control," see Ibid., p. 37f.

¹⁴ Figures based on the 1988 *Yearbook* of the United Church of Christ, p. 45.

¹⁵The 1988 *Yearbook* lists 1,662,568 confirmed members of the United Church of Christ and 6,395 congregations in the United States.

¹⁶Bonhoeffer, "Outline for a Book," *Letters and Papers from Prison*, p. 202.

¹⁷ Abraham Joshua Heschel, *The Insecurity of Freedom*, (New York, Schocken Books, 1972).

¹⁸ *The Church is All of You: Thoughts of Archbishop Oscar Romero*, ed. by James R. Brockman, S.J. (Minneapolis, Winston Press, 1984) p. 59.

¹⁹The need for a recovery of the "teaching ministry" of the church is critical. As this is done, the theological seminaries occupy a vital place. What we need are not only candidates for ordination who are equipped to offer pastoral counseling. We need good teachers and faithful preachers and pastors who understand the liturgy as a gift of God both for the renewal of the human soul and the renewal of human courage amidst the resistance to social justice that abounds in society.

²⁰Bonhoeffer, p. 202.

²¹Martin Niemoeller died at the age of 92 years in Wiesbaden on March 6, 1984. He was a submarine commander in World War I and became known as "the Scourge of Malta" for his exploits. Active in the Confessing Synod of Barmen (1934), he was an important figure in the resistance within the Evangelical Church to Hitler. He was arrested in 1937 and was sent to Sachsenhausen; then to Dachau, where he remained until 1945 as one of Hitler's "personal prisoners." From 1961 to 1968 he was a president of the World Council of Churches. "Live according to the Gospel, without fear or fail" Niemoeller advised his congregation at Dahlem-Berlin, and he embodied his own preaching. He became a pacifist in the "nuclear age" and was a harsh critic of United States involvement in the Vietnam War.

²²Heschel, p. 7f.

4

FAITH AND SOCIAL MINISTRY IN THE PRESBYTERIAN CHURCH (USA)

Barbara Hargrove and Dana Wilbanks

One encounters a number of difficulties when describing the social ministry of the Presbyterian Church. Should one approach the study through an historical analysis or through focusing on contemporary trends and developments? Should one examine official documents of the denomination or rely on the attitudes and practices of local congregations? Should one identify the denomination's normative teachings on topics of social ministry or seek to describe the patterns of social engagement at the various levels of church life? Should one seek to articulate as clearly as possible the denomination's approach to social ministry or should one engage in a critical evaluation of its approach?

We suspect, at best, that our study should represent a "both-and" response to the above questions. We shall proceed with this understanding of our task. In doing so, however, we acknowledge not only the complexity of the questions but also our struggle with which methods will elicit the most appropriate generalizations. As ethicist and sociologist, we shall especially seek to stress the interaction of normative and descriptive characteristics of social ministry in the Presbyterian Church.

Theological and Sociological
Understandings of Faith

The Presbyterian Church is within the larger family of Reformed churches, originating historically from the time of the Protestant Reformation and the theological and organizational influence of John Calvin. There are clear theological characteristics of the Reformed tradition that have had profound affects on the church's engagement with societies. For Calvin, as for Martin Luther, faith is a trusting relation with God that is a gift of grace through Jesus Christ. It is through faith alone and not through moral activity that persons are reconciled to God. Human sinfulness is so deep and pervasive that human beings are incapable of accomplishing anything of worth apart from the powerful and all-determining will of God.

Many commentators have been bewildered that these theological convictions have not bred passivity in Reformed churches but instead have fostered vigorous activity and impulses toward societal transformation. Part of the reason, theologically, is that moral activity has not been seen in opposition to or in contrast with faith but as a necessary accompaniment to faith. Faith will be expressed in works, so works in a vital way have been regarded as a sign of salvation, as a manifestation of authentic faith.[1] Moral activity, then, has functioned as a kind of visible test, though imperfect, of divine election as well as an essential outgrowth of faith as grateful response to the incomprehensible gift of God's grace. Moral seriousness and earnestness, positively manifested in persistent and courageous efforts for social reform and negatively in tendencies toward arrogance and self-righteousness, continue at various times to characterize Presbyterian social ministry.

Another reason for the activism of Calvinists is their emphasis on the sovereignty of God. There is no area of life untouched by God's rule. All things are subject to God's authority and will. In the Presbyterian theological tradition, God's sovereignty encompasses the whole creation including all the nations and peoples of the earth, therefore providing the basis for a distinctively international orientation. Alan Geyer writes: "It is more than coincidental that studies of voting behavior in the United States, both at the polls and in Congress, consistently disclose a stronger internationalist sentiment among Presbyterians than among most other mainline denominations."[2]

God's sovereignty clearly also includes governing authorities and social institutions. Calvinists believe they are called to shape human communities in ways that reflect the divine purposes of the sovereign God. God's purposes do not apply only to the church and individual believers but extend to every area of human life. The service of God requires obedience to God's will in society and throughout the world as well as in individual behavior and in church life.

These views were doubtless influenced and reinforced by Calvinists' historical experience with power. Unlike many Protestant denominations, Reformed churches can trace their history to times when they have been closely aligned with states in wielding religious and political authority. Like Episcopalians, Catholics, and Lutherans, then, Presbyterians have been influenced by their history to take seriously their responsibility for society. Although Calvinist Christians have experienced religious persecution in various times and places, they generally have not drawn members from oppressed or deprived groups, as do many more sectarian churches, but from educated groups that have achieved a certain status and access to power. It is not surprising, sociologically, that Presbyterians have emphasized the importance of order in their relation to society. The appropriate way to worship and serve the sovereign God, whether through ritual or social involvement, is "decently and in order."

Theological and sociological factors have led Presbyterians to have a more positive view of government and social institutions than some other traditions. There is a certain "common grace" available to persons to shape social institutions for the common good and not merely to restrain human sinfulness. God ordains governments and governing authorities to secure a just order for human communities. Presbyterians' commitment to order and orderliness tends to give rise to a keen sense of justice. They are likely to exhibit a readiness to question any given order that is deemed to violate divine principles of justice. There are possibilities for justice that Christians and non-Christians may seek together which are not dependent on "saving grace" alone. Presbyterians are encouraged to serve God and neighbor through the exercise of civic responsibility, including the choice of political vocations.

At the same time, there is the "realistic" awareness that no human institutions or authorities may claim absolute authority. Because of human sinfulness power may become corrupted and abusive, and Christians may be called to resist centers of power because "God alone is lord of the conscience."[3] Christians' ultimate allegiance to God always carries the seeds of tension in relation to human institutions. Even at best, human constructs are provisional and imperfect, requiring continuing criticism and reform under the dynamic impact of the Word of God. As Reformed Christians have often supported critically their social order, they have also on occasion participated in revolutionary struggle against dominant authorities and institutions. Presbyterians seek to apply "their motto *ecclesia reformata semper reformanda* (a church reformed, always needing to reform) to the totality of human existence and experience."[4] If the negative expressions of these convictions are theocratic tendencies, excessive and legalistic preoccupation with order, and unwarranted certainty about God's will for society, the positive manifestations are critical and persistent public engagement with social structures aimed at their qualitative transformation.[5]

Historically, the Bible has been regarded as the primary, sometimes exclusive, source of knowledge of God's will. The authority of scripture is still central to Presbyterians' faith, although there is vigorous debate and even bitter conflict over how scriptural authority is to be interpreted. Normatively, the Bible contains the history of God's self-disclosure and, above all, the decisive revelation of God's will in Jesus Christ. For guidance about the meaning of the Bible, Calvinists turn to historical creeds and edification through prayer, preaching, studying and debate under the guidance of the Holy Spirit. Most Presbyterian clergy and lay leaders interpret the Bible with the aid of historical and literary methods of modern scholarship and draw on insights from other academic disciplines and historical experience in seeking to understand God's will for the church and society.[6]

Although faith for Presbyterians is not in the first instance cognitive (it is relational, volitional), Presbyterians value greatly the articulation of their faith in cognitively clear, coherent and credible statements. This characteristic goes hand in hand with their historic emphasis on the importance of education and the church's teaching ministry. They are a *confessional* church, basing their understandings of Christian faith on a number of written historic confessions of the church. These confessions together, for Presbyterians, provide the authoritative witness of the historic church to the truth contained in scripture. They provide a dynamic and pluralistic authority for contemporary belief and action.

The most recent confession (Confession of 1967) gives doctrinal primacy to reconciliation as a way to understand God's activity in Christ and the church's life and mission. Reconciliation clearly refers not only to persons' relation with God and with one another in the church but also to racial, economic and international relations. In the contemporary style of Presbyterians, it is characteristic to develop a biblical, theological and ethical basis for the church's involvement with whatever social issue is being considered. This may represent at times excessive confidence in the influence of ideas to move people to action. At its best, it expresses the high valuation that Presbyterians give to thinking clearly and deeply as an activity of faith that contributes to obedient and effective social ministry.[7]

In Presbyterian churches, faith is nurtured in various ways. Participation in corporate worship is central, yet all facets of the church's life and ministry feed and express the faith of its members. Private spiritual disciplines of prayer and Bible study, though important, do not replace the centrality of public worship and the necessity for participating in the shared life of the believing community. Service within the church and in the wider community, Bible study groups, the educational program, evangelism efforts, committee meetings on the budget, counseling and supporting relationships, and social action for justice and peace are various dimensions of the whole life of the church. It is the totality of congregational life rooted in corporate worship that nourishes and challenges the faith of the church's members. Moreover, there are implications for social ministry in each of the various dimensions of church life.[8]

Understanding of Social Ministry

Presbyterians in America, like most of their fellow citizens, have been affected by the generally individualistic definition of religion in our culture. This is expressed in understandings both of the nature of worship and the church, and of social ministry. Private acts of service and charity are rated high by most Presbyterians. But as a church, they do not stop there. A high percentage of the social ministry undertaken by Presbyterians is, in one way or another, institutional. As a consequence, it is important to understand the

structure of the denomination in order to understand its way of
dealing with social ministry. The Presbyterian Church is a "connectional church," with a strong pattern of representative government
and corporate responsibility which involves both the clergy and the
laity. With a fine Calvinistic sense of human frailty and a consequent
suspicion of human motives, the Presbyterian system has instituted
a series of checks and balances that strives to keep power in the
church from falling into the hands of any particular group. The
presbytery is the basic governmental unit of the church. Every
minister belongs to some presbytery, and is expected to attend its
meetings regularly to assist in the governance of the church. However, every presbytery meeting is supposed to include an equal representation of the laity, chosen from among those lay leaders who
have been ordained elders by their local congregation. Thus neither
clergy nor laity are supposed to exercise dominance. However, there
tends to be a rotation among elders in attendance at presbytery
meetings, while ministers are always there. Thus the reality is that the
ministers know more of what is going on, and tend to exercise more
influence. However, ministers in the Presbyterian system are "called"
by the local congregation, and are dependent upon it and its governing board, the session (composed of those lay elders) for salary and
job security. So there is a kind of rough parity between the two
groups.

Sessions are vested with responsibility for the life of local
churches. Pastors and elders, who are elected by the congregation
and ordained to this office, constitute the membership of the session.
It is these elders who also may become delegated not only to
presbytery but to the national *General Assembly*, which is the highest
governing body of the Presbyterian Church (U.S.A.). It meets
annually and consists, again, of an equal number of clergy and elders
who are elected representatives from each presbytery. The General
Assembly provides organizational leadership, coordination, guidance, and resources for the denomination's diverse ministries. It is
served by a variety of agencies, committees, and councils. Laity as
well as clergy are involved in these groups, as well as in continuing
committees at the level of the presbyteries as well as the synods
(regional organizations).

This structure of Presbyterian government ensures a connectional relationship between local churches and wider units of govern-

ance. It protects the leadership role of laity in church decisions from the ecclesiastical elitism of the clergy. It further provides for the exercise of church authority through the election of representatives and the action of corporate entities.[9] It is a matter of considerable pride to Presbyterians that authority is not vested in a "bishop." Indeed, Presbyterians often refer to the presbytery as a "corporate bishop." Because church decisions involve corporate procedures, Presbyterians give considerable energy to the establishment of clear rules for deliberation, debate, and action. Rules recognize the value of vigorous debate in decisionmaking and seek to ensure that discussions are fair, open, orderly, and expeditious. In Swanson's terms[10] Presbyterians assume a social order that is associational rather than a social system, where there are a variety of different interests that must be adjudicated. There is no expectation that total agreement on any issue is either possible or required. Given this understanding of church and society, the theological basis for the emphasis on corporate decision making is that, negatively, power is less likely to be abused, and positively, the church is most likely to discern faithfully the will of God through orderly patterns of conflict and consensus.

It is necessary to understand characteristic features of Presbyterian polity because its approach to social ministry is strongly institutionalized. Authoritative principles and patterns of church government are written in a constitution called the *Book of Order*. The responsibility of the church to be in social ministry is not only articulated at the theological level, but is also identified in the *Book of Order* as one of the responsibilities of elders and ministers of local congregations:

> ...[they should] equip and renew [the people] for their tasks
> within the church and for their mission in the world, visit
> and comfort and care for the people, with special attention
> to the poor, the sick, the   lonely, and those who are
> oppressed. (G-6.0304)

This is clearly construed not only as social service but also structural change: "They should inform the pastor and session of those persons and structures which may need special attention." (G-6.0304)

The institutionalization of social ministry is most clearly seen at the General Assembly level of the Presbyterian Church. In the former United Presbyterian Church (USA), a functional distinction was built into the structure of General Assembly organization between social policy development and program implementation.   The policy development council (Advisory Council on Church and Society) was given a certain independence within the organization to provide an institutional place and role for prophetic challenge to the church in its social engagement.   It was also given direct access to the General Assembly and its agencies to insure significant institutional impact of the General Assembly's social policy.

Denominational social policy in this structure was developed in intentional contrast with the conventional church mode of making "pronouncements."   Pronouncements often imply "speaking out" on particular public issues.   Social policy, however, includes a carefully developed analysis of a broad issue (e.g., energy policy, Central American policy) with biblical, theological, and ethical bases for church response.   It includes the general stance of the General Assembly on the issue and a wide variety of specific recommendations designed to ensure the implementation of the policy institutionally throughout the church and in the church's engagement with society and public policy.   Social policy must be adopted by the General Assembly and is intended to stimulate and guide the church's involvement with particular social issues and to contribute to the church's identification of its mission in the world. Frequently, social policy recommendations include both social service and public advocacy ministries (e.g., the policy on abortion calling for counseling services for persons struggling with unintended pregnancies while also advocating support for laws which protect women's right to make decisions about their pregnancies.[11])

In this church organization, program units were established to develop resources and mechanisms to implement policies adopted by the General Assembly.   In 1983, the two major branches of the Presbyterian Church, United Presbyterian Church USA ("northern branch") and the Presbyterian Church US ("southern branch") were reunited. In 1988 the structures of this church were put in place. The distinction between policy and program functions was continued in the structures of the reunited Presbyterian Church, yet the policy unit (Committee on Social Witness Policy) is more closely linked to a program unit (Social Justice and Peacemaking) than in the former

UPCUSA structure. The importance in the Presbyterian Church of providing institutionally for both social policy development and effective implementation in church and society is evident in the organization of General Assembly entities in the reunited church.

Both previous Presbyterian streams included units specifically constituted to deal with women's concerns and with racial and ethnic concerns. This pattern was continued in the reunited church. The intent is to ensure the church's special responsiveness to theological and ethical commitments to sexual and racial justice both within the church and in the wider society. Moreover, the Presbyterian Church has institutionalized several priority areas of social ministry. One is a Hunger Program, established in the 1970s, and another is a Peacemaking Program, established in the early 1980s. The attempt in both these cases is to provide sufficient institutional resources and energy for the denomination to develop justice and peace ministries as central to its mission. Again, social ministry is understood to be both service related and advocacy related, interpersonal and systemic, pastoral and prophetic. Peace and justice commitments imply not only stands on particular public policy questions, although they certainly involve these elements, but they are also seen as affecting every facet of the church's life, from congregations to the General Assembly, and from worship and pastoral care to social action committees.[12]

Probably for most members of the Presbyterian Church, it is the local congregation which is the setting for most of the social ministry about which they know or care. Local congregations are understood to be social institutions whose role in their communities should contribute to the quality of life and the development of persons. On the whole, Presbyterian church members are likely to occupy positions of comfort if not leadership in their communities. They are likely to experience at least some measure of that sense of belonging to the establishment that tends to define order in terms of maintenance of the status quo. They tend to be highly supportive of programs that provide services to people in need, and to have a sense of responsibility toward those who might be excluded from the expected order of things. They may be much less sanguine about attempts to deal in systemic change, although they have a tendency toward reform of systems which seem "out of order." For the typical church member, those systems are most likely to be perceived locally.

Social ministry defined at that level tends to emphasize both the Christian call to private charity and the kind of public responsibility that is exercised through voluntary associations. Congregational committees develop plans for ministries to various areas of hunger, poverty, health, justice, and education, as examples. At the local as well as more inclusive levels, then, social ministry for Presbyterians more often than not is defined institutionally.

Both observation and the reading of statements about the ministry to which local congregations wish to call pastors indicate that most Presbyterians expect their ministers to be involved in leadership circles of the local community, mirroring to some extent their members' interests in voluntary and civic betterment associations, including those that are ecumenical in nature.

This is a comfortable role for many ministers. At the same time, clergy undergo some tension. The Presbyterian demand for well-educated ministers often leads them to adopt the critical stance most often offered in institutions of higher education at this period of history. This has been intensified in recent years, since ministry as a profession has become a less high status position than in the past.

Again, laity in leadership positions in the denomination are more likely to subscribe to a "cosmopolitan" rather than a "local" view of the world,[13] and to be less tied to the local establishment than many in the pew. Those who are able to devote a significant amount of time to committee meetings are likely to be professional persons in control of their own time, retired people, or homemakers, who may be currently experiencing less of the sense of being part of the local scene than most Presbyterian members.

It would not be surprising, then, to find that leadership in the denomination would be more likely to define social ministry in the mode of social change than would be the case of the majority in the pew. At the same time, Presbyterians have had a long history of taking very seriously the education of their members, including study papers on issues of social ministry. Thus there are mitigating circumstances within the structure that soften the potential division within the denomination and provide shared definitions.

Relationship Between Faith and Social Ministry

The Presbyterian Church in its normative self-understanding regards social ministry as an integral dimension of its life and mission. It is viewed as a vital element in the Christian life of individual members and as a responsibility of the corporate bodies of congregations, presbyteries, synods, and the General Assembly. Social ministry, in Presbyterians' theological heritage and institutional shape, involves works of both compassionate service and vigorous efforts at systemic change. For example, General Assembly policy on Mexican migration (1981) called for programs to meet the needs of Mexican immigrants in such areas as housing, food, education and health services; and it also called for fundamental change in United States immigration laws. Presbyterian social ministry is often characterized by a strong pragmatic flavor with the assumption that words and deeds that do not bear fruit in beneficial results may well be hollow.

Presbyterian social ministry also generally has an ecumenical orientation. Organizationally the Presbyterian Church (USA) is an active member of the National Council of Churches (USA) and the World Council of Churches. Moreover General Assembly staff work closely with staff of other denominations in social policy development and program strategies. For example, a Presbyterian office in Washington D.C. works cooperatively with staff from other denominations in communicating the churches' views to government leaders and in mobilizing an ecumenical social action network involving interested members of various denominations all over the U.S. Ecumenical also means cultivating a global perspective on social ministry, drawing on insights from church communions in various places in the world. Nationally and locally, Presbyterians are often in the forefront of efforts to institutionalize ecumenical approaches to social ministry and to develop coalitional strategies for engaging social structures.[14] Such strategies include secular social service and action groups as well as church related groups.

Historically, Presbyterians have articulated their theological convictions much more thoroughly than their social ethics, even as they have often been socially active. Yet over the course of many years, a body of social teachings has been developed as General Assemblies have sought to relate the church's faith to questions of social responsibility. Generally, more attention has been given to particular policies and stances than to the character of the social ethics tradition that is being created through such actions. Recently, however, a study was undertaken to interpret and systematize the Presbyterian Church's social teachings.[15] This study seeks to identify the principles of social ethics that provide a bridge between the theological vision and the concrete social circumstances to which the church is responding. The social ethics method which undergirds and informs the church's social ministry draws from both biblical/ theological and contextual analysis and moves in a dialectical fashion from one base to the other and back again toward a decision about policy and action.

This study claims: "If there is one social principle which is the basis for Presbyterian social teachings as a whole, it is the right of individual conscience."[16] On the one hand, Presbyterians believe that Christians are called to serve God in society; but, on the other hand, they recognize Christians may conscientiously disagree about what God's will requires. Sometimes this double affirmation has led to a social praxis in which the clergy will articulate the theological content of faith (e.g. love and justice of God) and leave the social implications to the consciences of members (e.g. what to do about racial segregation). Optimistically, this might imply that faith rightly preached and taught will be expressed in society through the lives of members as each one struggles with the will of God. Rather more cynically, this praxis may be a way of avoiding the potential conflicts and tensions created by pursuing corporately and concretely the social implications of Christian faith. At best, the Presbyterian Church's emphasis on the right of individual conscience leads to respect for conscientious disagreement, an unwillingness to adopt a highly prescriptive morality, to an emphasis on moral education, and to support for a social order in which personal responsibility for decisions is protected against restrictive public regulation. Still this principle is in tension with convictions about the importance of corporate church involvement in struggles to achieve justice for the poor and powerless which requires changes in socio-economic structures.

As the theological tenet of conscience is related to social issues, *Social Teachings* identifies five "middle-range principles." An example of such a principle is the following: "The church affirms that not all moral choices are equal, that such choices have grave ramifications, but that the circumstances and conditions of the individual are often of such a determinative character as to necessitate a full measure of freedom consistent with Christian responsibility."[17] For example, the Presbyterian Church has maintained that members might conscientiously choose either to participate or not to participate in the military service of the United States. Either stance may be authentically rooted in faith and conscience. The Presbyterian Church also has maintained that members ought to be supported in acts of conscience, even though others might disagree with the content of their actions. For example, in the context of the civil rights movement, the General Assembly of the Presbyterian Church (US) held that the church "should give the support of Christian conscience to any member who, following his conscience in obedience to the Word, engages in civil disobedience."[18]

The *Social Teachings* encompass four broad areas: the rights and dignity of persons, bread and justice, international peacemaking, and issues in the life of the nation. In each section, the theological basis for the teaching is elaborated, the contextual challenges are identified, and the middle-range principles are lifted up for special attention as the content of Presbyterian social ethics. In recent teachings, the moral claims of the oppressed in their struggles with the privileged and powerful have been supported and given special emphasis. If there is a conflict between the rights of the poor and the rights of the rich, General Assembly teaching has sided with the poor.[19]

Church policy in recent years also has emphasized racial and sexual justice in both church and society. It has enunciated the principle of economic justice and sought to elaborate its implications for international and domestic policies. In the last decade major developments have occurred in the General Assembly's teachings on issues of war and peace, focusing increasingly on the meanings and implications of "just peace" for U.S. foreign policy. Contextual challenges, then, continue to require fresh theological and ethical reflection in a dynamic praxis of experience and reflection, social engagement and theological understanding. Although faith has at times wrongly been identified solely with the reflective pole in this dialectic by some Presbyterians, faith encompasses and is expressed in both reflection and action in the social teachings of the Presbyterian Church.

Normative social teachings provide a thorough and coherent framework for pursuing social ministry, yet the influence of these teachings on church life is uncertain. Various efforts have been made institutionally to nurture and stimulate social ministry in Presbyterian churches. One way is to involve persons at local church levels in the process of policy formation. For example, a teleconference format was used to obtain suggestions about policy on a "just political economy." Also, a deliberate strategy was developed to enlist churches and presbyteries in studying and responding to a controversial study paper on "Presbyterians and Peacemaking: Are We Now Called to Resistance?" as a part of a policy development process.[20] Currently, a task force of the Committee on Social Witness Policy on eco-justice is convening meetings in geographically appropriate parts of the United States to consider such specific issues as sustainable agriculture, cleaner water, and community toxics. These discussions will contribute to the preparation of social policy on eco-justice for debate and action by the General Assembly.

A second way is to identify socially active congregations and to share their stories broadly throughout the church to provide models and challenges for other churches. An example of this was the establishment of a network of those Presbyterian churches involved in sanctuary ministry along with efforts to stimulate wider church support. Hessel has argued that the development of social policy at the General Assembly level needs to be linked more closely to the congregation context which is the primary, though not sole, location for social ministry.[21]

A third way is to build strategies of implementation into social policy recommendations, (e.g. provision for money, staff, materials, organization). For example, the policy on peacemaking included provisions for a special peacemaking program to be funded through a special offering with a distribution of funds to local and presbytery levels as well as to the General Assembly office. The policy on issues arising out of the presence of Mexican undocumented workers in the United States included provisions for special ministries in border areas.

The fourth way is through the preparation of study materials on various social policies. Each social policy adopted by the General Assembly is accompanied by an extensive study document which then is made available to churches for their own study. For example, studies are available on such policies as Central America, Mexican migration to the United States, and energy. Often these are accompanied by other kinds of resources both on the issues and on how to involve churches in social ministry in these areas of social concern.

A fifth way is to use existing programs and structures to emphasize social ministry. A current project of the Committee on Social Witness Policy is to bring together professors of social ethics from various seminaries, primarily Presbyterian, to deal with, in part, the seminary's opportunities to educate clergy for leadership in social ministry. Certainly the seminary's role is pivotal in reflecting on the relation of Christian faith and the church's engagement with society. Also, conferences involving synod and presbytery leadership are being held to develop more effective ways to involve Presbyterians in social policy development and implementation.

Most presbyteries have church and society committees which seek to provide leadership and support for local churches. Large presbyteries may even have staff persons who are able to give significant time to the task of nurturing social ministry. In local churches, there also may be church and society committees, or mission committees which encompass responsibility for social ministry. Especially important in local church life historically has been the leadership role of women's organizations in social education and action. Again, as befitting its sociological character and theological convictions, the Presbyterian Church emphasizes the importance of education and of organizational strategies in seeking to implement its commitment to social ministry.

The actual patterns of social ministry at the congregational level are many. Churches engage in all kinds of social service projects responding directly to diverse areas of human need: visit the sick and those who are in prison, provide shelter for the homeless, provide day care for pre-school children, work in drug and alcohol abuse programs, minister to women who have been abused and battered, volunteer on suicide prevention hotlines, provide food for the hungry, etc. Churches are less often involved in social action, but there are still many around the country involved in imaginative and creative efforts to change society: in prison reform, supporting the nuclear freeze, confronting racism and sexism in public life, seeking changes in U.S. policies in Central America, etc. In both social service and social advocacy, churches frequently encourage members to express their Christian discipleship by participating as volunteers. Sometimes members volunteer for such work with little or no encouragement from their church, but they are motivated by their own sense of Christian responsibility.

It is clearly a part of the Presbyterian ethos to stimulate members to participate in the public life of their communities. Many will do this in their occupations which, in Calvinist understandings, are regarded as vocations, that is, as callings through which persons use their interests and abilities to serve their neighbor and the common good as a response to God's love. At various levels of intentionality, then, Presbyterians will see their work and their voluntary participation in diverse civic organizations, service associations and advocacy groups as social ministry. For Presbyterians, social ministry does not take place only in the church or under the auspices of the church but in the varied facets of life in contemporary society.

The Experience of the Church in Social Ministry

Descriptions of the normative and programmatic understanding of the Presbyterian Church in regard to social ministry seem fairly orderly and direct. However, as one might suspect, the story of Presbyterian social ministry is not this neat and unambiguous. Presbyterians are often frustrated by the seeming chasm between General Assembly actions and church life in congregations and presbyteries. They may question whether it is because the national level of church organization is out of touch with rank and file Presbyterians, or because the infrastructure of church organization is not nurtured in ways that enable the connectional system to function well, or because effeorts to implement General Assembly policies are inadequate (e.g., insufficient money, staff, or poor strategies). Some say it is because too much effort is given to social policy and not enough effort to developing and supporting models of congregational social ministry. Each of the above theses has an array of vigorous proponents in Presbyterian circles. Fewer, perhaps, take seriously some of their root theological concerns in sociological context, that would assume different interests to be in competition within the church at all levels, yet such a consideration must be taken into account.

Inherent in the discussion above are contradictory forces impacting on the performance of Presbyterians in social ministry. Presbyterians are not immune to general social influences that tend to reinforce a definition of religion as a personal activity within the private sphere of life, even though both their official theology and the structure of the church tend toward a more corporate and public approach. The social class background of the majority of Presbyterians tends toward a vested interest in the status quo, yet positions of leadership and responsibility may lead toward a strong desire for a just social order as a matter of identification and pride.

In general, the orientation toward a strong public and corporate social ministry is strongest among those who are full time servants of the church, and among those placed in the more central parts of its structure. The tendency toward private acts of charity as social ministry is found most clearly among the rank and file, the people in the pew. However, the church is well organized to provide study materials and other forms of communication from the central structures to the local people, and their influence is felt as well through the structures of representation. Thus the observable action of the Presbyterian Church reflects both orientations.

Fortunately, Presbyterians also have been in the forefront of maintaining research about processes within the denomination. In particular, since 1973 the United Presbyterian Church has done continuing panel surveys among 3500 to 4000 selected members and clergy, in later years extended to include the Presbyterian Church in the United States (the southern branch) with which it was united in 1983. Some of those surveys have dealt specifically with issues of social ministry, and the findings in them may be used to test the goodness of fit among the different expectations developed above.

One of the factors that needs explication before the specifically social ministry issues are addressed has to do with the authority of the church to promulgate its understanding of these issues. The primary explanation for Presbyterian opinions about social issues given here has been sociological, related to their position in and experience with the society. That, of course, is not the primary explanation they themselves or denominational leaders give. The denomination engages in extensive educational and communicative effort to enlist members in programs and emphases in social ministry that are developed at the national level. It would seem evident that denominational leaders would hope that members would find the church and its publications an important source of information and authority on which members' opinions and actions might be based. When panelists were asked about that in 1978, however, the majority noted that the primary source of their opinions concerning controversial issues was the Bible. Articles in church publications were considered important resources by only about 10 percent of members and one elder in seven. TV evangelists and preachers received the least amount of recognition as sources of decision-making.

The Bible as a resource was not treated by most Presbyterians as a literal guide to life, but rather "more than three-fourths of the respondents in each group say that 'The Bible contains insights which provide general guidance for all of the problems of contemporary life.'" More generally, a clear consensus emerged that "religious beliefs and/or affiliations" exerted "a great deal of influence" upon their decisions concerning controversial social issues. Their perceptions, then, are that the church and its teachings do exercise an important influence on their opinions and involvement in social issues. The evidence, however, would indicate that that influence is felt selectively, with clergy most likely to exhibit its power, and the rank and file of the laity the least.

Among the subjects covered by the panel which fall under the rubric of social ministry are political involvement (referred to in the denomination as "social witness") issues of racial and ethnic justice, peacemaking, and crime and criminal justice. In the more general "social witness" area, in 1979 the report reads:

> The *Panel* clearly rejected the idea that our congregations should take no role in dealing with social problems. Seventy-five percent or more of the members, elders and pastors believe that providing direct services to persons in need is one of a congregation's most important role [sic.] in dealing with social issues, and approximately 60% of members, elders and pastors see support of community organization and development as among the most important congregational roles. Lobbying for particular legislation falls at the low end of this spectrum, affirmed as among the most important roles of the congregation by fewer than one member in every twenty, and by less than one of every ten in the other [clergy and elder] samples.(p.2)

Thus there is some confirmation here that the most approved social ministry is the kind that eases the pains of the current order, rather than changing it, particularly among the rank and file as compared with the more involved leaders and clergy. Again, the difference between clergy and lay groups was noted in the statement,

"With the exception of the clergy groups, study and/or action by United Presbyterians in any of the particular social policy areas has been minimal." (p. 2)

While issues of racial justice had been central to much of the social witness of the church during earlier times, by August, 1980, the panel reported that respondents felt that most of the white middle class members of the denomination would choose the words, "weariness," "apathy," and "frustration" to indicate their response to the issue. The word most often reported as "unlikely" in this context was "enthusiasm." More ministers than lay people expressed dissatisfaction with the denomination's involvement in racial issues, but most of all groups thought that it was about the right amount. In other words, by the 1980s social ministry in the area of racial and ethnic justice was not in the forefront of the consciousness of the majority of United Presbyterians.

Peacemaking became a strong focus of the denomination as a whole in the 1980s. Again, however, there were differences between clergy and laity in the amount of importance they attached to that issue:

> When asked about the sense of urgency they attach to peace making as a concern of the Presbyterian Church during 1982, lay persons are fairly evenly divided between those who view peacemaking as "an urgent concern," and those who feel peacemaking is "an important but not an urgent concern." Most clergy respondents see peacemaking as "an urgent concern."

However, the teachings of the church would seem to have had some effect on congregants:

> Presbyterians in each of the *Panel* samples more often favored meetings between the United States and the Soviet Union on nuclear disarmament than did the 1,519 adults surveyed in the Gallup Poll. In addition, panelists more often said they would be in favor of agreements "not to build any more nuclear weapons in the future" and "to destroy all nuclear weapons that already have been built"— even though the lay panelists are somewhat more likely

than the general public to think that the Soviet Union would not abide by such agreements. (p. 3)

Again, by 1984, there had been a slight decrease in the numbers of panelists who reported that their congregations or communities had engaged in *no* peacemaking activities, and Presbyterian panelists were more likely to oppose further military aid to El Salvador than the US public in general, thus indicating a general disagreement with some of the military stance of the nation.

In the February 1985, report, over 50 percent of the panelists are reported to agree that "the defense budget should be cut before cuts are made in human service programs for the poor or in social security for the elderly."

Support for the idea that Presbyterian laity are more involved in the institutional systems of the country than are clergy comes from reports in that 1985 panel on reactions to the "sanctuary" movement:

The majority of members and elders are *opposed* to congregations using their buildings to provide refugees from Central America with sanctuary from U.S. immigration Officers. However, a majority of the clergy *support* such actions. (p. ii)

The vast majority of those who say they oppose the use of church buildings as sanctuaries for Central American refugees give as a reason for their position that they "believe it is against the law and the church should not break the law in these circumstances." (p. iii)

Interestingly, "There is little support among Presbyterians for stopping the flow of refugees and immigrants to the United States" (p. iii). Thus it would seem that the issue of law breaking is a primary one in this case.

On the matter of crime and criminal justice, one of the rather surprising findings was that nearly one in every ten lay Presbyterians on the panel was involved professionally in the criminal justice system through their jobs or professions. Most panelists reported a feeling that the criminal justice system was doing about all it could,

victims of crime or families of inmates to be adequate. Says the report:

> These differences are rather startling if one began with the
> expectation that exposure to the criminal justice system
> through professional service or congregational ministry
> would tend to make a person more aware and more critical
> of existing efforts. The opposite seems to be true. It may
> be that, among the members at least, professional or
> volunteer involvement in the criminal justice system
> tends to increase a person's identification with the system
> and those who serve it, rather than increasing identifica-
> tion with prisoners and those served by the system. (p. 3)

Of all the results of the panel studies, this one may offer the
clearest support for the assertion that Presbyterians are affected by
their placement of leadership within the institutional structure of the
society. Again, this issue also speaks clearly to the division between
professional clergy and laity within the denomination:

> Policies of the church related to capital punishment clearly
> divide the clergy and the laity. Majorities of the elders
> *reject*, often with strong dissent, the call to work to repeal
> the death penalty and to prevent the executions of those
> under the sentence of death. Majorities of the pastors *agree*
> with these policies, and often do so strongly. The panel has
> recorded few policies, if any, which have so divided pastors
> and lay persons, or caused so many in both groups to hold
> more polarized opinions. (p. 3, Jan. 1983, *Panel*)

The division between clergy and laity is not necessarily the most
important cleavage in the Presbyterian church. The most basic one
may well cut across clergy and laity, congregation, presbytery and
General Assembly. This division is well documented by Dean Hoge
in *Division in the Protestant House*, and understood by him as basically
theological.[22]   There are those in the Presbyterian Church who
believe that social ministry occupies entirely too major a place in the
denomination's approach to mission, especially at the General Assembly level. Theologically, they believe the gospel is a matter of

For other critics of Presbyterian social ministry, such as the widely circulated *Presbyterian Layman*, the objection is often stated in theological terms, and yet involves sharp differences in viewpoint about the content of General Assembly's policies rather than such issues as that of personal salvation. For them, the question is not *if* the church ought to be involved in public advocacy but *what* it should advocate. Louis Weeks' generalization about Presbyterians in the early life of the United States still rings true: "The vast majority of Presbyterians, however, seem to have approved of some corporate political action and opposed other such activity."[23]

Still other critics of Presbyterian social involvement would agree that social ministry is one element in the church's mission, but they want to lower its priority and reduce its influence. They believe the church would be stronger and more unified if it deemphasized what the tasks of social engagement. For them, the controversial character of this ministry requires more institutionally cautious approaches.

Those committed to strengthening the vitality of social ministry in the Presbyterian Church believe there are both theological warrants and institutional capacities for the challenge. Yet they believe themselves to be in a time when the denomination's commitment is uncertain. It is uncertain in terms of both the church's theological self-understanding and institutional priorities. For them, the future of social ministry requires theological reflection and struggle. It also requires vigorous efforts to nourish the kind of church organization that will support and further its engagement with the world.

Notes

[1] Alan Geyer, "Reformed Faith and World Politics," *Reformed Faith and Politics*, edited by Ronald H. Stone. Washington, D.C.: University Press of American, 1983, p. 159.

[2] Idem.

[3] Westminster Confession, *Book of Confessions*, C.XX,2; 6.101.

[4] "Social Teachings of the Presbyterian Church," *Church and Society*, LXXV (November/December, 1984), 9.

[5] See H. Richard Niebuhr's categorization of John Calvin's theological ethics under "*Christ the Transformer of Culture*," New York, Harper and Brothers, 1951.

[6] See the recent statement of the General Assembly of the Presbyterian Church (USA) entitled "Presbyterian Understanding and Use of Holy Scripture," 1983; also "Presbyterians and Biblical Authority," *Journal of Presbyterian History*, 59 (Summer, 1981).

[7] See the volume of essays published under the title, "Reconciliation and Liberation—The Confession of 1967," *Journal of Presbyterian History*, 61 (Spring, 1983).

[8] See Dieter T. Hessel, *Social Ministry*, Philadelphia: Westminster Press, 1982.

[9] See Max Stackhouse's analysis of the convenantal type of ecclesiology in *Ethics and the Urban Ethos*. Boston: Beacon, 1972, pp.160-162.

[10] Guy E. Swanson, "An Organizational Analysis of Collectivities," *American Sociological Review*, 36:9 (August, 1971), pp. 607-624.

[11] See "Covenant and Creation: Theological Reflections on Contraception and Abortion," New York and Atlanta: Office of the General Assembly, 1983.

[12] See the constructive and thorough proposal of Hessel, op.cit.

[13] See Robert K. Merton, *Social Theory and Social Structure*. Glencoe, IL: The Free Press, 1957.

[14] Presbyterian Church (U.S.A.), *Book of Order*, G-15.0101-0105.

[15] *Social Teachings of the Presbyterian Church, op. cit.*

[16] Ibid., 11.

[17] Ibid., 20.

[18] *Minutes of the General Assembly of the Presbyterian Church U.S.*, 1965, p. 160.

[19] *Social Teachings of the Presbyterian Church*, op.cit., p. 23.

[20] See study booklet with above title by Dana W. Wilbanks and Ronald H. Stone, New York: Advisory Council on Church and Society, 1985; also accompanying volume of essays, Ronald H. Stone and Dana W. Wilbanks, eds., *The Peacemaking Struggle: Militarism and Resistance*, Lanham, MK: University Press of America, 1985.

[21] Dieter Hessel, "Ethics and Social Ministry," *The Annual of the Society of Christian Ethics*. Vancouver: The Society of Christian Ethics, 1984, pp.45-48.

[22] Dean Hoge, *Division in the Protestant House*, Philadelphia: Westminster, 1977.

[23] Louis Weeks, "Faith and Political Action in American Presbyterianism, 1776-1918," Stone, op.cit., p. 104.

Bibliography

"Covenant and Creation: Theological Reflections on Contraception and Abortion," New York and Atlanta: Office of the General Assembly, 1983.

Geyer, Alan. "Reformed Faith and World Politics." In *Reformed Faith and Politics*, ed. by Ronald H. Stone. Washington, DC: University Press of America, 1983.

Hessel, Dieter. "Ethics and Social Ministry," *The Annual of the Society of Christian Ethics*. Vancouver: SCE, 1984, pp. 45-48.

Hessel, Dieter T. *Social Ministry*. Philadelphia: Westminster Press, 1982.

Hoge, Dean. *Division in the Protestant House*. Philadelphia: Westminster, 1977.

Merton, Robert K. *Social Theory and Social Structure*. Glencoe, IL: The Free Press, 1957.

Minutes of the General Assembly of the Presbyterian Church U.S.A., Atlanta: 1965.

Niebuhr, H. Richard. *Christ and Culture*. New York: Harper and Brothers, 1951.

Presbyterian Church (U.S.A.) *Book of Order*.

Presbyterian Church (U.S.A.) *Book of Confessions*.

"Presbyterian Understanding and Use of Holy Scripture." New York: General Assembly of the Presbyterian Church U.S.A., 1983.

"Presbyterians and Biblical Authority." *Journal of Presbyterian History*, 59 (Summer, 1981).

"Reconciliation and Liberation—The Confession of 1967." *Journal of Presbyterian History*, 61 (Spring, 1983).

"Social Teachings of the Presbyterian Church." *Church and Society* LXXV (Nov./Dec., 1984).

Stackhouse, Max. *Ethics and the Urban Ethos*. Boston: Beacon, 1972.

Stone, Ronald H. and Dana W. Wilbanks, eds. *The Peacemaking Struggle: Militarism and Resistance*. Lanham, MD: University Press of America, 1985.

Swanson, Guy E. "An Organizational Analysis of Collectivities." *American Sociological Review* 36:4 (Aug., 1971), pp. 607-624.
Weeks, Louis. *"Faith and Political Action in American Presbyterianism, 1776-1918."*
Wilbanks, Dana W. and Ronald H. Stone, *Presbyterians and Peacemaking: Are We Now Called to Resistance?* New York: Advisory Council on Church and Society, 1985.
The following issues of *Presbyterian Panel*:
> February, 1979: "Social Policy: Activities and Attitudes among United Presbyterians."
> January, 1980: "United Presbyterian Views on the Nature of Biblical Authority and the Use of Scripture."
> August, 1980: "United Presbyterian Attitudes Toward Racial Ethnic Ministries and Racial Justice Issues."
> January, 1982: "Panelists' Attitudes Toward Peace and Peacemaking."
> January, 1983: "Criminal Justice Concerns."
> September, 1984: "Peacemaking: Presbyterian Attitudes and Involvements in 1984."
> February, 1985: "Attitudes toward the Sanctuary Movement, War, Social Issues and Political Involvement of Pastors."

5

FAITH AND SOCIAL MINISTRY:
UNITED METHODISM

Philip A. Amerson and Earl D. C. Brewer

United Methodist Approach to Faith

Methodism began as an emphasis on personal faith based in rigorous behavioral disciplines. It emerges from the convergence of several religious traditions and social phenomena. John Wesley, Anglican priest and missionary, and founder of the movement, was deeply influenced by the piety of the Moravian tradition, the sacramental character of his own Anglican heritage and the emphasis on holy living found in the writings of William Law, Thomas A'Kempis and Jeremy Taylor.

Many consider the beginning point of the new church to be May 24, 1738. This is when Wesley "broke the faith barrier" in what has become known as his "heart warming experience at Aldersgate" (Wood, 1978: 67). There were certain patterns or "methods" for daily expression of faith which Wesley had sought to live by from the time he was a student at Oxford, hence the name "Methodist" was given to Wesley and his followers. The "Aldersgate Experience" added the personal, affective dimension to this disciplined lifestyle.

However, other crucial events are often overlooked "shaping moments" for early Methodism. Outler (1971) points to another "sign event" of Wesley's conversion — the embarrassing decision by Wesley on April 2, 1879 to do field preaching. Wesley describes this decision to preach in the open-air, among the lower classes, as a submission to "become more vile." His text? Luke 4: "the Spirit of the Lord is upon me to preach good news to the poor..."

As Methodism evolved from the 18th century pietism preached by British traveling evangelists and lay preachers in the fields surrounding the industrial cities to American circuit riders of the 19th century, it frequently changed its focus and audience but never its stress on personal faith. In Britain and America, Methodists emphasized a call to a holy life with participation in small groups known as "class meetings." From the beginning, there was a focus on personal piety; there also were other, more communal, understandings of faith. These are reflected in the social outreach emphases of the revival and in "tests for faith" which are known as the "Wesley Quadralateral" (c.f., Snyder, 1980).

It has been frequently conjectured that England was spared the violent equivalent of the French Revolution because of the ameliorating effects of the Wesleyan revival (c.f., Halvey, (1971). Others argue Methodism was a radical, even revolutionary, influence contributing to social change (c.f., Semmel, 1973, or Vincent, 1984). Was Methodism a cohort and contributor to radical societal change or a diversion, a "release valve" for the social and political pressures in which it emerged?

In North America, where Methodism appeared as a phenomenon emerging in remarkable congruency with the Revolutionary War and new nation state, what was the influence of Methodism? Radical or reactionary? And in the contemporary world, in the places of rapid Christian growth amid dramatic social change, what is the character and contribution of Methodism?

The Social Dimension

A clear sign of the social dimensions of early Methodism is found in its meeting places. They were located in densely populated, core-city poverty areas. Wesley admonished his preachers to go where there were those most in need. In 1739 Wesley took a building which was "bombed out" and turned it into the first Methodist chapel in London. (The building, a munitions factory, had been badly damaged in an accident forty years earlier.) Wesley and followers took this arms foundry and established in it a medical clinic, book room and preaching center.

Similarly, the New Room in Bristol and the orphanage in New Castle were centers for preaching, study and also for care of widows and orphans, literacy and food programs and clinics. The work that went on in the three cities of London, Bristol and New Castle are powerful symbols of the implicit social dimensions of the earliest history. Wesley kept a personal apartment in each of these three centers. A place of arms production, in the midst of urban poverty, was transformed into a center for healing and education. Other abandoned places ware transformed into places of child care, food distribution and social aid.

Certainly personal holiness (agentic or intrinsic faith) was the starting point for this "social ethic," but social it was indeed. "Christian Perfection" or in Wesley's words, "perfect love" was the ethical ideal which asserted "God's love once shed in our hearts overflows in our love for our neighbor." This notion of "perfection" was drawn directly from the writings of Law, A'Kempis and Taylor.

"Perfect love" involved relationship with someone other than oneself; it was always communal. This was the rationale behind the establishment of regular small group meetings known as "classes" or "bands." Class members were to learn to live in covenant with others in the group and act together in charity toward the prisoner, widow and impoverished. Acceptance of the teaching of holiness was to find expression in words and specific actions with regard to the neighbor.

From the beginning, the Wesleyan movement was with the poor. H. Richard Niebuhr (1957: 72) called Methodism "the last great religious revolution of the disinherited in Christendom." Many persons of rank and wealth found Wesley's theology and ministry scandalous. The notion that all persons were equally in need of salvation and that even the poorest might live "a holy life" created numerous conflicts for Wesley and the early Methodists. Yet, Methodism was never fully a "church shaped by the poor" and took a different polity and style from other earlier churches of the disinherited, such as the Quakers and Mennonites.

While headquartered among and focused toward the dispossessed, Methodism was never a church entirely led by the poor. Niebuhr (1957: 67) writes, Methodism "remained throughout its history in the control of men who had been born and bred in the middle class and who were impressed not so much by the social evils from which the poor suffered as by the vices to which they had succumbed...Wesley was more offended by blasphemous use of the name of God than by a blasphemous use of His Creatures."

Although a pietist, Wesley understood the social nature of human make-up. For him faith was always personal, but never private. He argued (1872: 321) "'Holy solitaries,' is a phrase no more consistent with the Gospel than holy adulterers. The Gospel of Christ knows of no religion, but social; no holiness but social holiness. 'Faith working by love' is the length and breadth and depth and height of Christian perfection."

Wesleyan General Rules and Quadrilateral

Theology and doctrinal reflection for Methodists are to be done in terms of free investigation and inquiry out of four main sources or guidelines. These four elements, known as the "Wesleyan Quadrilateral," are: scripture, tradition, experience and reason. The task of theologizing is said to be never ending, carried forth out of these four dimensions. This contrasts with the "tripartite," or three-fold (scripture, tradition and reason) basis for theological reflection taught by the Church of England. Methodism added the forth component, human experience. Of course, this experience is both personal and social. In this way Methodism played a central role in introducing ethical and experiential elements into the Protestant views of the 19th and 20th centuries.

Wesley charged the society members not to separate faith from good works. He therefore gave 'directions' or 'rules' to the leaders. Ethics and emotion were linked. The primary instructional volume for Methodists is not a catechism, creed, pastoral letter or institute but *The Book of Discipline*. This book contains the polity, articles of religion, creeds and "the rules."

Noteworthy among these rules is a pamphlet published in 1743, "The Nature, Design and General Rules of the United Societies." Faith is understood as more affective than doctrinal. Catechisms, creeds and articles of religion were not touchstones of this movement.

Wesley took the 39 Articles of Religion of Anglicanism and reduced them to twenty-one. These articles were placed in the historical section of the "Discipline" and then rarely appealed to by church leadership or laity. Piety and experiential faith were more central among "Wesleyans." Society members were expected to pray together, hear exhortation, watch over each other in love so that they might help each other to "work out their salvation" (p. 67).

At a gathering of "Anglican Methodists" in 1744, the role of Methodism was identified as "To reform the nation, particularly the church", and to spread scriptural holiness. The organization was seen as a reform movement within the Church of England. In this "working out of salvation" with a delineated rule or guidelines, the social activism of Methodism is most apparent. It is also the point where some have judged Methodism to be a new form of Pelagianism, meaning that believers may think salvation depends on a "works righteousness."

Based on this rule, "Methodists in every age sought to exercise responsibility for the moral and spiritual quality of society." *The Book of Discipline notes*, "Our historic opposition to evils such as smuggling, inhumane prison conditions, or slavery, drunkenness, and child labor was founded upon a vivid sense of God's wrath against human injustice and wastage. Our struggles for human dignity and social reform have been a response to God's demand for love, mercy, and justice, in the light of the kingdom. We proclaim no 'personal gospel' that fails to express itself in relevant social concerns; we proclaim no 'social gospel' that does not include the personal transformation of sinners. It is our conviction that the good news of the Kingdom must judge, redeem and reform the sinful structures of our time." (p. 49.)

Activism, humanism and greater empiricism were all products of this Methodist "faith-style." And so while Wesleyan practice and preaching was steeped in pietism, Methodism moved naturally and almost inevitably toward the social gospel tradition of the late 19th and early 20th centuries. The Methodist approach to faith, then, is one which historically was centered in deep personal piety and behavioral disciplines — the experience of the heart and the experience of the street. This piety and discipline was believed to inevitably result in concern for social justice, for the work of God's new realm on earth.

Modern Faith Approaches

Jameson Jones (1984:125) suggests the contemporary "United Methodist Church is a great circus tent, with all sorts of sideshows going on underneath and around it." Jones asserts that the sideshows have diverted the crowd's attention from the main events.

Membership for the denomination peaked at over twelve million members in the United States in 1968. This was the time of merger between the Methodist and Evangelical United Brethren Churches. In recent years membership has declined to 8,944,000 (1989) and United Methodists have taken second place in denominational membership to the still growing Southern Baptist Convention. For more than a century, Methodism had been the largest of the Protestant denominational families with more local congregations than U. S. post offices. Methodism was the most ubiquitous and diverse of the Protestant groups. This characteristic has proven to be both a great strength and a weakness.

Methodism from its origins was a diverse, almost paradoxical, phenomenon as compared with other religious movements. It had elements which were "sectlike" and other dimensions which were clearly "church." It was evangelical in spirit, yet catholic; personal, yet communal. Thus Methodism was the ideal seedbed for a denomination with "many sideshows" or as United Methodists often describe themselves, a "pluralistic church."

The continuing decline in membership has resulted in several critiques of the denomination (e.g., Wilke, 1986; Willimon and Wilson, 1987). There are any number of new programs in "evangelism," "church growth" and "planting new churches," and "congregational redevelopment." The 1984 General Conference of the church set a membership goal of twenty million by the turn of the next century. Most annual conferences have developed specific programs which seek to reverse the pattern of declining membership. Despite these efforts and goals, membership losses continue and were approximately 70,000 for 1987 and 1988 (*Newscope*, June 30, 1989).

Three factors (two demographic and thus more easily measured, and a third, more cultural and evolutionary) appear as cohorts of this decline. First, a high percentage of United Methodist congregations are located in regions such as the Midwestern "rustbelt" which have experienced dramatic decline in total population. Second, United Methodists have failed to hold onto their children as adult members with the same success as the more Fundamentalist, pentecostal or evangelical groups.

A final corollary of the decline is seen in the very pluralism and openness which is celebrated by United Methodism. United Methodism has not appealed to many people in the decades of the 1970s or 1980s when personal faith choices appeared to rest at one end or the other of the extremes of increasing secularity or doctrines of certainty. In terms of numerical growth and societal appeal, at least, the recent openness and lack of strictness or doctrinal certainty found many United Methodist congregations in the "wrong place at the wrong time with the wrong message." (See: Roof and McKinney, 1987; Wuthnow, 1988).

The United Methodist Approach
to Social Ministry

Clearly the Methodist approach to social ministry is not simply individualistic. Organized activities of charity were found in the earliest stages of the movement. In the early years, these tended to stress sharing or acts of mercy rather than justice or endeavors which sought change. Today the various boards and agencies of the church are aware of the importance of development and social advocacy efforts which may accompany expressions of mercy. The United Methodist Committee of Relief is an example of an agency with this new breadth of understanding. While UMCOR provides emergency assistance, it is also involved in development and justice activities such as resettlement efforts for Central American immigrants, to the dismay of politically conservative groups within the church.

Contemporary United Methodist leaders have been involved actively in the conciliar movement of the Christian church. The attendant justice activities of ecumenical organizations such as the World Council of Churches have created problems of interpretation among conservative constituents. The *Reader's Digest* published articles in the early 1970s suggesting linkages among World Council of Churches member denominations, including Methodism, and "Communist terrorist" organizations (c.f., Hall, 1971).

A more recent example of such "press investigations" is the 1983 interview on CBS Television's "60 Minutes" with United Methodist Bishop James Armstrong, who was serving as the president of the National Council of Churches of Christ ("The Gospel According to Whom?", January 23, 1983). Interestingly, this television inquiry followed the second series of articles questioning the radical tendencies of United Methodism in *The Readers Digest* in the fall of 1982.

From the 1784 Christmas Conference in Baltimore, the founding conference of American Methodism, it was agreed God's purpose in raising up the people called Methodists was "to reform the continent and spread scriptural holiness over these lands." The words "particularly the church" in the 1744 rationale of the Anglican reformation have been dropped from the American version. Circuit riders crossing the North American frontier had a much different ministry from that undertaken in the slums of London, Bristol or New Castle or from the field preaching in mining or newly industrialized communities. The tackling of national social justice issues is not a new phenomenon for Methodism, no matter the suggestions of the current popular press.

American Methodism became linked to the experience of the frontier, and, then, the new nation state. In these New World beginnings, Methodism struggled with the social dimensions of faith. A predominant concern was still personal piety, but there were new issues pressing on the church, matters of patriotism, military service, church state relations and, of course, slavery.

The 1780 General Conference judged slavery as "contrary to the laws of God, man, and nature, and hurtful to society; contrary to the dictates of conscience and pure religion." Following the American revolution, however, Methodism spread through the "slave states." This led inevitably to conflict within the new American denomination. Divisions surfaced in 1844 when Orange Scott petitioned the General Conference to bring a resolution against slavery. Debate ended with the denomination divided, North and South. Daniel Webster, upon hearing of this schism, is said to have wondered how much longer it would be until the new nation was similarly rent apart. Like it or not, Methodism in America has been caught up in the great social justice struggles of the continent.

As in England, the church established institutions of charity and education, but the destiny of this church was closely interlocked into the destiny of the new nation state— even to the point of serving as a forum or more ominously, a harbinger, of future national events. Early circuit riders, who moved behind, along with, and, at times, even ahead of the settlers, farmers, trappers, merchants and hunters, proclaimed a personal faith, but it was increasingly linked with the social issues of the time.

Methodist figures were active thereafter in the great social struggles of the 19th century: slavery, suffrage, peace, child labor, and alcohol abuse. This ethical opposition was reinforced by a personal pietism, but increasingly there were new commitments to social structural change. By the beginning of the twentieth century, leading figures in the Methodist Church in America were involved in the "social gospel movement." Although the resultant "modernist/ fundamentalist controversy" has never been completely resolved, socio-economic understandings of Christian action were accepted by many lay and clergy leaders within the church.

Emphasis on social and political renewal was expressed by the denomination's "Social Creed". The first such creed was approved by the northern church in 1908. At this conference, a major part of the Episcopal address was devoted to "liquor traffic, child labor, international peace, working men, immigration and labor unions" (Piepkorn, 1978: 582). United Brethren accepted a similar document in 1913; by 1914, Southern Methodism adopted the creed; and in 1916, the Methodist Protestant Church followed (Piepkorn, 1978: 582). This creed was revised at the 1939 Uniting Conference of the northern and southern branches of the church.

Methodism, except for infrequent waves of concern for international peace and support for the conscientious objector, has been a highly nationalistic church. During the civil rights period of the late 1960s and early 1970s, Methodist churches were involved at least as actively as other mainline denominations in the pursuit of racial justice.

Since the General Conference of 1968, the first of the new United Methodist Church, there has been published *The Book of Resolutions* which contains resolutions "approved by the General Conference" which "state the policy of the United Methodist Church on some of the current social issues and concerns" (*The Book of Resolutions*, p. 5). By 1984, it contained 145 resolutions on topics ranging from the use of alcohol and drugs to school busing to collective bargaining to gun control to the Christian family, global racism, human sexuality, and resolution on events in such nations as Afghanistan, El Salvador, South Africa, Korea, and the Philippines.

What does this signify? It appears the denomination is both conserving and radical at once. It seems to carry the seeds of commitment to both the status quo and support for radical social change. Is Methodism a denomination suffering from schizophrenia or do we miss some other dimension?

The Relationship between Faith and Social Ministry

The most comprehensive contemporary investigation of United Methodists and social issues was conducted by the General Council on Ministries and reported in the book *Continuation or Transformation* by Earl D. C. Brewer (Abingdon, 1982). The volume reports on the survey of 1,273 local, regional and national church leaders which measured the extent to which persons agreed with the various social positions espoused by the United Methodist Church.

Twenty-five statements about social issues were tested in 1980 samples of local laity and pastors and by connectional leaders (bishops, district superintendents, and general board staffs and members). Overall agreement ranged from a high of 95 percent for "Favor the elimination of personal and institutional racism" to a low of 45.4 percent for "Favor a guaranteed annual income which permits each person to live with dignity." On most social issues, the local church leaders (laity and clergy) were more conservative than connectional leaders. Bishops and theological school faculty were among the most liberal on most issues.

Methodists were stronger in verbal support of social concerns than in a willingness to take appropriate actions to work toward the resolution of issues. The most frequently mentioned strategy for dealing with a social concern was for the elderly and persons with handicapping conditions to "modify church and other buildings for easy access for the elderly and persons with handicapping conditions." The least popular social strategy was to "practice civil disobedience in the social witness of the Christian faith."

There was a remarkable shift among laity from 1958 to 1980 regarding the chief aim of mission for the church. In response to the statement that the aim of mission was "to release in both individuals and society the redemptive power of God disclosed in Jesus Christ, so that all human life may be made whole," in 1958, 23.8 percent of the laity voted for this and in 1980, support for this had increased to 53.9 percent. (Eighty-one percent of the clergy in 1980 favored this aim.)

There also was a dramatic change in the belief in equal rights for women. In 1958, 34.1 percent of the laity affirmed equal rights, this doubled to 68.6 percent by 1980. Three fourths of the clergy in 1980 agreed. The statement "social change is of equal importance with individual transformation was approved by 25.5 percent of the laity in 1958 and by 34.0 percent in 1980." Two thirds of the clergy in 1980 favored this view. In terms of self identification of theological position, 60.6 percent of the total group claimed to be moderates, 17.6 percent liberal, 15.4 percent conservative, and 1.9 percent fundamental.

So what is the identity of North American Methodism? It is moderate, "middle of the road," yet with significant percentages of liberals and conservatives. It is changing. Moving, perhaps through a cycle toward an increasing linkage between faith and social justice. One sees such patterns in the history of the church — at the time of the Revolutionary War, just prior to the Civil War, and during the progressive era of the early 20th century. What is seen today is the manifestation of a breadth, a pluralism which nurtures both personal and social faith perspectives and sees institutional manifestations which are both radical and reactionary. The emphasis shifts but the duality of this faith pattern continues.

The Conditions Effecting the Nurture of Faith and the Promotion of Social Ministry

There have been obvious recent shifts in the self-perception of United Methodists and in their view of mission. The data from the research cited above is but one of many indicators of this shift toward a greater openness to social ministry and an expanded vision of faith as social as well as personal. Conditions which affect United Methodism's ability to nurture faith and promote social ministry are many.

United Methodism in the United States

We have noted the uniquely national character of American Methodism; certainly the parochial quality of this nationalism will be challenged by increasing awareness of global realities. While the percentage of persons who identify their religious preference as "Methodist" has dropped in national surveys (from 14 percent in 1967 to 7 percent in 1984, Gallup, 1985: 27), United Methodism remains a nationally distributed membership. And, while the membership is predominantly white, middle income, and more heavily concentrated in the southern and midwestern states, it is, none-the-less one of the more racially and culturally diverse of the mainline Protestant groups. The most rapidly growing sector of the denomination is among ethnic minority congregations.

United Methodism, along with several of the other mainline groups may play a particularly important role as a "post colonial church" in a "post colonial America." As U.S. dominance is diminished around the world, the denomination may help in discovering new identities based less on dominance and superordinance and more on mutuality. Many of the congregations are older: the members, the buildings and parish locations. A high percentage are in rural and inner city locations and have seen the composition of membership of past generations change dramatically. The new populations, often immigrants from around the world, now surround the church, and in many cases are becoming new participants. They provide both a threat to past traditions and an opportunity for future congregational life.

World Methodism and World Issues

A recent study of World Methodism deals with diverse views of global issues and social ministries (Brewer and Jackson, 1987). There are nearly 300 Methodist-related denominations around the world with a reported membership of 25.1 million persons.

A survey of opinions yielded a total of 2,466 responses from world Methodists. These were located in all major regions of the world: Africa, 237; North America, 632, Latin America, 279; Asia, 535; Europe, 739 and the Pacific, 44. Lay persons accounted for 1,382 respondents and clergy 1,084. By gender, 813 were women and 1,653 were men. By age, 145 were under 20 years of age, 986 were between 20 and 40, 889 were between 40 and 60, and 446 were 60 years of age or older. By type of community in which the respondents lived, 1,441 lived in urban areas and 1,025 lived in rural settings. By leadership position, 1,539 were leaders in local congregations and 752 were in the positions of denominational leadership. Some claimed no leadership position.

Six church and world issues and six church strategies for dealing with them were developed into a questionnaire which was distributed through denominational leaders. The questionnaires were translated into several languages. The responses do not constitute a sample of world Methodist people. They are the opinions of those who responded. They are interesting in terms of the ways the Methodist traditions have worked themselves out in contemporary Methodism on a worldwide level.

Table 1 shows the average rankings of all respondents or the issues and strategies. The highest ranking issue related to religion and dealt with the lack of belief in God. The others, in order of importance, dealt with poverty and starvation, discrimination, lack of a sense of holiness, war and peace, and the misuse of the earth's resources.

The church strategies for dealing with these issues were proclamation of God's love, stewardship of earth and resources, work for a world without oppression, join the poor, join with others in struggles for peace and relate the Wesleyan tradition of reformation and holiness to present-day conditions. These opinions may be seen in relation to the characteristics of the respondents and in relation to Wesleyan traditions.

Table I

Average rankings of importance for church and world issues and church strategies by 2,466 respondents, world Methodism and world issues study, 1986.

Item	Average Ranking of Importance
Church and World Issues	
1) Lack of belief in God as sustainer of daily life	4.57
2) Starvation and poverty	3.97
3) Discrimination, exploitation or oppression based on race, sex, age, economic class, religion, ethnic or national rights	3.30
4) Lack of a sense of holiness	3.23

Item	Average Ranking of Importance
5) Wars and arms races (conventional and nuclear)	3.10
6) Misuse of earth's resources	2.82
Church Strategies	
1) Proclaim God's love in Jesus Christ to all people, with invitations to become disciples	4.52
2) Develop stewardship beliefs and practices which care for God's holy earth, feed the hungry, and share earth's resources with all people everywhere	3.80
3) Work for a world without discrimination, exploitation, and oppression	3.33
4) Join the poor in struggles for survival and or economic and social justice	3.18
5) Join with others in urging all nations to move toward peace	3.17
6) Through study and action, relate an historic Wesleyan tradition of reformation and scriptural holiness to present-day conditions	3.02

[1]Rankings on a 1-6 scale. The higher the number, the higher the importance.

In this context United Methodists have established a tradition of links between personal and social concerns. This is seen in a breadth of perspective and involvement among Methodists and an openness to innovative efforts at theologizing and concrete acts of witness. Again the place of human experience is honored. The 1984 *Book of Discipline*, in the section "Our Theological Task," includes the following paragraphs:

Theological reflections do change as Christians become aware of new issues and crises. The Church's role in this tenuous process is to provide a stable and sustaining environment in which theological conflict can be constructive and productive. Our heritage and guidelines support this position. United Methodism in doctrinal lockstep is unthinkable...

Of crucial current importance is the surfacing of new
theological emphases focusing on the great struggles for
human liberation and fulfillment. Notable among them
are black theology, feminist theology, political and ethnic
theologies, third-world theology, and theologies of human rights. In each case, they express the heart cries that
dehumanization has produced. They are theologies born
of conflict. They reflect the consequences of tragic victimi-
zation and deep natural yearnings for human fulfillment.
More positively, they agree in their demands for human
dignity, true liberty, and genuine community (p. 82).

Thus a "method" for approaching faith during the rapid changes
occurring among the working classes of the industrial revolution
now survives to the time of the technological revolution and the time
when new peoples are expressing their place in the global order.
There appear to be new "Methodist" ways of proceeding: evangelical, yet catholic; personal, yet communal; conservative, yet radical.
Such is the anomaly of Methodism, such is the character of a
contemporary "mainline" denomination. At once it appears to
reinforce the dominant social order and at the same moment call it
into question. It is perhaps in this "post-colonial world" that this
puzzling, strange mixture will serve as the seedbed for new expressions of faith which honor the personal and the social, the revolutionary and the existential. One waits to see.

Thus, world Methodists, especially those in North America, are
still trying to work out their faith in relation to crucial social issues.
At times this is clearly precipitative of social change, at times this is
profoundly conserving of existing social order. Perhaps, this Methodist pattern of faith and social concern was best expressed in
questions and answers form in the first Methodist Conference in
1744. (Minutes of the Methodist Conference, 1744. Volume I, p.3.)

Question: What may we reasonably believe to be God's
design, in raising up preachers, called Methodists?

Answer: To reform the nation, more particularly the
church; to spread scriptural holiness over the land.

Bibliography

Baker, Frank. *John Wesley and the Church of England.* Nashville: Abingdon, 1970.

Brewer, Earl, D. C. *Continuation or Transformation.* Nashville: Abingdon, 1982.

Brewer, E. and Jackson, M. *Wesleyan Transformations.* Atlanta: S.T.C. Press, 1987.

The Book of Discipline of the United Methodist Church. Nashville: United Methodist Publishing House, 1984 and 1988.

The Book of Resolutions of the United Methodist Church. Nashville: United Methodist Publishing House, 1984.

C.B.S. 60 Minutes, "The Gospel According to Whom?" with Bishop James Armstrong, January 23, 1983.

Gallup, George, Jr. *Religion in America: 1985.* Princeton: Princeton Religious Research Center, 1985.

Genovese, Eugene. *Roll, Jordan, Roll.* New York, Pantheon, 1987.

Halvey, Elie. *The Birth of Methodism.* Chicago: University of Chicago Press, 1971.

Hall, C. W. "Must Our Churches Finance Revolution?" *The Readers Digest,* 99:95-100, October 1971.

Jones, Jameson. "United Methodism: A Cautious Mood" in *Where the Spirit Leads.* New York: Seabury, 1984.

Newscope, (National Weekly Newsletter for United Methodist Leaders). Nashville: The United Methodist Publishing House.

Niebuhr, H. Richard. *The Social Sources of Denominationalism.* New York: Meridian, 1957.

Miller, James F. *A Study of United Methodists and Social Issues.* Dayton, Ohio: United Methodist Church, 1983.

Outler, Albert. *Evangelism in the Wesleyan Spirit.* Nashville: Tidings, 1971.

Piepkorn, A. *Profiles in Belief, Volume II.* New York: Harper and Row, 1978.

Roof, Wade Clark and William McKinney. *American Mainline Religion.* New Brunswick: Rutgers University Press, 1987.

Runyon, Theodore. *Sanctification and Liberation.* Nashville: Abingdon, 1981.

Semmel, Bernard. *The Methodist Revolution.* New York: Basic Books, 1973.

Snyder, Howard. *The Radical Wesley.* Downers Grove, Illinois: Inter-Varsity, 1980.

Vincent, John. *Christ and Methodism: Towards a New Christianity for a New Age.* Nashville: Abingdon, 1965.

Vincent, John. *O.K., Let's Be Methodist.* Epworth Press: London, 1984.

Wesley, John. *The Works of the Rev. John Wesley.* Thomas Jackson, ed. London: Wesleyan Conference Office, 1872.

Wilke, Richard. *And Are We Yet Alive?* Nashville: Abingdon, 1986.

Willimon, William and Robert Wilson. *Rekindling the Flame.* Nashville: Abingdon, 1987.

Wood, A. Skevington. *The Burning Heart.* Minneapolis: Paternoster Press, 1978.

Wuthnow, Fobert. *The Restructuring of American Religion.* Princeton University Press, 1988.

6

FAITH AND SOCIAL MINISTRY:
IN AMERICAN LUTHERANISM

Ross P. Scherer

Historical Introduction

Lutherans have been a part of the United States since the middle of the 18th century, coming first to the states of New York and Pennsylvania. Lutherans came in force during the great German migrations of the mid-19th century settling in the East and the North Central regions. By the beginning of 1987, Lutheran church members in the United States numbered approximately eight and a half million, making them the fourth largest American denominational family after the Roman Catholic Church, various Baptist groups, and Methodists. As recently as the time of World War I, roughly three generations ago, Lutherans were divided into more than a dozen separate bodies, mainly along ethnic lines. But by 1988 about 99 percent of America's Lutherans became included in just three separate religious bodies—about 63 percent have been combined into the new Evangelical Lutheran Church in America (ELCA) as of January, 1988; 31 percent are in the Lutheran Church—Missouri Synod

(LCMS); and about 5 percent are in the Wisconsin Evangelical Lutheran Synod (WELS). The remaining 1 percent are distributed among 14 other tiny groups (Lutheran Council in the U.S.A. statistics, cited in the LCMS Reporter, November 3, 1986, p. 4).

The recent history of American Lutheranism has been dominated by two events: the schism in the 1970s within the LCMS and the founding of the ELCA beginning January 1, 1988. At its formation, the ELCA membership totaled about 5,342,000, being a merger of the former Lutheran Church in America (LCA—with membership in 1987 of about 2,900,000), the former American Lutheran Church (ALC—in 1987 about 2,332,000), and the former Association of Evangelical Lutheran Churches (AELC—in 1987 about 112,000).

Thorkelson (1978: 9) considers the LCA to have been the most Americanized, urban, ecumenical, and socially conscious of all the Lutheran bodies. While originally somewhat decentralized and tinged with pietism, under the leadership of the late Franklin Clark Fry, and subsequently Robert Marshall and James Crumley, the LCA became more centralized and committed to social justice and to becoming a bridge between American Catholicism and the other Protestant bodies in America. The ALC has been a solid, moderate combination of German and Norwegian groups located in the upper Midwest with the Norwegian elements seemingly leading. In the three decades of its existence, the ALC moved from pietism and toward serious grappling with issues of public policy. The AELC represented a serious brain drain of the most creative, ecumenical, and liturgically conscious circles from the Missouri Synod. When it found itself being pushed out of the LCMS in the mid-1970s, it made its mission to be the catalyst for a merger of the ALC, the LCA, and itself, and it has succeeded.

The LCMS continues as the oldest of the organizationally extant Lutheran bodies, being formed in 1847 in the Midwest out of evangelizing missionaries from Germany and elements of the Saxon migration (undertaken as a reaction to the alleged theological liberalism of the early 19th-century German territorial church).

Benne (1983: 171-173), has made an interesting comparison of the church polities of the LCA, ALC, and LCMS. He writes that the LCA at one time was organized along "federalist-pluralist" lines, with strong identification with the regional synods simultaneous with strong leadership by the national church's central program boards.

The ALC, on the other hand, was characterized by a "centralized-mass" structure with weak regional units (districts) and a measure of populism. The LCMS has operated with a "traditional-communal" structure based upon familial-ethnic solidarity, strong theological consensus, and rational organizational practicality. The LCMS' gemeinschaft-type solidarity allowed a great deal of regional district autonomy and local circuit vitality (among a district's dozen or so congregations). LCMS practicality has also been evident in its widely known encouragement of the development of voluntary parade-nominational associations in education, youth work, and social action (see below). Viewing their recent histories, one might hypothesize that the LCA and ALC, having undergone two previous mergers each in the last 60 years, have possibly been forced to become more rationalized in self-understanding, social outlook, and church organization over the years. The formation of the ELCA will probably further accelerate this process.

The Wisconsin Synod, while originally somewhat moderate, has become the most conservative Lutheran body. It was formed in 1917 by merger of three smaller, upper midwestern synods. The WELS was for many decades in formal (but not really very operative) fellowship with the Missouri Synod, suspending this relationship in 1961 as the LCMS began to moderate and develop closer ties to the other Lutheran bodies (Thorkelson, 1978: 51-55).

Contemporary American Lutheranism thus boils down to the "big two": the newly formed, moderate-conservative Evangelical Lutheran Church in America and the smaller and more conservative Lutheran Church—Missouri Synod. On the side stands the sizeable but small and ultra-conservative Wisconsin Synod.

How Lutherans Understand "Faith"

Because the Lutheran bodies differ in some specific emphases in their understanding of faith, it will be necessary for us to describe the Lutheran understanding in terms of a single ideal-type model. Despite the fact that Lutherans share many theological elements with other Christians, an ideal-type presentation will undoubtedly highlight many aspects in which Lutheran emphases are different. Another point—structure. We shall assume that modern denominations are "open systems," which means that they are generally in frequent if

"open systems," which means that they are generally in frequent if not constant interaction with their surrounding environments, cultural and sociopolitical. The degree and timing of such openness, of course, varies with internal attitudes and also external events.

As heirs of the vanguard of Reformation "protestants," modern Lutherans share much of their faith with Roman Catholics (their mother church), as well with their co-reforming Protestants. Also because of the exigencies of carrying out and practicing that faith in non-established, pluralistic America, Lutherans also share many similarities in ecclesiastical practice with their other fellow Americanized religious bodies. In the U.S.A., Lutheran groups adhere to the same Lutheran confessions, including the major Augsburg Confession. The ELCA differs from the Missouri Synod mainly in its avoiding the major shibboleth of "inerrancy" to describe its view of the Bible's accuracy, preferring to term the Bible "the written Word of God" and "inspired by God's Spirit..."; and also in certain areas of policy and practice (e.g., the ordination of women [which it practices] and ecumenical relations and memberships [which it cautiously favors]).

Since their 16th-century origins, Lutherans have put a lot of emphasis upon theological formulation and have seen themselves as a "confessional" church, which to some extent sets them off from other denominational traditions. On the other hand, in theory at least, they have been pragmatic with regard to religious organization (polity) and ministry. The earliest Lutherans saw themselves as a confessing movement within the universal church, and contemporary Lutherans (in the ELCA) are again reexamining this self-image within the present ecumenical age. While theological conservatives tend to limit such "confessing" only to doctrinal formulations, political liberals direct their confessional protesting toward the public realm and civil authority if need be. As Troeltsch has pointed out, Lutheranism was derived from a "church"-type (monopoly establishment) in Europe, which has set limits to the kinds of accommodations it has been willing to make with American pluralism.

The reformer Martin Luther developed his idea of "faith" as a reaction to the lack of spiritual consolation he experienced in his mother Catholic Church. In his soul, Luther could never feel really forgiven via the Catholic system of sacraments and penances. Luther's concept of faith developed as a relationship of trust and a concern over the state of "sin," rather than "sins." His discovery of "justification by faith alone—without works" in the New Testament book of Romans later became unfortunately adulterated, by some Lutherans, into "justification by belief." In Luther's formula, faith became a trusting relationship to God established by the suffering, death, and resurrection of Jesus Christ and implemented by the inspiration of the Holy Spirit. Faith thereby is not just an intellectual apprehension but a life of total commitment. Faith includes belief in the unworthiness of one's own efforts and yet the possibility of divine acceptance of self through the work of Christ. Luther in his own life provided his followers a model of faith as a struggle.

The watchwords of the Reformation became Faith Alone, Grace Alone, Scripture Alone. One could not earn salvation by works, but works were expected to follow. The ideal is a faith-active-in-love. As an Augustinian monk, Luther was anti-Pelagian (i.e., man had no inherent worthiness); and also anti-infused grace (i.e., man could not merit salvation even via divinely inspired works). His theology leaned heavily upon St. Paul. Luther was at home with mystery and paradox; he fought hard to activate the "presence of God" among the faithful. He elevated the "theology of the cross" with its positive value of suffering over a "theology of glory."

Another distinction. Lutheran theology has traditionally put a strong emphasis on the tension between what it calls Law and Gospel. The Law condemns and kills, while the Gospel—the Good News of forgiveness in Christ—gives life. In the Missouri Synod all children going through the process of confirmation, from about 1900 until 1950, were taught that the "three functions of the Law" were as a curb, a mirror, and a rule (Missouri Synod President Henry Schwan's *A Short Explanation of Luther's Small Catechism—LCMS*, 1943: 85-86). Perhaps an unintended side-effect of emphasizing the terrors of the Law (in order to make one mindful of sin and so receptive toward forgiveness) was to make one overly pessimistic about trying to change society so as to become more kind or just.

Troeltsch (1911/1960: 515-576) alleged that Martin Luther had "spiritualized" the idea of the church in a utopian way, allowing it to become subjected to the state. Troeltsch held that Luther actually propounded a dualistic understanding of Christian ethics whereby the individual Christian was held to the highest standards of Christ's Sermon on the Mount, while the state and other social institutions were allowed to function according to realistic needs of the human situation. Luther, in fact, envisioned many intersections between the church and the world so that, in his own mind, social justice would necessarily flow from faith. Troeltsch was bothered by the fact that, to him, German Lutheranism had become too quietistic and politically passive in the centuries after Luther, and Troeltsch abandoned any hope of reversal. Contemporary Lutheran ethicists, however, are reiterating Luther's idea of faith-as-struggle and are reexamining the Augsburg Confession, especially its Article XVI which deals with church and state. Strieter, for example (1986), has examined several critical incidents in recent Lutheran church history where church leaders and members felt compelled to dissent from both political and ecclesiastical authorities—the Barmen Declaration adopted by members of the German confessing church against Hitler; Dietrich Bonhoeffer's life of protest against the Nazis; the protest by moderates within the LCMS against its conservative administration in the 1970s and the subsequent walkout by the faculty and student body of Concordia Seminary—St.Louis (Seminex); and the recent Denominational Ministry Strategy controversy within the LCA (Long, 1985 and 1987—see below). Richard Niebuhr in his classic *Christ and Culture* characterized Luther's outlook as "Christ and culture in tension" (1951: 149-189), a characterization which many Lutherans would term apt.

The Reformation Experience As Backdrop for Lutheran Social Ministry

The central Lutheran theological-ethical problem for defining the relationship of the Christian to society has been the so-called "doctrine of the two kingdoms," which originated as an improvisation in the 16th century but did not become institutionalized until the 18th. The problem concerns the relations of the church to the state and the concepts of compliance employed. Ideally, within the church the persuasive Word of God was to be employed; whereas in society, the coercion of law had to be the ultimate norm for the state. Luther insisted, while the territorial authorities had to provide a political umbrella for the reformers and the new evangelical movement, the state was not to interfere in specifically religious affairs. While Luther himself was not afraid to talk back to rulers and princes in his day—to "speak truth to power"—his less prophetic successors were more fearful before late medieval and early modern authority figures. Thus, the Lutheran preoccupation with the core of faith may have resulted in a too casual underappreciation of the complexities of church order and the problems of applying the faith to everyday decisions within social institutions and to the quest for social justice in general. Only since World War II have American Lutherans begun to address the role of the church in "social action" in any significant way.

As noted, Troeltsch (1911/1960: 515-576) criticized what he regarded as the abdication of the early 20th-century German church from responsibility over against the public realm. He held that the reformers unfortunately accepted the existing political arrangements as "given" in alleged "natural orders of creation." That is, while the Lutheran reformers must be credited with having made big breakthroughs in the core of faith, they neglected to see the need for checks and balances within a late medieval political system which was basically undemocratic and authoritarian.

Historically, the Lutheran concept of ministry leaned to emphases upon preaching the Word of God, administering the sacraments, and the personal "cure of souls." While Luther tried to make everyone into a "universal priest," much of the church work over time became delegated to the professional pastors. In the latter 17th and early 18th centuries, in reaction to the sterility of Lutheran orthodoxy after Luther, Philip Spener and August Francke created a movement known as pietism which infused emotion into the life of faith, stressed discipline in the practice of Christian love, and established institutional programs for the expression of mercy via medical care, economic support, and social service (termed "inner missions"). Francke founded a virtual Lutheran "Boys' Town" in Halle, Germany (Kuenning, 1987: 21). The voluntary nature of these programs of mercy was to have its real payoff in Lutheranism within the voluntary culture of the New World in the second half of the 19th century.

The Relationship of Faith and Social Ministry

As stated earlier, the traditional Lutheran position has been that the human person is not saved by works, but works are expected to follow as fruit of faith and forgiveness by Almighty God. The relationship between faith and social ministry, therefore, is dialectical. While European Lutheranism initiated the whole movement of works of mercy, American Lutherans became even more active in these services, aided and abetted perhaps by the American "voluntarization" of religion. The first concern of these American Lutherans on the 19th-century frontier was social service for their own kind. While the ascetic, anti-pleasure aspects of pietism were fairly widespread, although not among German-background Lutherans, all Lutheran groups became involved in the "works of mercy" aspect.

After the Civil War, American Lutherans became very active setting up paraparochial homes for children and old people, hospitals, and later on foster care and adoptive services (Lueking, 1968, for the history of welfare in the LCMS). Today both the new Lutheran Church and the Missouri Synod sponsor vast networks of health and welfare institutions which minister not just to Lutherans but to persons of all faiths. The ELCA (see Constitution, chapter 16) is structured to operate by means of six major program divisions: congregational life, education, global mission, ministry, outreach, and social ministry organizations. In addition, among the supportive commissions are important Commissions for Church in Society, for Women, and for Multicultural Ministries. (The Division for Social Ministry Organizations was originally listed as being allocated eleven full-time positions plus fourteen support staff; and the Commission for Church and Society about the same staff number— ELCA, Report and Recommendations, p. xxi). Bloomquist has commented on the widespread permeation of the ELCA staff structure and program with social emphases and the attendant difficulty of identifying the exact numbers of staff involved with social policy and programs.

More recently, local and national Lutheran agencies (hospitals, social service agencies) have been moving into providing centers for rehabilitation of alcoholics and drug addicts, family counseling, world relief of famine (Lutheran World Relief), immigration and resettlement, and transnational adoptions. As "service" agencies, the above ministries tend mainly to be remedial and to leave structures as they are.

Old Lutheranism tended to view government primarily as a check upon evil and not enough as a force for positive good. It also tended to view social problems as caused primarily by individual sins, and the solutions likewise were thought to be individual. Contemporary Lutheranism is more positive about the necessary role of the state in bringing about a more just social order. While there are theo-

state in bringing about a more just social order. While there are theological disagreements about the appropriateness of the third use of the Law (as a rule) for individual Christians, American Lutheran church bodies in the last 20 years have given much attention to formulating and issuing "Social Statements" on social issues of public importance. In relation to ethnic exclusiveness, the ELCA in particular in its formation has made conscious efforts to expand its membership beyond its basic German and Scandinavian-background core. In addition, official as well as unofficial agency representatives have become engaged in public lobbying and sociopolitical action with state and federal government officials. Stimulation for the development of such public pronouncements has come from staff members of Lutheran agencies in the field, as well as from a new breed of theologians and social ethicists in Lutheran seminaries and full-time staff persons in denominational offices for church-in-society questions. As noted, the ELCA has structured an entire unit, the Commission for Church in Society, for the development of policies toward social issues.

Sherman (1984) raises some strategic questions concerning the issuance of such statements and opines that their issuance may be a sign of American Lutheranism's finally coming of age, as well as being a reaction to the passivity of the German church in the face of the Nazi holocaust. He thinks the church might best couch such statements on a level which is both not overly general nor overly specific, since their authority is basically limited and advisory. Lutz (1987) has noted how the ALC from 1960 to 1987 moved from a posture of individual to corporate church responsibility and shifted its focus over time from church-state matters at first to race, gender/sex/abortion, and most recently to foreign policy questions. (For a similar history of LCA experience, see Klein [1989]). Lutz notes that ALC social statements tended to be drawn up by staff and board members who were more politically liberal than ALC rank and file; that they generally received overwhelming convention support (except for the issues of abortion and apartheid disinvestment, which passed by only 57 percent and 65 percent majorities); but that only 1-3 percent of the ALC congregations actually offered any feedback on pronouncements when specifically asked to do so.

Offices of the LCA, ALC, and LCMS have made available copies of the social statements adopted by the general conventions or governing councils of these bodies. These number close to 50, and since the mid-60s have dealt with recommended church stands on the following topics:

—church and state, religious liberty, civil disobedience,
peace and human rights
—environment, ecology, farm management
—public schools and religion, tuition tax credits
—church and human welfare, the aged
—socioeconomic justice, poverty and tax policy
—capital punishment and crime
—the American Indian, racism, apartheid
—sexism, abortion, marriage and the family, human
sexuality, pornography
—gambling
—nuclear disarmament, war and peace, conscientious
objection
—medical technology and terminal illness, death
and dying

Up to their merger in 1988, the LCA and ALC had generally taken moderate to left-of-center stances on public issues, e.g., supporting cooperation between church and state (institutional separation and functional interaction); supporting tuition tax credits but no formal prayer in public schools; supporting (with limitations) the right of citizens to civil disobedience, as well as conscientious objection; taking a middle-of-the-road position on abortion; opposing "any use of weapons of mass destruction"; and violations of civil and human rights. These statements may not have become widely known to the general public, but they have been used as guides for writing educational materials for parish use and also for reference in lobbying legislators and government agency officials. Until the ELCA adopts its own statement, the past statements of the LCA and ALC provide interim social ethical guidance.

In 1989, the ELCA Churchwide Assembly adopted a set of "Principles and Procedures" for producing such statements. "Teaching Statements" (which are more general and advisory) are to take three years to develop and adopt and require a two-thirds vote of the ELCA Churchwide Assembly; "Social Practice Statements" (aimed at guiding day-to-day practices of ELCA agencies) are to take at least one year and also require a two-thirds vote of the ELCA CWA or a three-fourths vote of its Church Council (between conventions executive board). District synods are to receive the statements at least six months prior to Churchwide Assembly consideration, and summaries of significant dissenting viewpoints are to be included. Criteria for ELCA Social Statements include the following: be consistent with Lutheran theology; be "persuasive, not coercive"; foster "ethical reflection"; result from an official study process; guide church life and advocacy activities; and be relevant to the constituency's needs (ELCA, Commission for Church in Society, 1989).

The Missouri Synod also has adopted selected position statements, but these have leaned more to the right-of-center. For example, the LCMS has officially disapproved of abortion (except in danger to the life of the mother), women's ordination, an Equal Rights Amendment to the U.S. Constitution, and pornographic materials. It also has given cautious approval to capital punishment and the removal of life supports when they no longer assist a dying person's recovery.

Prior to 1988, the LCA, ALC, and AELC supported an active Washington office of the Lutheran Council in the U.S.A., which effort has now been incorporated into the new ELCA with five to six full-time staff. The LCA belonged to the National Council of Churches, the World Council of Churches, and the Lutheran World Federation. The ALC joined the latter two, as did the AELC. The ELCA plans to follow the LCA policy of wide ecumenical memberships, and it confirmed this at its first Churchwide Assembly in 1989. The Missouri Synod at one time participated in several agencies of the NCC and once was a full member of LCUSA; but in the 1970s the LCMS cut back on NCC participation and limited its LCUSA participation (LCUSA ceased its existence as of 1987). The ELCA and LCMS have worked out a new arrangement for what the latter terms "cooperation in externals," through a number of inter-Lutheran organizations—Lutheran World Relief, Lutheran Immigration and Refugee Services, the Lutheran Educational Conference of North America (for higher education), the Lutheran Resources Commission, and Lutheran Film Associates. The heads of the ELCA and the LCMS also have arranged for regular consultations between their staffs and for providing ad hoc task forces for specific kinds of social

action.   All the above is monitored by a Committee on Lutheran
Cooperation (CLC) composed of the top officers of both bodies
(LCMS Reporter, 13 November 2, 1987: 2-3).

An additional comment needs to be made about selected para
denominational action movements and voluntary agencies that are
important but not part of the official structure of American Lutheranism. For example, the Lutheran Human Relations Association of
America emerged originally in the Missouri Synod in the early 1950s
to promote the cause of racial and ethnic social justice; in the 1970s
it became a pan-Lutheran voluntary action agency. Currently in the
ELCA there are a number of caucuses promoting special causes, e.g.
black awareness, women's roles, and the welfare of Hispanics, Native
Americans, and Asian-Americans. There is also a caucus of Lutherans
Concerned with Gay and Lesbian Persons. The new ELCA has
specifically built into its Constitution (chapter 5: 17-18) a requirement that at least 50 percent of the members of its various boards
shall be female; and that at least 10 percent of such members "shall
be persons of color and/or persons whose primary language is other
than English" (the so-called quota rule). There was considerable controversy over the adoption of this rule within the deliberations of the
Commission for a New Lutheran Church; and it has not been easy to
implement, at least in terms of personnel for the very top levels of the
denomination.

There are several Lutheran fraternal insurance agencies which
devote much of their profits to the causes of Lutheran higher
education, theological education, church social service, and social
scientific research on ministry, parish life, and religious policy
questions. The insurance companies serve almost as quasi-research
and development agencies for the Lutheran bodies when they need
resources and ideas for developing policies for new directions. Historically, the Missouri Synod had a policy of encouraging local congregations, or coalitions of them, to initiate the formation of special
service agencies, which over a long period of time were formally
adopted by the denomination and incorporated into its official
program structure.   This worked well economically and almost ap-
proximated a market approach to the rise and fall of auxiliary
services.

With the formation of the new Lutheran Church in 1988,
American Lutheranism enters a new era. In order to see how contem-

and social ministry, it will be helpful to look at the basic purposes of the ELCA as enunciated in its Constitution. The six purposes of the ELCA can be summarized as proclamation of the Gospel, evangelism, human service and social action, worship and celebration, education, and fellowship and ecumenism. These are generic church functions which all denominations normally have to come to terms with. However, it is interesting to note that rank and file church members in the United States tend to give highest priority to proclamation, worship and celebration, child and adult education, and ministry to human needs; but universally, they give much lower priority to social action, support of the church-at-large (and the denomination), and ecumenism. This seems to be true for all denominations. Conversely, it is general church officials and at least many clergy who highly value social witness and oneness with other Christians (see below; also Leege, et al., Notre Dame Study of Catholic Parish Life, 1984-1986).

In Chaper 7 of this volume, Richard Jones describes the churchly tasks of social ministry under four separate subfunctions: (1) social service (both congregational and agency); (2) social education; (3) social witness; and (4)social action. The ELCA's Statement of Purpose makes reference to each of these social ministry activities. The cause of social ministry is forwarded not only by official agencies and pronouncements in this direction but also by the liturgy and hymnody, programs of religious education, and a whole panoply of voluntary agencies active alongside the local congregations.

Sociological Observations

In this section we will make some sociological observations as to the present plight of American Lutheranism vis a vis the relation of faith to social ministry and the Christian life. Then we also shall summarize and interpret a number of national sociological surveys of Lutheran laypersons and clergy.

As stated earlier, Lutheranism is basically a transplanted ecclesia. While originally the reformers could only visualize religious monopoly and church- state establishment, their successors eventually accepted religious toleration and multiple establishments. Weber (1930/1958: 79-92) and Troeltsch (1911/ 1960: 569-576) were partly correct in attributing to German Lutherans an oversocialization to correct in attributing to German Lutherans an oversocialization to "authority." Early migrant American Lutherans thus may have had some problems in adjusting to and accepting democracy and America's system of denominational pluralism. Recent Lutheran theologians are uncomfortable with such churchly detachment and are trying to disengage American Lutheranism from passivity toward the state. However, their writings do not seem to touch much upon the strategies and tactics (e.g., for civil disobedience to misguided government decisions [see Strieter, 1986]).

Lutheran church government in the U.S. has leaned to the congregational model, with the central denomination merely assisting local congregations via the production of educational materials and the education of pastors. Since World War II, however, the functions of the general church have been widening (viz., the change in labeling from "synod" to "church," synod now being reserved for state and metropolitan-level church organization). In the Missouri Synod, social service has been primarily a regional responsibility. The new ELCA seems to be more centralized and perhaps necessarily so, although the increased number of program divisions reporting to the top may make for more board autonomy. In the ELCA, seemingly the more central LCA model won out over the more local gemeinschaft pattern of the ALC. The recent LCMS situation is confused, having moved from decentralization to gross political centralization in the 1970s, but perhaps only temporarily.

Organizational sociologists have noted that in large, geographically dispersed organizations there often is a "leakage" of policy. That is, the distance from the top leadership to the grass roots may be very far, with each going into opposite directions. This may be even more true in voluntary organizations like churches since church members are not paid as are employees; but on the contrary, they contribute and expect to "have a say" in policy direction.

Laity generally give a medium priority to social service ministries and a low one to social action—they may even be strongly opposed to churches' taking stands on certain subjects. Wood (1981), however, suggests that American lay people will accept pastoral leadership on controversial social policies provided that the pastor can refer to national denominational policy statements, time is allowed for adequate education, and the people feel they are receiving adequate and competent traditional kinds of pastoral care.

A Tragic Case of Local Lutheran Community Social Action

Long (1985 and 1987) has described an interesting, but stressful, case of the fragility of church decision-making and conflict resolution in a critical situation. It illustrates how well-intentioned efforts can end in tragedy. The case deals with deindustrialization and plant shutdown in the Pittsburgh metropolitan area and the failure of action by an LCA regional synod to reverse the situation. In the late 1970s, the Western Pennsylvania Synod of the LCA set up an Alinsky-style church-renewal community program at the behest of certain local pastors (which eventually became interdenominational and was known as the Denominational Ministry Strategy—DMS). The situation, however, got out of hand, and the synod officials backed off as certain of its pastors used unusual tactics and were labeled as radicals. Long implies that there was disagreement over policy and action tactics.

First, the synod leadership and certain self-styled "prophetic" pastors seemed to be in disagreement over the church's basic functions and goals. Synod leaders seemed to view the church's external social role to be palliative and adaptive. The job of pastors was mainly to be liturgical and pastoral and only secondarily to engage in social action. In a sense, the regional majority of Lutherans seemed to accept the industrial shutdowns as bad but probably something they could do little about. The dissident pastors, on the other hand, sought to roll back the situation to the preexisting socioeconomic situation.

Second, in terms of tactics, the synod leaders deemed it appropriate to use only persuasion and ordinary due process in appeals to civic and corporate leaders. The dissident pastors, on the other hand, considered it necessary to use disruption, civil disobedience, and violence (e.g., picketing, spraying of skunk oil, insertion of dead fish into the Mellon Bank's night depository, disruption of official meetings—"dirty tricks"). In other words, what originally was a church vs. industrial establishment dialogue turned into a collision course between church hierarchy and prophetic pastors. The pastors lost, with two being suspended from the ministry of the Lutheran Church. Meanwhile all became diverted from their original focus, trying to rectify the external industrial situation. Alinsky organizers, it is said, became somewhat dismayed with the distortions and excesses which DMS activists introduced into their approach.

Thus, there seems to have been confusion over means and ends, especially among the dissident pastors. The case illustrates that, externally, churches may lack political and economic know-how to engage in the nitty-gritty of local socioeconomic social action. In the light of this case, some opine that it is better for churches to limit their actions to general social criticism and restrict their use of power to religious persuasion when dealing in civil affairs. Internally, in the decision process in this case, the major policy goals seemed to get sidetracked (producing goal-displacement), as the major players encountered dilemmas and decision-making became paralyzed and ineffective. The moral may be that church organization inherently seeks harmony and cannot handle internal dissidence and conflict very well. (Thompson and Tuden [1959] refer to the difficulties connected with the use of "inspirational" decision strategies, which flow from a lack of consensus on both ends and means). The above interpretation of Long's case is the present writer's. However, Long himself states that the voluntaristic federalism of church structures, together with their ideological bases, inevitably tend to make church decision-making ambivalent and ineffective when used for clarifying civil community issues. One must, however, be cautious in over generalizing from a single case of regional church social action.

A concluding note to this discussion. With regard to the social action subtype of social ministry, Lutherans may be termed as having been "drowsy" but now as being aroused. They are perhaps not emerging from their sociocultural enclave mentality as rapidly as are current Roman Catholics—Roman Catholics are having simultaneously to undergo rapid theological aggiornamento but also organizational voluntarization, which Protestants had to face in America a long time ago. Lutherans also may suffer from a psychotheological problem of fearing to be compromised when attempting to perform "good works." Evidence of this has surfaced in recent surveys on Lutherans in the U.S. To these surveys, and their implications for mission, we now turn.

Comparisons of Lutherans with Others

We shall now briefly report on a number of sample surveys, mostly national in scope, completed on American Lutherans in the last 25 years. We shall review them in temporal sequence, and at the end, summarize their overall findings. In this section we look at three studies presenting comparative data on Lutherans in the U.S.; in the final section, we look at some studies directed at Lutherans only.

Scherer (1965) reported on a 15-denomination random sample survey of local Protestant clergy done under the sponsorship of the NCCC in 1964. While geared toward clergy financial support, the survey included respondents' rankings of a number of ministerial functions. The 5,623 returns included 1,095 from parish pastors of the LCA, ALC, and LCMS. While all clergy generally ranked worship and preaching, religious education, and evangelism as major tasks and social action and ecumenism at the bottom, there are some interesting intra-Lutheran variations. Of all 15 denominations, LCMS pastors were second highest on adult evangelism and last on social action; the ALC ninth on both evangelism and social action; and LCA fifth on evangelism and seventh on social action. (United Church of Christ ministers were highest on social action and Southern Baptist on evangelism). Evangelism and social action were pretty well inversely correlated.

Stark and Glock (1970) reported on the theological leanings of 3,000 laymen in nine Protestant and (the) Roman Catholic denominations surveyed in 1964 in the San Francisco area (supplemented by another 1,976 respondents nationwide). The LCMS had the highest church attendance next to Roman Catholics (1970: 86) and was high on biblical literalism and "orthodoxy." In general, the ALC and LCA respondents were revealed as moderate in theology and the LCMS as more conservative.

Roof and McKinney (1987, passim) have compiled the most comprehensive, comparative study of data on American denominations, based to a great extent on general national sample surveys. Since these national surveys sample people who self-identify themselves according to a general denominational tradition rather than as church members, their responses tend to be more liberal and perhaps less organizationally committed than the responses given in the church-member surveys summarized below. In the general American social surveys, Lutherans (subgroups not identified) present themselves as generally "moderate" (perhaps as conservative moderates). About 45 percent say they regularly attend church; and about 55 percent say their religion is "important" to them, which parallels most Presbyterians, Methodists, and Roman Catholics. In social class, Lutherans are in the middle (along with the Reformed, Methodists, Catholics, and Disciples; but below Episcopalians, UCC, Presbyterians, and Jews). America's Lutherans are disproportionately located in rural and smaller urban places but equally to others in metropolitan suburbs. They are among the most ethnically homogeneous of all denominations, with 69 percent from German and Scandinavian stocks, and 1 percent each from Hispanic and black. They are among the most indigenous, with 75 percent born as Lutherans (vs. 43 percent average for all denominations).

On ethical attitudes, Lutherans are generally also in the middle (along with Roman Catholics) on civil liberties scales. They are not as liberal as Episcopalians, UCC, and Presbyterians but are more open than Disciples, Baptists, and Reformed. They are near the center on minority and women's rights and sexual morality. Roof and McKinney consider "moderates" to be more community-bonded and possessing resources for forging new syntheses.

Selected Sample Surveys of Lutherans Only

Kersten (1970) did a survey of 886 Detroit-area laity and 241 pastors in 1967. He surveyed them on women's equality, sexuality and birth control, abortion, minority attitudes, and church roles in social action along with other items. He generally found the laity to the right of center, with the WELS most conservative, followed by the LCMS, ALC, and LCA laity in that order. On the other hand, he found the WELS and LCMS clergy to the right of the whole body of laity, the LCA clergy to the left of and the ALC clergy closest to the laity. These results seem characteristic of the Lutheran picture nationally.

Strommen and associates (1972) undoubtedly executed the best designed and analyzed survey of all Lutherans in the U.S. in 1970, receiving 4,745 responses within 316 congregations nationwide. Not surprisingly, the authors found that Lutherans prefer an orderly, dependable, and controllable world but not detachment from it. They placed a lot of emphasis on their scale termed "the heart of Lutheran piety." Their results indicated that 60 percent of Lutherans have an intellectual understanding of the Lutheran ("justification") viewpoint but found the oldest and least educated respondents most guilty of "misbelief" responses (salvation by works). Ironically, LCMS respondents turned out to be lowest on misbelief and LCA highest.

The study found Lutherans making much more of the divinity of Christ than His humanity. Laity gave less approval to church and pastoral social involvement than did clergy; laity favored an individualist approach to social problems. Lutherans are stronger on "safe" issues—substance abuse, free medical care, better housing, and ecumenism; in 1970 they were somewhat wary of forcing integration of the races. Sixty per cent admitted that their own congregation was not very socially active. One fourth reported they were quite disappointed with the church, with such disaffection expressed mainly by the youth and those uncertain as to their faith (Strommen et al., 1972: 168). The authors reported being baffled that, while 75 percent of respondents said that faith in Jesus Christ was "necessary" for salvation, 40 percent did not feel they wanted to impose their own beliefs upon others. Their findings on a national scale appear to mirror Kersten's Detroit results which found the LCMS as the most conservative and the LCA most liberal on social issues. While they found Lutherans to be generally pious and active in their congregations, "apathy or noninvolvement describes the typical pattern for most laymen" (Strommen et al, 1972: 182). In 1970 at least, Lutherans were more willing to offer personal support and neighborliness than to favor community social action.

Reuss (1982) wrote up the results of an inter-Lutheran survey of all Lutherans in the United States conducted in 1980 (and funded by the Aid Association for Lutherans). The findings of the 1980 survey parallel those from 1970. The hallmark of Lutherans is "faithfulness" (paralleling Strommen's "order"). Lutherans are mainly born into their denomination, come from German and Scandinavian backgrounds, are active in their congregations but little outside them, and exhibit much piety in church and home. (This survey drew from 4,371 lay responses, 886 clergy, and 377 teachers).

Bondivalli (1986) directed a national survey of Missouri Synod Lutherans drawing responses from 1,377 laity, 512 teachers, and 475 clergy in 1985. The sample, however, was biased to rural and smaller congregations. The data revealed a great deal of latent male chauvinism in these congregations. For example, 55 percent indicated that they would be offended by being ministered to by women pastors; and 54 percent agreed that preschool children would be "likely to suffer" if their mothers worked outside the home. Only 23 percent approved of abortion if pregnancy were detrimental to the mother's health; but 70 percent would approve if the mother's life were "severely endangered." Ironically, the more active the respondents were in church participation and giving, the more chauvinistic were their replies; conversely, the more involved respondents were outside the congregation, the more liberal were their answers. External involvement appeared to promote more openness.

Johnson (1983) edited a volume sponsored by the LCA involving a dialogue between church theologians and consulting sociologists. This is a sophisticated book raising interesting questions concerning what some might term the "delivery of salvation." Robert Wuthnow, after examining the LCA Lutheran "Listening Post" survey data concluded that the "overwhelming majority" of both laity and clergy subscribed to orthodox views of sin, grace, Christ, the crucifixion, and the forgiveness of sins (Johnson, 1983: 15); and these views appear to have been stable for the preceding 20 years. While 74 percent of LCA clergy chose the phrase "my trust in God's grace" as giving the meaning of faith, only 40 percent of the laity did so. But Wuthnow wondered about the possible dysfunctions of Lutheranism's heavy reliance upon a doctrine of "faith and grace alone," since it "strips away the institution's capacity to manipulate the ultimate reward— salvation" (Johnson, 1983: 55). Thus, there may be risks in avoiding a faith built upon rules; the heart of Lutheran piety, therefore, is a gamble. In a complementary point, theologian Lyman Lundeen averred that distortion tends to result practically if too much consistency is demanded in the working out of faith-as-trust on a day to day basis, since Christian life is very often ambiguous and faith ultimately is a mystery (Johnson, 1983: 57-82). Faith means belief *in* and not just belief *that*. That is, for real spiritual creativity, there must be some "slack" for making mistakes and misjudgments in the hurly-burly of daily living. (While LCMS responses may be the most consistent, they may also be the least open).

Sociologist Mary Weber in the same volume (pp. 84-102) found that biblical literalism and a "works" orientation were strongly correlated with political and social conservatism. Laymen are a stronghold of moderate opinion, and on every measure the LCA clergy tended to be more liberal than their laity—on sexual questions, politics, human rights, criminal justice, economic equality, church advocacy, women's ordination and liberation. Historian Jerald

Brauer, in the same volume, is surprised that the LCA clergy were so open to social advocacy and thinks that the liturgical-sacramental and confessional theology developing in the LCA in recent decades has won out over any remnants of pietism.

Summary and Conclusions

As stated at the beginning, American Lutherans share very much with fellow Christians of other denominations; but they also have some unique traditions and also some unique problems in seeking to implement that faith into action. Lutherans basically are conservative moderates in theological outlook, social outlook, and general lifestyle. Their spiritual tradition, although somewhat narrowly Northern European in background, is rich in resources. Lutherans are generally faithfully loyal to their church, religiously devout, active in attending church, liberal in giving, and respectful toward their pastors and spiritual leaders. They have a strong commitment to the core of the Christian gospel and a strong sense of God's living presence in life. Vis as vis some others they show a higher sense of spiritual "otherworldliness."

There is a flip side, however, to these strengths. To sustain the believer's sense of faith, the Lutheran is counseled against putting too much reliance upon "human trust," which sometimes may have the unintended effect of dampening optimism about possibilities for changing this life and the enduring value of human works. But Lutheranism is changing, and the new ELCA's commitment to openness and its positive emphases on seeking to hold up the concerns of social justice, ecumenical sharing, and world peace—as well as the traditional values of good local pastoral care, education, and evangelization—suggest a rebalancing of priorities for American Lutheranism in the twenty-first century. As do members of other communions, Lutherans face the perpetual dilemma of how to maintain internal organizational loyalty and viability while simultaneously pointing people to openness and spiritual creativity toward the world. As Wood (1981) has pointed out, however, it is possible for modern churchmen to lead their people to greater openness to the environment, provided that the causes of social ministry and social action are given legitimacy by the parent communion and that the people experience dedicated and effective pastoral care.

Acknowledgments

The author wishes to thank the following for a careful reading of the manuscript: the Rev Karen Bloomquist, Ph.D., Director of Studies, Evangelical Lutheran Church in America, Commission for Church in Society; the Rev. Franklin Sherman, Ph.D., formerly of the Lutheran School of Theology at Chicago and now Muhlenberg College; Roger Finke, Ph.D., Department of Sociology/Anthropology, Purdue University .

References

American Lutheran Church, *Social statements*. Minneapolis, MN: Augsburg, 1966-1985.

Benne, Robert. "The Social Sources of Church Polity," pp. 169-183 in Carl E. Braaten, ed., *The New Church Debate, Issues Facing American Lutheranism*. Philadelphia, PA: Fortress Press, 1983.

Bloomquist, Karen. Director of Studies, ELCA Commission for Church in Society, Chicago, letter to author, July 6, 1989.

Bondavalli, Bonnie J. "Summary Report of the 1985 Attitude Survey of the President's Commission on Women" (of the Lutheran Church—Missouri Synod). River Forest, IL: Concordia Teachers College, 1986.

Brunotte, Heinz. "Barmen Declaration" (1934), pp. 190-194 in Julius Bodensieck, ed., *The Encyclopedia of the Lutheran Church*, 3 vols. Minneapolis, MN, 1965.

Evangelical Lutheran Church in America, Report and Recommendations of the Commission for a New Lutheran Church (includes Constitution and Bylaws). New York/Minneapolis/St.Louis: LCA, ALC, AELC, 1986. Adopted August 29, 1986.

ELCA, Commission for Church in Society. "Social Statements in the Evangelical Lutheran Church in America: Principles and Procedures." Chicago, 1989.

Groh, John E. and Robert H. Smith, eds. *The Lutheran Church in North American Life*, 1776-1976 and 1580-1980. St. Louis, MO: Clayton, 1979.

Johnson, Roger A., ed. *Views from the Pew—Christian Beliefs and Attitudes*. Fortress Press: Philadelphia, PA., 1983.

Kersten, Lawrence K. *The Lutheran Ethic, the Impact on Laymen and Clergy*. Detroit, MI.: Wayne State University, 1970.

Klein, Christa, ed. *Politics and Policy: Genesis and Theology of Social Statements in the Lutheran Church in America*. Philadelphia, PA: Fortess Press, 1989.

Kuenning, Paul P. "The Social Activism of German Pietism," pp. 20-25 in *Lutheran Partners* magazine, 3 (July-Aug.), 1987.

Leege, David et al. Notre Dame Study of Catholic Parish Life.
Notre Dame, IN: University of Notre Dame, Institute for
Pastoral and Social Ministry and Center for the Study of
Contemporary Society, 1984-1987. Reports 1-11.

Long, Theodore. "The Church and Labor Conflict in Post-Indus-
trial Pittsburgh," and "Religious Conflict and the Law in
the Pittsburgh Controversy over Unemployment" (both
unpublished). Merrimack College (Ma.), 1985 and 1987.

Lueking, F. Dean. *A Century of Caring, The Welfare Ministry among
Missouri Synod Lutherans, 1868-1968.* St. Louis, MO: LCMS
Board of Social Ministry, 1968.

Lutheran Church in America. *Social Statements.* New York, NY:
LCA, 1966-1984.

Lutheran Church—Missouri Synod Reporter, vol. 12 (Nov.3,
1986): 4; 13 (Nov.2, 1987): 2-3. LCMS, A Short Explanation of Luther's Small Catechism (by LCMS President
Henry C. Schwan). St. Louis, MO: Concordia, 1943 rev.

LCMS. Social statements, St.Louis, MO: LCMS, Commission on
Theology and Church Relations, 1973-1984.

Lutz, Charles P. *Public Voice:* 1960-1987. Social Policy Develop-
ment in the American Lutheran Church. Minneapolis,
MN: American Lutheran Church, Office of Church in
Society, 1987. pp.1-36.

Mead, Frank S. *Handbook of Denominations in the United States.*
Nashville, TN: Abingdon, 1970, 5th ed.

Neve, J.L. *Churches and Sects of Christendom.* Blair, NE: Lutheran
Publishing House, 1944.

Niebuhr, H. Richard. *Christ and Culture.* New York, NY: Harper,
1951. Reuss, Carl F. *Profiles of Lutherans in the USA.*
Minneapolis, MN: Augsburg, 1982.

Roof, W. Clark and William McKinney. *American Mainline Religion.
Its Changing Shape and Future.* New Brunswick, NJ: Rutgers
University, 1987.

Scherer, Ross P. "The White Protestant Denominations and Some
Central Tendencies and Variations in Their Clergy," paper
given at the American Sociological Association meeting,
Chicago, IL, 1965.

Sherman, Franklin. "Church Social Pronouncements—Open Questions," pp. 33-40, in Eckehart Lorenz, ed., *To Speak or Not to Speak, Proposed Criteria for Public Statements on Violations of Human Rights*. Geneva, Switzerland: Department of Studies, Lutheran World Federation, 1984.

Stark, Rodney and Charles Y. Glock. *American Piety: the Nature of Religious Commitment*. Berkeley, CA: U. of California, 1970.

Strieter, Thomas W. "Contemporary Two-Kingdoms and Governances Thinking for Today's World: A Critical Assessment of Types of Interpretations of the Two-Kingdoms Governances Model, Especially within American Lutheranism." Unpublished Th.D. dissertation, Lutheran School of Theology at Chicago, 1986.

Strommen, Merton P., Milo L. Brekke, Ralph C. Underwager, and Arthur L. Johnson. *A Study of Generations, Report of a Two Year Study of 5,000 Lutherans between the Ages of 15-65, Their Beliefs, Values, Attitudes, Behavior*. Minneapolis, MN: Augsburg, 1972.

Thompson, James and Arthur Tuden. "Strategies, Structures, and Processes of Organizational Decision," pp. 195-216 in James D. Thompson et al, eds., *Comparative Studies in Administration*. Pittsburgh, PA: University of Pittsburgh, 1959.

Thorkelson, Willmar. *Lutherans in the USA*. Minneapolis, MN: Augsburg, 1978 rev.

Troeltsch, Ernst. *The Social Teaching of the Christian Churches*. New York, NY: Macmillan, 1911/1960.

Weber, Max. The Protestant Ethic and the Spirit of Capitalism. New York, NY: Scribner's, 1902/1930.

Weissburger, Hans. "Confessionalism," pp. 567-572 in Julius Bodensieck, ed., *The Encyclopedia of the Lutheran Church*, 3 vols. Minneapolis, MN: Augsburg, 1965.

Wood, James R. *Leadership in Voluntary Organizations: The Controversy over Social Action in Protestant Churches*. New Brunswick, NJ: Rutgers University, 1981.

7

FAITH AND
SOCIAL MINISTRY:
AMERICAN BAPTIST VIEWS

Richard M. Jones

Introduction

This chapter provides initial insight into the life and history of American Baptists as this group has struggled, and continues to struggle, with the relation of faith and social ministry. Limited space allows only a surface view. There is a need, however, to provide some description of who American Baptists are and how they have faced the linkages of faith and social ministry and attempted to move toward wholeness in belief that expresses itself in word and deed.

American Baptists embrace a wide diversity of race, ethnicity, culture and theology. Over a third of our membership is Black, Hispanic, Native American or Asian. We range theologically from liberal to evangelical, conservative, and fundamentalist. Our strains include Roger Williams, a "short term" Baptist in the 17th century, who stressed separation of church and state; Walter Rauschenbusch, "social gospel" pioneer who pastored in Hell's Kitchen in New York City and later taught at Colgate Rochester Divinity School in Rochester, NY; Martin Luther King, civil rights activist and American

Baptist pastor; Helen Barrett Montgomery, Bible translator and "feminist;" Jitsuo Morikawa, Japanese "evangelist" emphasizing ministry of the laity, witness to the secular structures and holistic evangelism; Edwin T. Dahlberg, ecumenical mediator, who served as pastor in St. Louis and as President of the National Council of Churches of Christ; Harold Stassen, lawyer, world statesman, and President of ABC; and Harvey Cox, theologian and professor at Harvard Divinity School.

Our current ecumenical commitment reflects the biblical faith we share with the entire body of Christ. We embrace the historical heritage of the faith of Nicea and the definition of Chalcedon. Although we refuse to be bound by human creeds, we join with all the faithful in affirming the great themes reflected in the Councils. American Baptists are clearly trinitarian. We know the one true God as the Eternal Creator, Redeeming Savior and Holy Spirit. We recognize Jesus Christ as fully human and fully divine and faithfully acknowledge his sinless life, atoning death, mighty resurrection and triumphal return to consummate God's eternal reign.

We see the Bible as our final authority in all matters of faith and life. We affirm the Reformation emphases of grace alone, faith alone, Christ alone and scripture alone. In terms of the four sources of faith found in chapter one, American Baptists stress more heavily scripture and experience, less heavily tradition and reason. We see the community of faith as helping in support of the individual Christian as well as needed correction for interpreting the scriptures.

How is the Faith of American Baptists Expressed?

Although not a creedal church, there are some Confessions of Faith which, over the years, have helped to define who American Baptists are and what they believe. The most important one may well be the New Hampshire Confession of 1833. This Confession contains 18 statements expressing the convictions of the subscribers related to the divine inspiration of the Bible, the belief in the Trinity, the essential fallen and sinful nature of humanity, the work of Christ in providing salvation through his death and resurrection, the meaning of the community of faith as consisting of baptized believers who are associated by covenant in the faith and fellowship of the gospel, the emphasis on immersion of adult believers as the mode of baptism and the recognition that believers have a priestly accountability to one another as they share together in ministry.

For Walter Rauschenbusch, to be a Baptist was to stress the experience of faith. He states, "I am a Baptist, then, because in our church life we have a minimum of emphasis on ritual and creed, and a maximum of emphasis on spiritual experience and the more I study the history of religions, the more I see how great and fruitful such a position is."

As American Baptists have moved through frontier and sect-type manifestation of their life, the emphasis on experience has been tempered by education and reason. Harvey Cox struggles with this in his latest book, *Religion in the Secular City*, wishing to affirm both the impact of emotion and reason as an American Baptist and as a theologian for the whole church.

How do American Baptists View Social Ministry?

Trying to depict American Baptists' views of social ministry is no easier than trying to depict American Baptists' faith stances. Biblically, the linkage is found in James 2: 14-18; Hebrews 11: 1-39; and Luke 4: 15-19, etc. Nationally, regionally and in local churches the gamut of social ministry is engaged in. One typology for that which would apply to American Baptists comes from a helpful description prepared by the Capital Region Conference of Churches in Connecticut. The column on the left outlines four types of social concern. The column on the right provides illustrative programs in American Baptist national and local church life which fit these categories.

Types of Social Concern

Social Service: Direct assistance to persons in need. Here, help must be given in such a way that freedom and responsibility remain with those assisted.

Social Education: Informing persons about issues and concerns. This is distinct from social service in that it focuses on issues rather than on persons in need. It is distinct, as well, from social witness in that it attempts to give both sides. This does not assume that persons who participate in an educational experience will act upon what they learn.

Social Witness: The public declaration by word or deed of a conviction on an issue. This is distinct from social education in that it takes a public position on one side of an issue. It is also distinct from social action in that it is usually an individual and occasional effort.

Social Action: An organized effort focusing on the causes of a problem and dealing with its system in nature by changing policy and/or structures. Tactics used are program development, advocacy and empowerment.

American Baptist Programs

Refugee resettlement: Over 40,000 refugees settled since World War II; Homes and Hospitals: 150 facilities united in one association for common support and sharing; Domestic Disaster Relief: average of 150,000 per year to needs caused by all kinds of disasters; Christian Center work; barrier-free loans for churches; work with Church World Service, etc.

Office of Governmental Relations in Washington, D.C.; Advocacy with the President and Congress for support certain legislature; Office of the United Nations the Church; Peace Program; Community Development.

Social and Ethical Responsibility in Investments; Expressing American Baptist concern to corporations in relation to environmental justice, peace, and armanent issues; Policy Statements on Issues of Importance—enabling American Baptists to speak to the issues of the day.

Social and Ethical Responsibility in Investments; Sanctuary church movement: Local churches welcoming Central American refugees and providing support and protection; Peace/justice marches and mobilizations; Ministry of the Laity in the Workplace; bringing persons together on the basis of their occupation to consider implications of faith related to work life.

How do American Baptists Express Linkages Between Faith and Social Ministry?

American Baptists came into being because of a concern to relate faith to social responsibility. Prior to the Civil War, questions were raised by responsible Baptist bodies as to the propriety of a slaveholder serving as a foreign missionary. This led to a basic split between the southern states and the northern, and the creation of a new Foreign Mission Board which was anti-slavery. The Home Mission Board, the American Baptist Home Mission Society, faced the same question in relation to the appointment of a slaveholder as a missionary to the Cherokee Indians. After several months of agonizing, the Executive Board of the Society declared that "it is not expedient to introduce the subjects of slavery or antislavery into our deliberations, nor to entertain applications in which they are introduced;" and therefore the Board declined to consider the applicant's request (Brackney).

Later, in the 19th century, many American Baptists responded to the writings of Walter Rauschenbusch on social justice. In this century the liberty and freedom strain in American Baptist life was identifiable again in the life and ministry of Martin Luther King, Jr., who carried the torch for civil rights. We continue to be active in Central America, as illustrated by the Baptist involvement in many facets of the liberation struggle in Guatemala, Nicaragua, El Salvador, Eastern European countries and in the Soviet Union. The point is that American Baptists have always been a contemporary people, being shaped by, and shaping, every new future. That is part of our identity. Earlier brothers and sisters bore witness to the vision of the Kingdom of God in the social and political order in which they lived. Baptists cannot remain silent or be found among the absent on the great and oppressive issues of the current time, issues such as war and peace, world hunger, economic oppression and human rights. (Material drawn from unpublished manuscript prepared by American Baptist Identity Commission).

What Are Some of the Evidence of Linkages?

Evidence in denominational life of attempts to link personal-faith and social ministry are numerous. On the national, structural level, one of the major program agencies has organized itself so that program delivery units deal in their staff life, their resource planning and deployment, their conference planning and in their program delivery with the linkages between faith and social ministry. These units are described as follows:

Personal and Public Witness This unit plans and implements programs which express the wholeness of the church's task to "proclaim the gospel" to persons and institutions. The biblical function to which this unit relates most closely is the function of *kerygma*, which is most often translated "proclamation." This involves bringing together persons who are knowledgeable in enabling the church to express its concern publicly in terms of critical social issues. The forms of proclamation are shaped by uniting the personal and the public and learning new ways of sharing the gospel with others on a one-to-one and an institution-to-institution basis.

Church and Community Development This unit plans and implements programs which express the wholeness of the church's task to "build churches" or communities of faith and witness. The biblical function to which this unit relates most closely is the function of *koinonia*, which is often translated "fellowship" or "community." In this unit are persons who are knowledgeable about the local congregation as a vital, growing, renewing, witnessing body, persons who are concerned to enable regional bodies in working with these faith communities in terms of discipleship, renewal and new church extension. Also in this unit are persons who are knowledgeable about the communities in which congregations seek to minister—especially racial/ethnic concerns—who bring their expertise and knowledge of community need and concern to the way in which the church community structures itself for mission. The forms of the faith community are shaped by uniting the church with its setting and the needs of both as shapers and sharers of the gospel.

Individual and Corporate Responsibility This unit plans and implements programs which express the wholeness of the church's task to minister to persons of "special need." The biblical function to which this unit relates most closely is the function of *diakonia*, which is most often translated "service," but moves beyond providing "a cup of cold water" to raise the concern for "principalities and powers," which often create the needs in the first place. This involves bringing together persons who are knowledgeable about the needs of individuals who are hungry, homeless, oppressed, caught in the crisis of the political, economic and social changes of our time; persons who can marshal the forces of the church to respond to those cries of need; and persons who are knowledgeable about the ways in which the institutions and structures of corporate and governmental life work to create and shape injustice and human need and who can see the ways in which institutional practices can be changed which will allow response to human needs in more systemic ways.

Another manifestation of this concern for linking faith and social ministry was through a major emphasis of the denomination on "Grow By Caring." Grow By Caring was a six-year emphasis which concluded in 1990 and emphasized nine "marks" of a caring, growing church: personal witness, social witness, discipleship, leadership, congregational growth, service, stewardship, cooperation and identity. The emphasis was on the linkage of faith and action in a wholeness which leads to personal, congregational, missional, educational growth resulting from engaging in caring concern for others and the needs of the world.

Another manifestation was a major conference "Faith Faces Issues" held in Boston, MA, in September, 1989, which sought to link through worship, speakers, seminars and workshops, and specific actions with special focus on what local congregations can do. In addition, on the local congregational level, one of the attempts at gathering specific data on the linkage between faith and social ministry is through the use of the Congregational Profile System, a denominational data base managed by Dr. Norman Green. Each congregation in American Baptist Churches is asked to fill out forms relating the demographics of their membership, giving and program. Each five years a more extensive data instrument is prepared which asks further questions related to the life and ministry of the congregation.

Although there are no specific questions eliciting data on the faith stance of a congregation, there are some questions which make it possible to imply what some elements of a faith stance may be, such as:

"Church set a goal to develop 'spiritually vital church members'"
"Church set a goal to 'share Christ with unbelievers'"
"Church reported having a Preaching Mission or Revival in 1985"

There are also some questions which make it possible to imply ways in which a local congregation could be involved in social witness:

"Church set a goal to 'perform Christ's work in the community'"
"Church reported taking action concerning a community, state, national or world issue in 1985"
"Church is officially enrolled in Grow By Caring"

One specific control variable related to social ministry was chosen against which other variables were correlated. The control variable was as follows:

"Church set a goal in the past two years to perform Christ's work in the community."

Probing the data on an initial basis indicates that 1295 churches out of 5758 (22 percent) indicated that they had set a goal to "perform Christ's work in the community" in 1985. Of that number, 366 were composed of 100 members or less; 358 were composed of 100-199 members; 219 were composed of 200-299 members; 198 were composed of 300-399 members; and 154 were composed of 500 or over members. The predominant ethnic composition of these churches were as follows: White: 1139; Black: 115; Hispanic: 30; Asian: 8; Indian: 1 and Other: 2.

Comparing the 1295 churches committed to perform Christ's work in the community with other variables shows the following:

1123 out of 1295 set a goal to develop spiritually vital church members (a very high correlation of significance to the linkage between faith and social ministry).

1025 out of 1295 set a goal to share Christ with unbelievers
442 reported having a preaching mission or revival
740 reported taking action on an issue
751 reported official enrollment in Grow By Caring

Although too much cannot be made of this data, there is considerable indication that local congregations committed to social ministry also combine that with a concern for expressing faith in personal ways. This bears out the intention on the national and regional levels to see the gospel and its expression in whole terms and not to bifurcate the witness.

Conclusion

Perhaps no better words would summarize the concerns of this paper and the emphasis on faith and social ministry which characterizes what we seek to portray as an American Baptist view, than the words of Walter Rauschenbusch in *A Theology for the Social Gospel:*[1]

Faith once more means prophetic vision. It is faith to assume that this is a good world and that life is worth living. It is faith to assert the feasibility of a fairly righteous and (fraternal) social order. In the midst of a despotic and predatory industrial life, it is faith to stake our business future on the proposition that fairness, kindness and fraternity will work.

When war inflames a nation, it is faith to believe that a peaceable disposition is a workable international policy. Amidst the disunion of Christendom it is faith to look for unity and to express unity in action. It is faith to see God at work in the world and to claim a share in (his) job. Faith is an energetic act of the will, affirming our fellowship with God and (man), declaring our solidarity with the Kingdom of God, and repudiating selfish isolation...Other things being equal, a solidaristic religious experience is more distinctively Christian than an individualistic religious experience. To be afraid of hell or purgatory and desirous of a life without pain or trouble in heaven was not in itself Christian. It was self-interest on a higher level. It is not strange that (men) were wholly intent on saving themselves as long as such dangers as Dante describes were real to their minds. A (man) might be pardoned for forgetting his entire social consciousness if he found himself dangling over a blazing pit. But even in more spiritual forms of conversion, as long as (men) are wholly intent on their own destiny, they do not necessarily emerge from selfishness. It only changes its form. A Christian regeneration must have an outlook toward humanity and result in a higher social consciousness.

"The saint of the future will need not only a theocentric mysticism which enables (him) to realize God, but anthropocentric mysticism which enables (him) to realize his fellow-(men) in God.

The more we approach pure Christianity, the more will the Christian signify a (man) who loves (mankind) with a religious passion and excludes none. The feeling which Jesus had when he said, 'I am the hungry, the naked, the lonely,' will be in the emotional consciousness of all holy (men) in the coming days. The sense of solidarity is one of the distinctive marks of the true followers of Jesus."

Note

[1] The author of this chapter recognizes the exclusively male language which would characterize Dr. Rauschenbush's time. Therefore, the male references are in parentheses so that readers will themselves be sensitized, but still not violate the flow of Dr. Rausch-enbush's writing.

References

Brackney, William H., ed. *Baptist Life and Thought: 1600-1980.* Judson Press: 1983, 223-224.

Rauschenbusch, Walter. *A Theology for the Social Gospel.* New York: Macmillan, 1918: 95-109.

8

FAITH, SOCIAL MINISTRY, AND LINKAGE BETWEEN THE TWO IN THE SOUTHERN BAPTIST CONVENTION

William Jere Allen

My image of Southern Baptists is that of people who champion regenerate believers who hold freedom high in one hand and the Bible in the other. Out of this stance has evolved a tradition of concern for and practice of social ministry.

Because we Southern Baptists are a non-creedal people with a historic commitment to freedom, we are diverse both in belief and practice. However, generally we are conservative in theology and with regard to social ministry often say "changed people change society." As will be shown, we are strong in the practice of social ministry but have often been reticent in social action, except in selected areas.

Understanding Faith in the SBC Tradition

What Baptists profess to believe can best be traced through historical movements; influential theologians and confessions of faith.

Historical Movements

Walter Shurden, professor and chairman of the Christianity Department of Mercer University, teaches that four historical movements, which he calls "traditions," have shaped the Southern Baptist synthesis (Shurden, 1980, 1983).

Baptists' southern roots go back to Charleston, S.C., where William Screven migrated with a Baptist congregation from Kittery, Maine, between 1683 and 1696(Wamble, 1958: 8). Later, the churches, in association in the Charleston area, adopted the Philadelphia Confession of Faith, with minor deletions. This group, which fathered the *Charleston Tradition*, reflected English Calvinistic Puritanism with importance given to religious experience and the authority of Scripture. The Charleston churches practiced stately order in worship, as distinguished from spontaneous emotional excess. Emphasis was given to an educated ministry. Shurden refers to them as "semi-presbyterian." (Shurden 1983: 19).

The *Sandy Creek Tradition* grew out of the Great Awakening of the 1740s. Shubal Stearns, Separate Baptist in New England, migrated south with a congregation to Sandy Creek, North Carolina, in 1755 (Wamble, 1958: 11). Leery of confessions of faith, they were opposite, in many ways, to the Charleston group. They had a "red hot" religion characterized by spontaneity, revivalism and the visible moving of the Holy Spirit. Their belief included literal interpretation of the Bible. A major priority was winning people to Christ, characterized by an identifiable religious experience. They had a strong belief in personal freedom out of which came their sentiment for religious liberty and separation of church and state. Stearns did not encourage an educated ministry. They are referred to as "semi-pentecostal" (Shurden, 1983: 19).

Shurden lists two other traditions. The *Georgia Tradition*, for where Southern Baptists were founded in 1845, represented cooperation as a denomination and Southern regionalism. The *Tennessee Tradition*, for where J.R. Graves fostered the Landmark Movement, emphasized local church successionism and exclusivism (Shurden, 1983: 19-20). Though Landmarkism was rejected by Southern Baptists, its influence remains strong.

Southern Baptists' faith and practice has emerged out of these four traditions.

Influential Theologians

Southern Baptists have produced at least five theologians (some add J. R. Graves, J. M. Pendleton and Carl F. Henry) who have written systematic theologies (McBeth, 1987: 675-6). They are John L. Dagg (1794-1884), James P. Boyce (1794-1888), Edgar Y. Mullins (1860-1928), Walter T. Conner (1877-1952) and Dale Moody (1915-   ). Dagg and Boyce were influenced by Charles Hodge and the so called "Princeton Theology" which, in turn, was influenced by Frances Turretin and the Scottish school of theology. Mullins adapted some of these views, giving more emphasis to the substance of scripture and Christian experience, drawing on the work of Friedrich Schleiermacher. Conner was a student of Mullins and studied with Augustus H. Strong. Moody, influenced by modern American and European theologians, builds on the writings of all the men above (McBeth, 1987: 676).

Possibly the most influential of all Southern Baptist theologians was E. Y. Mullins, who defined faith as:

> Saving faith...we may analyze into at least three elements. ...First, faith contains an intellectual element. We believe the truth of the gospel...We accept...historical facts...The second element is assent. The sinner convicted of his (sic) sin and need and his (sic) dependence recognizes in the provisions of the gospel the divine answer to his (sic) needs. This necessarily includes an element of feeling as well as of knowledge. But it is not even yet the faith....The third element...is volition. In the last resort faith is an act of will (Mullins, 1917: 371-2).

The most distinctive element of Mullins' theology was the concept of soul competency. "What then is the distinguishing Baptist principle?... it (is) the doctrine of soul freedom, the right of private judgment in religious matters and in the interpretation of the Scriptures. . . Religion is a personal matter between the soul and God" (Mullins, 1908: 50 and 54). To him, Baptist belief in the priesthood of the individual Christian, autonomy of the local church, separation of church and state and religious liberty for all people found their rootage in soul competency.

Confessions of Faith

Since the founding of the Southern Baptist Convention in 1845, there have been but two official statements of faith adopted by the Convention—in 1925 and 1963. Both were produced in the crucible of controversy.

Baptists in the South in their earliest years had adhered to the Calvinistic Philadelphia Confession of 1742; it had served as a unifier of Regular and Separate Baptists. As this confession receded in influence, churches and associations turned to the New Hampshire Confession of Faith, written in 1833, with Calvinism stated in more moderate terms. It was popularized by J. M. Pendleton, a leader of the Landmark Movement in his *Church Manual*, published in 1867 (Lumpkin, 1969: 360-1). However, there was no official statement of faith adopted at a Southern Baptist Convention from its founding in 1845 until 1925.

Prior to the adoption of this first confession was controversy over evolution, Modernism and biblical inspiration (Shurden, 1979: 72). E. Y. Mullins, the chairperson of the committee that drew up what is called a statement of the Baptist Faith and Message, was opposed to having such a document, fearful it would eventually lead to creedalism. This statement was an adaptation of the New Hampshire Confession of Faith, with notable additions. The introduction stated that the sole authority for faith and practice among Baptists is the Old and New Testaments; confessions were considered guides in interpretation, having no authority over the conscience. This first confession had relatively little impact on Southern Baptist life (Carter, 1964: 171), though many local churches either adopted or adapted its content for their own use. It had no binding effect on denominational employees, churches or individual; it expressed the consensus of messengers present at the 1925 SBC.

In 1963 a revised Baptist Faith and Message was adopted by the Southern Baptist Convention, prompted by the "Elliott Controversy." Broadman Press, the denominational publishing house, had published a book on Genesis by Ralph Elliott, professor at the SBC sponsored Midwestern Baptist Theological Seminary, utilizing the historical-critical method of biblical interpretation. The chairperson of the group that presented this 1963 revision to the Convention was Herschel H. Hobbs, pastor at the time of First Baptist Church in Oklahoma City. Hobbs is the protege of E.Y. Mullins and the most influential practical theologian among Southern Baptists today.

This 1963 confession has had significant influence on Southern Baptists (Carter, 1976: 71), though it made few substantial changes from the 1925 confession. (The most significant change was to dilute Landmark influence by acknowledging the word *church* can be used in the universal as well as local sense.)

Section I of the 1963 Baptist Faith and Message on the Bible states:

> The Holy Bible was written by men divinely inspired and is the record of God's revelation of Himself to man. It is a perfect treasure of divine instruction. It has God for its author, salvation for its end, and truth, without any mixture of error, for its matter. It reveals the principles by which God judges us; and therefore is, and will remain to the end of the world, the true center of Christian union, and the supreme standard by which all human conduct, creeds, and religious opinions should be tried. The criterion by which the Bible is to be interpreted is Jesus Christ.

Periodically this statement has been reaffirmed by the Southern Baptist Convention. "Conservatives" generally interpret this to mean inerrancy in all areas—historical, scientific, theological and philosophical; "moderates" generally interpret "without any mixture of error" as relating to the message of the Bible. A Peace Committee composed of conservatives and moderates brought a report to the SBC in 1987 that was overwhelmingly adopted. It states:

> Although all Southern Baptists do not understand the Baptist Faith and Message Statement on Scripture the same way, this diversity should not create hostility towards each other, stand in the way of genuine cooperation, or interfere with the rights and privileges of all Southern Baptists within the denomination to participate in its affairs.

Section IV on salvation in the 1963 confession reads:

> Salvation involves the redemption of the whole man, and is offered freely to all who accept Jesus Christ....Repentance

and faith are inseparable experiences of grace. Repentance is a genuine turning from sin toward God. Faith is the acceptance of Jesus Christ and commitment of the entire personality to Him as Lord and Savior.

Faith Development and Programs That Promote/Nurture Faith

Southern Baptists' children are nurtured in the faith through the home and church. A growing number of Southern Baptist churches have dedication services for parents of infants during Sunday morning worship. When a child has a profound sense of God's love and his/her lostness, the child usually talks to an adult (parent, Sunday school teacher and/or pastor), openly expressing repentance and faith, then presents him/herself before the congregation for baptism and church membership. Immersion is symbolic of death to sin and resurrection to new life (Romans 6). Though conversion of children is normally calm, as opposed to cataclysmic, there is considered to be a definite time when one moves from death to life. Most do not recall the exact moment but do remember the time when they accepted God's salvation and committed themselves to God.

Unlike churches that practice pedobaptism, there are no confirmation classes upon which satisfactory completion leads to a ritual of passage. For children reared in a Southern Baptist church, the age of baptism is normally between ages 9 and 11. The nurturing activities are not significantly different before and after believers baptism. Following baptism, there is usually a new members class on the meaning and responsibilities of church membership.

It is often said among Southern Baptists that a Christian has been saved (at a specific time), is being saved (a lifelong process) and will be saved (following death). Salvation is considered a process of development, rather than a one time event. After a religious experience one is nurtured, not in order to be saved, but because one has been saved. It is generally believed that once true conversion has taken place, the believer will persevere to the end with God's grace. There may be temporary lapses but a complete falling away indicates false conversion. Obviously reformed theology has had its' influence.

In a fully developed church nurturing program, there will be a great number of activities and emphases for the faith development of members from pre-school through senior adults. The following is a listing of *some* of these, minimizing Southern Baptist terminology. (l) Sunday school is both for outreach and Bible study for all age groups, including adults. In many churches the attendance in Sunday school equals that in worship. With nearly eight million enrolled, it is viewed as the premier program for faith development. Vacation Bible school and January Bible study are a part of this program. (2) Discipleship and leadership training take place primarily on Sunday evenings before evening worship. Its' curriculum includes systematic theology, Christian ethics, Christian history, church polity and organization for general discipleship training, as well as leadership training for specific ministries. Daily Bible reading is promoted for each member. A doctrinal study book is promoted each May and has a growing following. A convention wide book study program with diplomas is a vital part of leadership training. (3) Mission programs are provided for males and females of all age groups. Often mission programs are the most significant activities in the life of a child regarding salvation and gift discovery. In recent years, adult and youth groups have been involved in mission trips; this often includes a week in the summer to construct churches or houses or to lead in vacation Bible schools, revival services or door-to-door visitation. Each year more than 33,000 volunteers serve in construction or ministry projects through the Home Mission Board; 1,000 plus are serving one year or longer. (4) A music program offers choirs for all age groups and instruction in worship. (5) Worship services are usually conducted on Sunday mornings and evenings and prayer services as a part of a Wednesday evening family night program. Though revival services have lost some of their vitality in some urban areas, they remain a major event in many churches. (6) A deacon ministry plan assigns each deacon a number of families and provides training in various kinds of ministry. Deacons are available during the various crises and victories of life for his/her assigned families.

Generally, Southern Baptists have supported the public schools, but there are notable exceptions to this. Baptist state conventions sponsor 52 colleges and universities with an enrollment of 115,000. There are campus ministry programs involving 1,042 colleges or universities involving 143,000 students. An in-service guidance program is conducted on college campuses for students choosing a full-time church related vocation.

We Southern Baptists are an activity-oriented denomination sometimes criticized for explaining ourselves in terms of programs rather than liturgies or content (Rosenberg, 1989: 51-2). Due to the size of the SBC, the amount and diversity of literature available is possibly without equal among Protestant denominations in the United States.

However, programs and literature alone will not assure faith development. A concern of Southern Baptists is the movement from the extended family in a closely knit rural and manageable size environment to a nuclear type family in a relatively depersonalized urban setting, and the resulting effect on faith development of children.

Social Ministry in the SBC Tradition

Southern Baptists' view of social ministry can be approached by considering official documents of the SBC, resolutions of the convention messengers, and a brief history of Southern Baptists involvement in social ministry.

Official Documents

Article II of the first SBC constitution in 1845 stated that the design of the Convention was to promote foreign and domestic missions and other objects of God's kingdom and to combine for this purpose "a general organization for Christian benevolence...." The stated purpose at present is the "promotion of Christian missions at home and abroad and any other objects such as Christian education, benevolent enterprises, and social services...for the furtherance of the Kingdom of God." Social ministry has been at the heart of Southern Baptist thought, though secondary to evangelism and missions.

The 1963 Baptist Faith and Message Article XV on "The Christian and the Social Order" reads:

Every Christian is under obligation to seek to make the will
of Christ supreme in his (sic) own life and in human

society. Means and methods used for the improvement of society and the establishment of righteousness among men (sic) can be truly and permanently helpful only when they are rooted in the regeneration of the individual by the saving grace of God in Christ Jesus. The Christian should oppose in the spirit of Christ every form of greed, selfishness, and vice. He (sic) should work to provide for the orphaned, the needy, the aged, the helpless, and the sick. Every Christian should seek to bring industry, government, and society as a whole under the sway of the principles of righteousness, truth, and brotherly love. In order to promote these ends Christians should be ready to work with all men (sic) of good will in any good cause, always being careful to act in the spirit of love without compromising their loyalty to Christ and His truth.

Herschel H. Hobbs, chairperson of the committee that drafted this 1963 revised statement, commented on Article XV in his book *The Baptist Faith and Message* (1971: 129-30):

Baptists generally do not believe in a social gospel or that the kingdom of God can be established simply through social reform of the individual or of society as a whole. But Baptists do believe in a spiritual gospel which has social implications...Since all social injustice is rooted in sin in the human heart, efforts for improving the social order and establishing righteousness must begin in the regeneration of the individual person...(Jesus) began with the individual and worked out into society....Jesus rejected all efforts to establish his kingdom by violence or by forced reform from without (Matthew 11: 12). Rather he proposed to redeem men (sic) and then to send them into society to change it into God's will and way.... Jesus was opposed to every form of man's (sic) inhumanity to man (sic). He recognized the evil systems which violated the dignity of human personality (such as slavery). But he attacked them from within, seeking to change men's (sic) hearts so that redeemed men (sic) would live together in peace and love.

Social ministry is written into the official documents of the SBC, calling for changed persons to change society through involvement in social ministry and action.

Resolutions

The resolutions passed at annual conventions reveal a broad based consensus of Southern Baptists' belief in regard to social ministry.

For the 12 year period 1978-1989, five types of resolutions have been passed for five or more of those years. Remarks are selected from the latest resolutions. (1) *Pornography*. Calls for working actively for the passage of federal legislation against obscenity. (2) *Alcohol*. Expresses "total opposition to the advertising, manufacturing, distribution, sale, and consumption of alcoholic beverages." (3) *Abortion*. Upholds the sanctity of life and opposes abortion "except to prevent the imminent death of the mother." (4) *Peacemaking*. Favors nuclear disarmament providing it does not compromise national security. (5) *Hunger*. Calls for working with other denominations and governmental agencies in resolving the issues which cause poverty and homelessness.

Other frequently passed resolutions during the above 10 years have been in the areas of gambling, family life and human sexuality, handicapped, domestic violence, and the Christian and the state. It is obvious that resolutions have been most often in areas that involve personal morality. This reflects the strong individualism of Southern Baptists.

Brief History of Southern Baptists'
Involvement in Social Ministry

Southern Baptists began in the midst of social upheaval when 328 delegates from Baptist churches in the South met in Augusta, Georgia, May, 1845. This convention formed, along with other Southern Protestant denominations, over the issue of regional factionalism, precipitated by slavery. A respected Baptist historian, Robert Torbet, said Southern Baptists "did not attempt to defend the evils in the slavery system, but described the institution as an inherited disease to be cured slowly" (Torbet, 1972: 309).

That which ushered Southern Baptists into "a broader sense of social responsibility was associated immediately with the prohibition movement" (Eighmy, 1972: 55). Though Baptists in the South in the early 19th century did not censure members for drinking alcoholic beverages, by mid-century total abstinence was the prevailing view. Churches, state conventions, and finally the Southern Baptist Convention took action on prohibition in the late 1800s (Eighmy, 1972: 51-2). The first resolution ever passed by the SBC was in 1896 and it was against alcoholic beverages (Parham, 1989: 4). After the passage of a constitutional amendment on prohibition, the Southern Baptist Convention temperance committee evolved into a social service committee with a broader social agenda.

For some years the convention had expressed concern over mob violence and lawlessness in the South. A 1907 resolution concerning these problems proposed a special mass meeting on "civic righteousness" in conjunction with the next convention. Out of this special meeting came a statement urging Southern Baptists to "redeem society" by working for the abolition of "every wrong, public and private, political and social." In language characteristic of the social gospel, the delegates were challenged to become "aggressive builders of the new order" in preparation for the consummation of the kingdom (Parham, 1989: 81).

Eighmy gives three factors that keep Southern Baptists from being progressive in the area of social action: (1) A congregational polity that requires broad consensus before the denomination becomes active in social action. (2) A conservative theology that gives emphasize to a religious individualism/privatism that is not balanced with a broad range of social issues. (3) A cultural captivity to a rural Southern mindset.

In 1953, the Southern Baptist Convention social service committee produced the Christian Life Commission (CLC). It has served as the moral conscience of the SBC, though constantly under attack for its moderate stand on moral and justice issues. Some say the CLC has reflected the New Deal philosophy of Franklin D. Roosevelt. In 1988-89, a more conservative board of trustees, reflecting changes in the direction of the SBC over the past decade, made significant alterations in the staff of the CLC to assure greater emphasis will be given to the resolutions of a more conservative SBC, especially in the area of abortion.

Two of the more progressive statements made by the Southern Baptist Convention in the modern era were in 1954 and 1968. In 1954 a resolution was adopted that recognized the Supreme Court decision on desegregation of schools as "in harmony with the constitutional guarantee of equal freedom to all citizens, and the Christian principles of equal justice and love for all men." The statement must be assessed in the light of the date and the geographical residency of those who adopted the statement. In 1968, "A Statement Concerning the Crisis in Our Nation" was adopted. It spoke of injustice, heartless exploitation, slum housing, poverty, and Southern Baptists' responsibility to action in pursuing equality and rights for all, irrespective of race. "We will strive to obtain and secure for every person equality of human and legal rights." It was a public declaration of wrongdoing in which Southern Baptists admitted to having "allowed cultural patterns to persist that have deprived...black Americans...of equality...(in) education, citizenship, housing, and worship."

Ellen M. Rosenberg, in *The Southern Baptists: A Subculture in Transition* (1989), writes that the new conservative SBC leadership of the past decade has ties with the New Religious Political Right (NRPR). She says some of the key agenda items of the NRPR have paralleled those of the new SBC leadership group: abortion, school prayer, pornography, homosexuality, anti-ERA, etc. Rosenberg cites instances of close connection of these SBC presidents with the Religious Roundtable, Moral Majority and American Coalition for Traditional Values (ACTV), groups which she says have attempted to influence evangelicals of various denominations toward the social agenda of the Republican party (Rosenberg, 1989: 180-214). Pressure is being exerted to alter the direction of both the Christian Life Commission and the Baptist Joint Committee on Public Affairs toward this agenda. Southern Baptists are a dynamic body reflecting the changing patterns of grassroots conservative constituents.

Agency Involvement

The lead role in social ministry in the United States for the SBC has been assigned to the Home Mission Board. It is required to work with and assist churches, associations and state conventions to express Christian love and to provide a Christian witness through mission ministries, specifically through church community weekday ministries, mission centers, rescue missions, homes for unwed mothers, homes for the aging, child care institutions and programs, adoption centers, youth and family services, day care, literacy ministries, migrant ministries, disaster relief, and rehabilitation work with alcoholics, drug addicts and ex-prisoners. Personnel includes 327 Christian social ministry missionaries funded by the Home Mission Board in 38 different state conventions. They distribute a million dollars in hunger relief funds and a hundred thousand dollars in disaster relief funds annually. Southern Baptists, through state conventions and associations, serve human needs through 22 hospitals, 27 retirement facilities and 23 children's homes.

The Woman's Missionary Union and the Brotherhood Commission has been a major force for ministry in the SBC. They involve all age groups in "mission action" to persons with special needs who are not members of the church or its programs. Undoubtedly, this has further led to systemic change at the root level in their respective cities and towns.

The agency of the SBC charged with major responsibility in the area of social concern is the Christian Life Commission. Its purpose statement reads:

> To assist Southern Baptists in the propagation of the gospel by (1) helping them to become more aware of the ethical implications of the Christian gospel with regard to such aspects of daily living as family life, human relations, moral issues, economic life and daily work, citizenship, world peace, and related fields; and by (2) helping them create, with Gods' leadership and by his grace, the kind of moral and social climate in which the Southern Baptist witness for Christ will be most effective. This emphasis in the field of applied Christianity is pursued with the full awareness that the chief concern of the Christian Life Commission is in the area of Christian social ethics, which is understood to mean the application of Christian principles in everyday living. The Commission seeks (1) to assist the churches by helping them understand the moral demands of the gospel, and (2) to help Southern Baptists apply Christian principles to moral and social problems.

A standing committee of the SBC is the Public Affairs Committee, which works directly with the Baptist Joint Committee on Public Affairs (BJCPA), a group supported by several Baptist denominations, with headquarters in Washington, D.C. The objective of the BJCPA is "To conduct, promote, counsel, and advise with leaders of the cooperating conventions in study and research concerning the meaning of Baptist heritage and practice with respect to contemporary public policy and to provide them with continuing research facilities and opportunities from the vantage point of the nation's capital." They are especially active in the area of speaking to the national government in regard to church-state issues. The BJCPA has been under heavy criticism recently for their moderate stand in such areas as school prayer and abortion. Attempts are made at the SBC annually to decrease their budget and establish a strictly Southern Baptist presence in Washington, DC that will reflect the agenda of a more conservative SBC.

There are coalitions of churches and individuals, not officially tied to the agencies of the SBC, which are taking a prophetic stand on justice issues. Two of these are SEEDS, which deal with hunger, and Peacemakers, which has combined with other Baptists in a North American Baptist Peace Fellowship. They encourage churches to become involved in influencing government on these respective issues.

Relationship Between Faith and Social Ministry in the SBC Tradition

There is a consistent voice among Southern Baptists calling for individual Christians to become involved in social ministry and social action. E. Y. Mullins, our most influential theologian of the past, interprets the relationship of what some would see as an individualistic faith with social ministry: "The doctrine of the soul's competency...goes further than individualism in that it embraces capacity for action in social relations as well as on the part of the individual. ...The idea of the soul's competency embraces the social as well as the individual aspect of religion" (Mullins, 1908: 55). To Mullins a social conscience and social concern spontaneously evolve from regeneration. It is a high and idealistic view of conversion.

Herschel H. Hobbs, protege of Mullins, believes that "improving the social order and establishing righteousness" on earth will begin with the regeneration of persons (Hobbs, 1971: 129). Changed individuals will involve themselves individually and with "all men (sic) of good will" in social ministry and social action (1963 Baptist Faith and Message, Article XV).

C. Anne Davis, Dean Carver School of Social Work at Southern Baptist Theological Seminary, has a similar viewpoint: "Christian social ministry is generally defined as the activities carried out by redeemed individuals called by God to proclaim the good news, to minister to the needy, and to seek justice for all."

Delos Miles, Professor of Evangelism at Southeastern Baptist Theological Seminary, in the preface of his 1986 book *Evangelism and Social Involvement*, expresses the relationship of evangelism and social ministry in a manner that would be acceptable to most Southern Baptists:

> Evangelist Billy Graham defined evangelism in 1983 as "the offering of the whole Christ, by the whole Church, to the whole man, to the whole world." If the world-renowned evangelist was right, and I believe he was, then evangelism and social involvement are two wings of the same gospel bird. Evangelism and Christian social concern are two sides of the same coin. If one side of a coin is missing, that coin has lost its value. The lack of a social conscience impugns the reputation of the holy God and leads to societal failure. Evangelism is surely a blood brother to social involvement. Perhaps we need something like physicist Nils Bohr's 1927 Theory of Complementarity in Physics to help us view the essential wholeness of the gospel. E. Stanley Jones, an indefatigable evangelist, said: "An individual gospel without a social gospel is a soul without a body, and a social gospel without an individualized gospel is a body without a soul. One is a ghost and the other is a corpse (p. 7).

Southern Baptists' historical commitment to the Bible has consistently involved us in social ministry and social action. Southern Baptists have not ignored the social message of the Bible, especially as declared in the pre-exilic prophets and the gospels. We are more likely to interpret the truths of the Bible in regard to social concern on a biblical theology based on specific passages or on an accumulation of similar passages within their context than on a theology of social ministry based generally on the implicit rather than on the explicit thrust of the biblical revelation.

Samuel S. Hill, the premier interpreter of Southern Protestantism and a former Southern Baptist "preacher's kid," wrote in *Southern Magazine* how five Baptist leaders in the South relate religion and politics. All of these diverse views are present today among Southern Baptists: (1) The late Martin Luther King, a Progressive National Convention Baptist, dynamically interrelated the two, seeing both religion and politics as basic to Christian life and incapable of being ranked. Southern Baptists are the most ethnically diverse Protestant denomination in the U.S.; this view is prevalent among the leadership of our 1,100+ predominantly black churches. (2) Jimmy Carter, a Southern Baptist, accepts both piety (morality defined mainly in interpersonal and social categories rather than as private morality) and social justice responsibility as Christian qualities and thus interrelates the two. (3) Billy Graham, a Southern Baptist, compartmentalizes religion and politics, with evangelism viewed as the highest good; he believes the converted will bring about a moral order. (4) Pat Robertson, who is on the fringe of Southern Baptist life, believes God reveals to spiritually attuned persons His will in a detailed manner for a strong America. (5) Jerry Falwell, though not a Southern Baptist, is among the most admired within the right wing of the conservatives of the SBC; he believes the Bible has laws which apply to all people whether religious or not. Again, we Southern Baptists are a diverse people, unwilling to give up our personal freedom or local church autonomy.

In summary, Southern Baptists believe that regenerate believers will work inside and outside the church to meet human need and work for a just society. This belief closely links faith to social ministry, especially in areas of personal one-on-one ministry. Social action has evolved from faith among Southern Baptists, but not to the consistency of some mainline denominations on a broad agenda of justice issues. In recent years social action on various issues has been fostered on a national scale, but most significantly among the left wing of the moderates and the right wing of the conservatives. Social action in selected areas, such as gambling, pornography, and alcohol abuse has consistently occurred on a state and local scale.

How Southern Baptists Have, in Practice, Linked Faith and Social Ministry

The following are various research projects which reflect Southern Baptists' practice in regard to social ministry and action.

1. C. Anne Davis developed a "Mission Action Research Report" based on the period October 1986 to February 1988, that contrasted the adult members of Woman's Missionary Union (WMU) who were active in mission action with actual or potential members of WMU assumed not involved in mission action. The definition used in the questionnaire was: "Mission Action is ministering and witnessing to persons of special need or circumstance who are not members of the church or its programs; mission action is also combating social and moral problems" (p. 8).

The greatest self-perceived influence for their involvement in mission action were: (1) life of Jesus; (2) Bible; (3) discipleship; (4) needs of people; (5) purpose of the church. Davis concludes: "It is evident that the items which influence the most respondents are Biblical and theological issues...the nature of the church and the needs of people are next highest....beyond these, there is personal satisfaction" (pp. 57-8). Another answer reveals that women are more actively involved if their parents and/or siblings are or were involved in mission action.

The greatest mission involvement is to the poor, nursing homes, sick, hospital and families with problems. Davis argues that these are the needs most generally known and experienced by the public and the problem areas where WMU members themselves are most vulnerable. The areas listed that receive the least involvement are to military groups, drug abusers, runaways and latch key children.

2. Nancy Tatum Ammerman, assistant professor of sociology of religion, Candler School of Theology, developed an unpublished SPSS cross-tabulation based on 480 returned questionnaires mailed to a random sample of Southern Baptist laity in 1985. Among her findings: (1) 89 percent of Southern Baptist laity answered "very true" or "somewhat true" to the statement: "My church puts a lot of

emphasis on providing care for the needy." (2) Of the 45 percent who answered "very true" to the above question, 97 percent put "very true" or "somewhat true" to the question on whether their church put "a lot of emphasis on evangelism and soul-winning." (3) Only 23 percent (higher than the 22 percent average) of the churches that put "a lot of emphasis on evangelism and soul-winning" promoted "social change." Based on these findings Southern Baptist churches that emphasize evangelism also emphasize social ministry. Southern Baptist churches do not generally support social change; however, an emphasis on evangelism does not necessarily mean less emphasis on social concern.

3. A 1986 NFO Panels study of 40,000 homes isolated 3,358 Southern Baptists. The research is described as "the largest most solid picture...of Southern Baptists...in recent years" (Hayes, 1988: 49). Twenty-four "things which many people consider to be moral, or economic problems" were listed. Respondents were asked to check five of the items "which concern you most." The highest chosen were: use of drugs, child abuse, high divorce rate, abortion, drinking of alcoholic beverages, terrorism and parental neglect. The lowest were, beginning with the lowest percent: capital punishment, women's rights/opportunities, spouse abuse, racial discrimination and nuclear disarmament.

4. Harold Songer, vice president for academic affairs and professor of New Testament interpretation at Southern Baptist Theological Seminary, in the book *Ministry in America* (1980), interprets Southern Baptists in the extensive "Readiness for Ministry Project," based on 5,000 randomly selected seminary oriented laity and clergy entrances. He concludes that the significant dissimilarities Southern Baptists have with most mainline denominations are: "(1) an open and verbal acknowledgement of religious experience; (2) encouragement and maintenance of a relevant Biblical faith, as manifested by teaching the Bible as authoritative; and (3) an active concern for the unchurched showing itself in an assertive style of personal evangelism" (Schuller, 1980: 265-6). In these three characteristics Southern Baptists show similarities to the more evangelical groups in the study. But, we are unique in that we contrast with these evangelical groups and are more similar to the mainline denominations in our commitment to social action and involvement. "Southern Baptists interpret

this commitment as entailing both aggressive individual evangelism and social action..." (Ibid., p. 266). Thus, Southern Baptists are considered in this research as giving a balance to evangelism and social ministry to an extent not usually found among either evangelical or mainline denominations.

5. Murray H. Leiffer, in a 1969 book entitled *Changing Expectations and Ethics in the Professional Ministry* (pp. 99-108), gives comparative data on the opinions of ministers of five Protestant denominations regarding social ministry and social action. On the question: "The denomination should increase its support of special ministries, such as high-rise apartments, migrant workers, 'hippies' and drug addicts, etc," Southern Baptists were only behind the Presbyterians but ahead of Methodists and United Church of Christ in positive responses. But, regarding two statements, "The ministry must become increasingly involved in meeting and influencing the power structures of our society" and "In city areas where there is acute racial tension, ministers of all racial groups should engage actively in efforts at social construction," Southern Baptists scored the lowest.

6. Two reports indicate a correlation between size of church and social ministry. There is a relationship between the size of the church and whether it has a benevolence committee—from 15 percent with churches size 1 to 99 progressively up to 85 percent with 1,500 to 1,999 members (Baptist Sunday School report, "Size of Leadership Target Groups," RS-290, January, 1975). Larger churches (over 500 members) have an average 4.2 social ministries, medium size churches (200-500 members) have 2.4 ministries, and small churches (under 200 members) have 1.7 ministries. "The three top ministries for small churches were visitation to older adults, crisis services (rent payment, gasoline, referral) and family counseling. Medium-size churches offer these three plus food and/or clothing closets. Large churches tended to also offer day care in addition to the basic four types of ministries (February, 1985 Baptist Viewpoll with responses from 154 pastors and 238 ministers of education in "Percentage of Southern Baptist churches reporting Christian Social Ministries, 1985" by Clay L. Price, Research Division, Home Mission Board, SBC, October, 1985).

7. George W. Bullard, Jr., Director of Missions for the South Carolina Baptist Convention, in a study of Southern Baptist churches

in transitional communities for the period 1965 through 1975 discovered that: "Of churches perceiving their ministry emphasis or style as evangelism, only 47.6 percent...declined (in membership); of those perceiving a combination of evangelism and Christian social ministry 73.5 percent had declined, and of those perceiving a style of Christian social ministry 87.5 percent had declined." He maintains that this does not necessarily mean the first group had less social ministry activities, but their intentionality differed.

8. George Gallup Jr. (1985: 169-70) states: "Those in our surveys who fit our category of 'highly spiritually committed'...are vitally concerned about the betterment of society. They are, for example, far more involved in charitable activities than are their counterparts. A total of 46 percent of the highly spiritually committed say they are presently working among the poor, the infirm and the elderly, compared to 36 percent of the moderately committed, 28 percent of the moderately uncommitted, and 22 percent of the highly uncommitted." Though this category does not exclusively apply to Southern Baptists, we perceive ourselves this way. The same Gallup report (1985: 34) indicates 72 percent of Southern Baptists said religion was very important in their own lives; Lutherans and Presbyterians 55 percent; Methodists 56 percent; Episcopalians 37 percent. Early results from a spring 1986 "Church Planning Inventory" of Hartford Seminary's Center for Social and Religious Research indicates the same results. There is a direct correlation between those Southern Baptists who score high on evangelism and those who score high on social ministry.

9. I have had the opportunity of leading 115 churches and 22 associations in the development of missions strategies. The major event in this process is a retreat in which laity and clergy are asked to list needs in their churches and communities. Without exception, social ministry needs are surfaced and goals and action plans developed. Out of the faith of Southern Baptists in rural and urban churches, whether they be working class, blue collar or middle income, social concerns spontaneously arise.

There are several reasons why Southern Baptists score higher on social ministry questions than social action questions. First, involvement with people in social ministry is perceived as being more "people oriented" and offering a greater opportunity for "reaching persons for Christ" than that of involvement in changing social structures. Second, it is more difficult for lay persons to interpret the scripture as calling for the "transformation of corporate society" than that of demanding personal ministry. Third, the term social action is a "loaded term" with perceived negative connotations. Southern Baptists score higher when asked if they support organizations that are politically involved in moral and social concern issues. Fourth, many Southern Baptists believe that involvement in and activities dealing with the complexities of social evils takes energy and resources away from the main concern, which is evangelism.

Conclusion

Southern Baptists are an idealistic people, believing that, in a free and non-creedal environment, regenerate Christians guided and motivated by a biblical theology will voluntarily choose to minister to human need and work toward a just society. In congregationally controlled churches where the power to act arises from the grassroots, it often takes longer than in a "top down" system to act on justice issues, especially controversial matters that will result in significant social change. However, when Southern Baptist churches take action in regard to corporate injustices, our actions are honest. That is, the actions represent the majority of the church members and not the often more socially conscious denominational employees.

Eighmy was pessimistic about Southern Baptists in his day for not dealing adequately with some of the serious justice issues that had arisen from an industrialized society. However, he believed there was hope in the prophetic voices that have always been a part of Southern Baptist life.

Southern Baptists have a tradition of significant involvement in social ministry, but historically have been reticent about a broad based and balanced agenda of social action, except in selected areas. But, God is not through with us yet.

References

Bullard, George W. 1979. "What is Happening with Churches in Transitional Areas." In *Search*, Summer 1979 (*Journal of Sunday School Board*, SBC in Nashville).

Carter, James E. 1976. "American Baptist Confessions of Faith: A Review of Confessions of Faith Adopted by Major Baptist Bodies in the United States," in William R. Estep, ed., *The Lord's Free People in a Free Land* (Fort Worth, Texas: Faculty of the School of Theology. Southwestern Baptist Theological Seminary). In 1979 Shurden article listed below.

Carter, James E. 1964. "The Southern Baptist Convention and Confessions of Faith, 1845-1925 (unpublished Th.D. dissertation, Southwestern Baptist Theological Seminary, Fort Worth, Texas). In 1979 Shurden article listed below.

Eighmy, John Lee 1972. *Churches in Cultural Captivity*. Knoxville: The University of Tennessee Press.

Gallup, George Jr. 1985. "Religion in America." In *The Annals of the American Academy*, 480, July, 1985.

Hayes, Kenneth E. 1988. "1986 Survey of Southern Baptists." *Quarterly Review*, April, May, June.

Hill, Samuel S. 1986. "Billy, Jimmy, Pat and Them: A Layman's Guide to Religion, Politics, and the Southern Tradition." *Southern Magazine*, November, 1986.

Hobbs, Herschel H. 1971. *The Baptist Faith and Message*. Nashville: Convention Press.

Hobbs, Herschel H. "Southern Baptists and Confessionalism." In *Review and Expositor*, Vol LXXVI, No. 1, Winter, 1979.

Hudson, Winthrop S. 1979. *Baptists in Transition: Individualism and Christian Responsibility*. Valley Forge: Judson Press.

Leiffer, Murray H. 1969. *Changing Expectations and Ethics in the Professional Ministry*. Evanston: Garry Theological Seminary, Northwestern University Campus.

Lumpkin, William L. 1959. *Baptist Confessions of Faith*. Philadelphia: The Judson Press.

Lumpkin, William L. "The Nature and Authority of Baptist Confessions of Faith." In "Review and Expositor," LXXVI, No. 1, Winter, 1979.

McBeth, H. Leon 1987. *The Baptist Heritage*. Nashville: Broadman Press.

Miles, Delos 1986. *Evangelism and Social Involvement*. Nashville: Broadman Press.

Mullins, E.Y. 1908. *The Axioms of Religion*. Philadelphia: The Griffeth & Rowland Press.

Mullins, Edgar Young 1917. *The Christian Religion in its Doctrinal Expression*. Philadelphia: The Judson Press.

Parham, Robert 1989. "Am I My Brother's Keeper." In *Light*. A publication of The Christian Life Commission, SBC, April-June, 1989.

Religion in America 1984. The Princeton Religion Center, Inc. The Gallup Report No. 222, March, 1984.

Rosenberg, Ellen M. 1989. *The Southern Baptists: A Subculture in Transition*. Knoxville: The University of Tennessee Press.

Schuller, David S., Merton P. Strommen and Milo L. Brekke, editors 1980. *Ministry in America*. San Francisco: Harper & Row.

Shurden, Walter B. 1980. "The 1980-81 Carver-Barnes Lectures." Wake Forest, N.C., Office of Communications, Southeastern Baptist Theological Seminary.

Shurden, Walter 1983. "The Baptist Association: A Historical Introduction." In *Associational Bulletin*, November/December.1983, Vol 17, No. 10 (Journal of the Associational Administration Development of the Home Mission Board, SBC in Atlanta).

Shurden, Walter B. 1979. "Southern Baptist Responses to Their Confessional Statements." In *Review and Expositor*, LXXVI, No. 1, Winter.

Torbet, Robert G. 1950. *A History of the Baptists*. Philadelphia: The Judson Press.

Wamble, Hugh 1958. *Through Trial to Triumph*. Nashville, Convention Press.

9

NAZARENES AND SOCIAL MINISTRY:
A HOLINESS TRADITION

Michael K. Roberts

Introduction

The Church of the Nazarene is considered a part of the "evangelical" or "conservative" Protestant church. To the outsider looking in, the house of "conservative" Christianity mostly appears as one of disarray. Confusion often occurs when one tries to distinguish between fundamentalists, evangelicals, pentecostals, and holiness groups. William Abraham in his book, *The Coming Great Revival*, talks about a professor who defined the main difference between fundamentalists and evangelicals as "evangelicals are really `fundamentalists with good manners'" (Abraham, 1984:IX).

Frustrated and confused, most outsiders ignore the subtle differences and combine these traditions by labeling them with titles such as: sectarian Protestantism, conservative Protestantism, fundamentalism, evangelicalism, and "the religious right." Some of the major sociological studies have grouped these traditions together for the purpose of analysis (Pope, 1942; Johnston, 1961; Hunter, 1983). While some consolidation is necessary in some research, most consolidation is not justified and is often misleading (Smith, 1957 and 1962; Warburton, 1969; Dayton, 1975 and 1976; Nees, 1976). To ignore the important theological and sociological distinction between these traditions would be equivalent to ignoring distinctions among other major church traditions as Lutheranism and Roman Catholicism.

The Church of the Nazarene is a part of the "holiness" tradition. Historically, the church traces its roots back to the teachings of John Wesley, an Anglican minister in the 18th century, who was instrumental in the great social reform movement in England of that century. The church maintains that it stands in the direct succession of the teachings of John Wesley and "early" Methodism. More accurately, the church is a synthesis of the Methodist doctrine of "Christian Perfection" and the 19th century revivalism movement which dates back to Charles G. Finney.

In the last half of the 19th century, there was a widespread holiness revival movement not only in Methodism itself, but also among several Protestant denominations. Out of this movement grew numerous holiness papers, local camp meetings and associations, missions, and colleges. But the movement was by no means popular and opposition to its message and lifestyle arose. By the turn of the century, many of these groups and associations were forced to band together for mutual encouragement and support. It was out of this movement that the Church of the Nazarene and related holiness churches [the Church of God (Anderson, IN), Pilgrim Holiness Church] were formed.

The first Church of the Nazarene was founded in Los Angeles in 1895 by Dr. Phineas F. Bresee, a pastor and presiding elder of the Methodist Episcopal Church. Bresee had the unusual ability of forming intimate alliances with similar groups and associations across the country. Within 10 years, dozens of churches had been organized under the Nazarene name, not only on the West Coast but reaching far into the heartland of the United States. In 1907, Bresee's group united with an association from the East Coast to officially form the new denomination. In the next year, 1908, a large group from the South joined the new denomination, giving a truly national scope to the church. This latter date became the official "birthday" of the Church of the Nazarene.

Beginning with a little over 10,000 members in 1908, the Church passed the 100,000 mark by 1930, and by 1950, there were already 225,000 members. Today, the Nazarenes have over 5,000 churches and more than 500,000 members in the United States alone.

Compared with other denominations and faiths, the Church of the Nazarene is relatively small. But, if one were to add the membership of the Church of the Nazarene to that of its sister denominations in the holiness tradition (e.g., Wesleyan Church; Free Methodist; Salvation Army; Church of God, Anderson), the total membership would constitute the seventh largest family of Protestant churches around the world (Dieter, 1972). Another thing to consider is that holiness churches have strict membership requirements and therefore, church attendance is often much higher than membership. It is quite common for Sunday School attendance to be double the size of membership (Dayton, 1975). As a result, holiness churches claim a wide constituency of several million. A group of this size in American Protestantism cannot be overlooked.

To explore the relationship between the holiness tradition (specifically, the Church of the Nazarene) and social ministry, this chapter will focus on three main topics: the holiness conception of faith, the holiness tradition and social ministry, and the relationship between faith and social ministry.

The Holiness Conception of Faith

The holiness tradition, in general, and the Church of the Nazarene, in particular, were most profoundly influenced by the teachings of John Wesley. Wesley was not the creator of any "new" theology, rather his creativity was the synthesis of several traditions (e.g., Catholic, Anglican, Calvin, Lutheran, Moravian). George Croft Cell (1935: 347) best summarizes Wesley's work by stating "the Wesleyan reconstruction of the Christian ethic of life is an original and unique synthesis of the Protestant ethic of grace with the Catholic ethic of holiness."

One of the best examples of this synthesis is found in Wesley's conception of faith, an essential component of the holiness movement. Mildred Wynkoop (1972: 223), a Nazarene theologian, declares:

> He [Wesley] stood squarely in the Reformation tradition in
> his declaration of salvation by faith alone as an antidote to
> the Roman Catholic emphasis on works. But he was

equally emphatic about a vital correction to Reformation theology which he felt was biblical, that love was the antidote to faith as an end in itself without works.

Wesley accepted the Protestant reformers' view that people are justified by faith alone (sola fide). Faith is not the cause of salvation, but the condition of receiving it. "Our faith does not save us but we are saved by Christ in whom we have faith" (Wynkoop, 1967: 66). Wesley declared that because of the sinful nature of human beings, repentance is necessary before faith can be exercised. The Church of the Nazarene follows Wesley's thought by stating in its "Articles of Faith" (Manual, 1980: 29):

> We believe that repentance, which is a sincere and thorough change of the mind in regard to sin, involving a sense of personal guilt and a voluntary turning away from sin, is demanded of all who have by act or purpose become sinners against God. The Spirit of God gives to all who will repent the gracious help of penitence of heart and hope of mercy, that they may believe unto pardon and spiritual life.

Therefore, William Greathouse (a General Superintendent in the Church of the Nazarene) states, "The link between repentance and salvation is faith—trust in Christ and Christ alone...To believe is to put one's whole weight down upon Christ, to trust the merits of His life, death, and resurrection" (Greathouse and Dunning, 1982: 79).

Wesley proclaimed the great Protestant slogans of sola fide and sola scriptura, but he interpreted solus to mean "primarily" rather than "solely" or "exclusively" (Outler, 1964). Wesley (1968: 77) argued that faith was not one of assent but rather:

> ...faith itself...is still only the handmaid of love...Love is the end of all the commandments of God. Love is the end, the sole end, of every dispensation of God, from the beginning of the world to the consummation of all things.

For Wesley, faith is not an intellectual affirmation or belief. Faith must be dynamic rather than static. Faith is not the end but the means to the end of restoring God's love in the human heart. Love

means to the end of restoring God's love in the human heart. Love is a "by-product" of faith. Love and faith cannot be separated. Faith leads to love, a holy love of God and of one's neighbor.

Therefore, faith has an ethical implication. "It is a moral commitment with moral consequences" (Wynkoop, 1972: 236). For Wesley, faith means a realignment of one's life to please God. Faith is the foundation for the new love and obedience. This love and obedience is holiness, sometimes referred to as the holiness ethic. Holiness is the love and obedience which faith in Christ initiates and develops (Wynkoop, 1967).

Thus, for the holiness tradition, the most distinguishing and essential component of the faith is the holiness ethic. It is this component that differentiates the holiness movement from fundamentalism, evangelicalism, and pentecostalism. The holiness tradition is more oriented to the holiness ethic and the spiritual life than to a defense of doctrinal orthodoxy which tends to be the main concern of evangelicalism and fundamentalism (Dayton, 1975; Nees, 1976). That is not to say that doctrine is not important to the holiness movement; it has just not been given the prominent status that fundamentalism has given it.

The holiness ethic has received its central position in the church because the cardinal doctrine of "entire sanctification" as the "second work" of God's grace. This teaching encourages the Christian to seek the "higher" Christian life, free from original sin or depravity. This crisis experience is subsequent to conversion—the "first" work of grace. Sanctification brings the believer "into a state of entire devotement to God, and the holy obedience of love made perfect" (Manual, 1980: 31).

A believer is sanctified by receiving the "baptism of the Holy Spirit," who empowers the believer for life and service. However, the Church of the Nazarene, like most holiness groups, does not believe that this baptism is manifested through the speaking in "tongues." It is this difference that separates the holiness groups from the pentecostal churches. In fact, the holiness groups are among the strongest critics of the "charismatic movement."

The holiness ethic and its doctrine of sanctification have often been trivialized by outsiders who describe this ethic as "no smoking, no drinking, no gambling, no theater-going, etc." Although such standards are true of most holiness groups, such an image often hides from view an important and significant ethic and lifestyle that has had a profound effect on our social world.

This holiness ethic not only emphasizes the importance of one's relationship with God but also stresses the importance of one's relationship with one another. One cannot have one without the other. Contrary, the fundamentalists' and evangelicals' focus is on matters of belief or doctrine. A fundamentalist believes certain "doctrines." While the holiness tradition would not deny the importance of doctrine, those who subscribe to the holiness tradition would maintain that there is much more. Even Wesley spoke of the devils of being "orthodox;" they lack the true Christian faith which manifests itself in "repentance, and love, and all good works" (Wesley, 1968: 63).

This holiness ethic and its related doctrines must be subjugated to "tests" of truth: experience, scripture, tradition, and reason. The holiness tradition, along with Wesley, puts great stress on personal experience of faith. For Wesley, this is a direct reaction to "formal" religion which tends to stress the "form" of religion without the "power" of religion, which is God's love working through the lives of individuals. Wesley's sermons stressed the importance of "heart religion." For the holiness tradition, it is only through the inward witness of the Spirit that one can understand the meaning of true faith in Christ.

But experience alone is vulnerable to error. Therefore, all religious experience must be subjected to scripture. It is at this point that Wesley and the holiness tradition stands clearly with the classical Protestant view of the scriptures as the final authority in matters of faith and practice. Wesley was very cautious about a religion based upon feeling; therefore, he continually stressed that one should ground their religious experience on scripture.

But one must be careful of how she/he interprets the scripture and of his/her "personal" religious experience. Thus, Wesley and the holiness tradition have a great appreciation for the church's tradition. It is not surprising, therefore, to find churches in the holiness tradition participating in the Christian calendar, reading the creeds (e.g., Apostles' Creed), and observing the Christian sacraments (e.g., baptism, the Lord's Supper). One's personal experience is always subjected to the collective experience. The holiness churches are very suspicious of "peculiar" experiences (e.g., "speaking in tongues") and will suggest to such individuals who engage in such experiences to seek another congregation.

Finally, the last, but not least, test of truth is reason. For Wesley, religion and reason go "hand in hand;" all irrational religion is false religion. Thus faith must be a "reasonable" faith. Colin Williams (1969: 32) summarizes the Wesleyan position on the role of reason as:

> The importance of reason is not that it provides another source of revelation, but that it is a logical faculty enabling us to order the evidence of revelation; and that, with tradition, it provides us with the necessary weapons for guarding against the dangers of the unbridled interpretation of Scripture.

H. Orton Wiley (1967:147), a Nazarene theologian, compares faith and reason in the following way: "Faith honors reason...Reason approves the evidences upon which faith rests, and therefore in the whole economy of redemption, the Scriptures of revelation and the voice of sound reason blend into one perfect and harmonious whole."

Consequently, the holiness tradition sees no conflict between faith and learning. Since its beginning, the Church of the Nazarene has made a strong commitment to higher education. The denomination has established eight liberal arts colleges in the United States and over 200 other special schools around the world.

In addition to formal education, the Church of the Nazarene promotes faith development among its constituents by a number of means. First, it has maintained a publishing company, the Nazarene Publishing House, for over 75 years. The literature it produces is distributed to the constituents in the form of Sunday School materials, adult Christian reading, biblical study aids, and devotional materials. All of these materials are for the purpose of developing one's relationship with God and with one another.

Another means of promoting faith development is the strong emphasis the Church of the Nazarene has on world missions. The church supports more than 600 missionaries in over seventy world areas. The general church also finances a worldwide radio program, "Showers of Blessings." It is carried by over 700 stations, in more than thirty world areas, in at least a dozen different languages.

On the local level, the Church of the Nazarene promotes faith development in a variety of ways. First, faith is primarily developed through public worship. A typical Nazarene church has a morning worship service and an evening service every Sunday, plus a mid-week service each week. Although attendance varies from service to service, the norm is for every constituent to attend every service. In addition to these regular services, most congregations will have at least two special service events (revivals) each year which will last for a couple of days to two weeks in duration.

When attending a Nazarene church service, one finds a number of ways faith is expressed. The first is the centrality of preaching. In nearly all Nazarene churches, the pulpit is found in the center of the platform. The focus of the worship service is the reading of the scriptures and the proclaiming of the Gospel. Often sermons focus on encouraging the "righteous" to walk a "holy life" and/or persuading the "sinners" to commit their lives to Christ.

Another important faith development in public worship is singing. The Nazarene church has often been referred to as "the singing church." Every service is filled with different kinds of music (e.g., congregational singing, special solos, choir specials, instrumental music). Through music, people express their faith and commitment to Christ.

Finally, faith is expressed in public worship by giving. Offerings are a part of every service. As a result, the Church of the Nazarene has one of the highest per capita giving figures among all denominations. People give sacrificially as an expression of their faith in Christ.

Another example of how faith development is promoted at the local church level is through religious or Christian education. Most churches have Sunday Schools that emphasize faith development. Sunday School is not just for children, but for all ages. Classes are created for the everyone, from the babies to the oldest senior adult.

Finally, the local congregation promotes faith expression in numerous activities. These activities include: youth Bible quizzing, youth camps, Bible studies, retreats, church dinners, community outreach and service programs, and evangelism programs. All such activities stress the relationship of faith to the activity. If the spiritual side of such activities were omitted, the local congregation probably would drop that activity because it is too "secular" in nature.

These programs for faith development, both at the local and general level, were at one time more informal and spontaneous in nature. Today, they have become more institutionalized and have become common characteristics of the Nazarene church. The church will continue its present emphasis on faith development since it has ranked among the top denominations in growth for several years.

The Holiness Tradition and Social Ministry

Historically, the American holiness movement was at its very heart a social reform movement. Contrary to popular belief, the holiness movement did not grow out of a reactionary protest to the social gospel movement. In fact, similar social and theological positions gave rise to both the holiness movement and the social gospel movement (Smith, 1957). Both were responding to the new social problems of industrialism in the cities of the 19th century and the structural evils that industrialism had brought with it.

One of the first social issues that the holiness movement confronted was slavery. Most of the early holiness advocates were abolitionists. Early holiness groups such as Oberlin College, Wesleyan Methodists, and Free Methodists were explicitly abolitionists and worked on both the structural and individual levels for the abolishment of slavery (Dayton, 1976).

Closely connected to the issue of slavery were the rights of women. Again, the holiness movement was actively involved. Oberlin College became the first to accept women, of which several graduates became the most radical feminists of that era. The first women's rights convention was held in a Wesleyan Methodist church (Dayton, 1975). The holiness movement was among the first to ordain women. The Church of the Nazarene at its beginning, not only ordained women, but established a special ministry for women— the deaconess. Women were able to participate on any level of the church hierarchy. Some served as pastors, evangelists, missionaries, and educators. In addition to playing a very prominent role in the early years of the Church of the Nazarene, the church became a forum for advancing women's rights by officially supporting the adoption of the nineteenth amendment (Schwartz, 1984).

Another social problem that the holiness movement became directly involved with was the ministry to the "poor and oppressed." One meaning of the "free" in Free Methodist was the church's opposition to church pew rent, which served to exclude the poor (Dayton, 1975).

Phineas Bresee, founder of the Church of the Nazarene, left a socially elite church to minister among the poor of the inner city slums. The name "Nazarene" was chosen because it symbolized "the toiling, lowly mission of Christ," thereby identifying Nazarenes with the poor and oppressed of society (Smith, 1962: 111). One of the first buildings Bresee used for his new congregation was very plain. He defended his choice in an editorial in his paper (Bresee, 1899: 2):

> We want places so plain that every board will say welcome to the poorest. We can get along without rich people, but not without preaching the gospel to the poor. We do not covet the fine churches of our neighbors; we only long after a richer anointing with the Holy Ghost, that we may be committed to reach the poor and the outcast, for whom some care so little but for whom our Redeemer lived and died. Let the Church of the Nazarene be true to its commission; not great and elegant buildings; but to feed the hungry and clothe the naked, and wipe away the tears of the sorrowing; and gather jewels for His diadem.

The holiness movement supported a number of "relief" works in the cities with the Salvation Army as the best example. Many orphanages were formed and several homes for unwed mothers were established.

Several other social problems of the 19th century (e.g., support for prohibition, opposition to large corporations, opposition to war) could be cited to demonstrate the active involvement of the holiness movement. But what has happened to the holiness movement, in general, and the Church of the Nazarene, in particular, in the twentieth century concerning social reform and social ministries? Simple. It has made a complete reversal. Smith (1962: 318) describes this shift within the Church of the Nazarene:

> Consequently the social work which has inspired so much devotion in the early years suffered from steadily increasing neglect. Rescue homes and missions disappeared from district programs. Pronouncements on social issues, when made at all, were buried in the reports of committees on public morals whose real preoccupation was standards of personal behavior among church people. The order of

denomination, declined in both numbers and influence. Even the ancient commitment to prohibitionism was restated in terms of personal rather than social regeneration.

There are three basic reasons for this "great reversal." First, the fundamentalist/modernist controversy of the 1920s had a great effect on the withdrawal of the holiness tradition from social activism and social ministries. Although the holiness groups were not directly involved with the debate, they were forced to choose sides. By siding with the fundamentalists which stressed the importance of orthodoxy, the holiness groups put social ministries lower on the priority list.

Second, three secular events took place in the 1920s and 1930s that almost totally crushed all social reform and social ministries: (1) the destruction of World War I and, with it, the promise of a better world; (2) the failure of prohibition to reform society; and, (3) the Great Depression, which virtually "dried up" all available resources.

The third basic reason for the "great reversal" was the increase of wealth and affluence among the converts of the poor. No longer were the holiness groups confined to the small "storefront" churches of the inner city. New churches were built in the suburbs of the cities, where the members and their new found wealth were moving.

Evidence today would strongly suggest that holiness groups like the Church of the Nazarene have been extremely influenced, if not completely dominated, by the fundamentalist movement. For example, the church of the Nazarene no longer speaks out against racism. Also, the church no longer takes an active role in advancing women's rights. In fact, in 1980, the General Assembly adopted an anti-ERA platform. In 1908, approximately 20 percent of the church's ministers were women; in 1975, 6 percent (Schwartz, 1984).

With this evidence, it appears that the church has become a fundamentalist church. Its emphasis is upon personal action rather than social action; individual sin instead of social morality; and "vertical" relationship instead of "horizontal" relationships. It appears that all social ministry must be carried out by individual members and social reform must be avoided.

But, just when one might declare social ministries dead, several "rumblings" can be heard coming from the ranks. A survey was done by the denomination in 1982 of all Nazarene churches in urbanized areas. The questionnaire listed 10 areas of social ministries (i.e., job placement, housing renewal, housing placement, medical service, day-care, adult education, clothing and food distribution, immigrant counseling, alcohol/drug rehabilitation, and legal counseling) and asked each church to indicate on a scale of 0 to 10 (0 = not involved, 10 = very involved) how involved their church was in each social ministry. Six hundred twenty-one congregations out of 2,034 (31.1%) indicated they were highly involved in at least one of these social ministries at a level of six or above (See Table 1). This is a rather large percentage of churches involved in some type of social ministry, especially if one thinks of social ministries as being non- existent in conservative Christianity.

On the denominational level, the church created a new office in 1984 called "Nazarene Compassionate Ministries." In one of the brochures produced by this new office, its policy is stated as:

> Being under mandate from scripture, and compelled by our holiness heritage, the Church of the Nazarene will respond in the following areas through the utilization of resources provided by our people:
>
> 1. To alleviate the pressing human and physical needs arising from natural disaster, personal tragedy, and other acute need.
>
> 2. To seek ways and means to find longer range solutions to the problems confronting the needy.
>
> 3. To seek to do scriptural holiness as a practical demonstration of the love of Jesus Christ for all mankind.

In addition, a Nazarene Hunger and Disaster Fund, established in 1975, has offered immediate relief to acute needs around the world. What was started as a sincere attempt to respond to the victims of the 1973 earthquake in Guatemala has developed into a fund that is supported by contributions from individuals and churches. This fund in the last few years has increased dramatically (see Figure 1) and consequently, has branched out into several new areas of relief (see Figure 2).

Finally, the church is still actively involved in its missions program. While social ministries diminished here in the United States, the church continued its social ministries around the world. The church supports more than 31 dispensaries, 3 hospitals, and 197 day and special schools around the world.

As suggested by the title of the "new" office and its policy statement, the focus of the general church is on "charity" rather than upon social justice issues. While the Church of the Nazarene is increasingly becoming more involved in social ministries, it has yet to step out into the area of social reform—the area that helped nurture its birth.

The Holiness Ethic and Social Ministry

Anthony Campolo, in a recent address to the personnel of the Headquarters of the Church of the Nazarene, stated that the "Nazarenes were truly the `light of the world.'" But he added, "the problem with Nazarenes, as is true with all lights, is that they attract `bugs!'"(Campolo, 1984). The Nazarenes, as well as other holiness groups, had tended to attract the "bugs" of society; the socially disinherited, the poor, the outcasts, the "rejects" of society. But this was the mission or purpose of the church, to minister to the "bugs" of society. It was for this reason that the church began.

To the outsider, it is surprising to discover that the holiness tradition and the Church of the Nazarene were middle class movements (Jones, 1974; Nees, 1976), responding to the plight of the poor and the need for social reform. It is of little surprise that, when the Nazarenes quit appealing to and working with the poor, they became a typical middle class church.

As stated earlier, the holiness ethic is the distinguishing factor for the holiness tradition. Faith alone is not sufficient for God's redemption. Out of faith must come good works. The book of James is just as important for the holiness tradition as the Pauline Epistles— "faith without works is dead." The holiness ethic stresses "love" rather than just "faith;" "doing" rather than just "knowing;" and "being" rather than just "believing."

It is this component that distinguishes holiness groups from evangelicalism and fundamentalism. The holiness ethic was the motivating force behind the involvement of the early holiness movement in social reform.

In the past couple of generations, there has been a great dilution

In the past couple of generations, there has been a great dilution of the holiness ethic. The holiness ethic has been reduced to just a religious experience. Commitment is now given to living a "pietistic" lifestyle for one's own personal gratification, not for its social implications. Holiness is expressed in "inward" experiences rather than "outward" manifestations. Therefore, the holiness ethic and its relationship to social ministries has been severely damaged. Now, the dominant attitude among holiness groups is that social ministry is a nice thing to do for some people, providing it doesn't get in the way of their personal relationship with God. The holiness ethic is reduced to "don't drink, don't smoke, don't dance," because these things are "bad" for the individual.

Although the holiness tradition has narrowed and weakened its understanding of the holiness ethic, there still lies dormant a seed of social concern which could erupt in the near future, producing a crop of social activism which would send the holiness movement into the battle for social reform and justice. In all of "conservative" Christianity, the holiness people are most likely to take up an active role in social issues because of their holiness ethic.

While the majority of the Nazarene churches have little or no interest in becoming involved in social ministries, there is a surprisingly large percentage who are highly involved in at least one type of social ministry (Crow, 1984). But, how can Nazarenes, who share the same tradition, the same theology, the same holiness ethic, the same religious experience, sometimes the same congregation, take such different positions toward church involvement in social ministries? Two recent studies (Crow, 1984; Roberts, 1989) on the Church of the Nazarene have focused on this question. Three major findings from these studies strongly suggest some possible reasons for this phenomenon to occur. First, Crow (1984) discovered that one of the best predictors of why some churches are involved in social ministries was their location in the inner city. He found that the closer the church is to the inner city, the more likely it is to be involved in social ministries. It appears that structural conditions, such as church location, play an important role in promoting social ministry among Nazarene churches. The denomination has very few churches within the city limits of the major metropolitan cities in America. Most churches are located in the suburbs. This fact alone helps explain why the majority of Nazarenes are not involved in social ministries.

Second, Roberts (1989) obtained data from a survey of twelve Nazarene congregations located in various areas of the United States in the summer of 1985. Some congregations were highly involved in social ministries while others were not involved at all. A comparison was done, using 708 usable returned questionnaires (60 percent return rate). The major finding of this study pertains to the members' attitudes toward the cause of social problems. The more church members believe the root cause of social problems, such as poverty, lies within the social system, the more they want their church to become involved in social ministries. People who believe social problems are created by society tend to maintain that these problems must be addressed in a structural manner (e.g., the church), not just through individual efforts.

The third major finding also comes from Roberts' (1989) study. I found that Nazarenes who attend socially active churches want their churches to continue with their social ministries. It appears again that a structural condition (i.e., belonging to a socially active church) has an important effect on the individual believer.

As new interest in social ministries among Nazarenes continues to grow, more tensions and struggles are certain to arise between those who want to stress only faith development (and evangelism) and those who want to include a greater emphasis on social ministries. At present, there are no blatant battles being mounted. However, there are "quiet rumblings" involving those who fear movement toward social activism and the social activists who are pushing for increased social ministries. When the two camps clash, the battles of the 1920s could very well be relived.

Perhaps the new labelling of social ministries in the Church of the Nazarene as "Compassionate Ministries" has averted the confrontation, at least for the present. This label appears to have sidestepped the battles over terminology and emphasizes that these ministries are indeed expressions of one's faith.

If such a confrontation does develop, the two possible outcomes are: (1) acceptance of social activists as a viable part of the church; or, (2) expulsion of those especially interested in social ministries.

The first choice means understanding those interested in social ministries, interpreting their views for others who may disagree with them, and not "pitting" their views against those who may not want the churches to be socially involved. It would be important for church leaders to do all they can to integrate these "dissenters" and their views into the thinking and actions of the entire church from the grassroots level on up.

If the dissenters are not integrated, they will become increasingly alienated. Those who feel that social ministry is an important expression of their faith tend to be highly involved in their local church, are young people, and have a high level of education and abilities (Roberts, 1989). Considering these attributes, this would be a tremendous loss for the church.

Conclusion

The decline of social ministries and social reform in the Church of the Nazarene was a direct result of the church's decision to relocate away from the central cities to the affluent middle class suburbs. In doing so, the church and its membership moved away from its "structural" views of social problems and adopted the middle class view of explaining social problems from an "individualistic" perspective. The Nazarenes even changed their "holiness ethic" to conform with their "individualistic" world view. The holiness ethic was reduced to include only the individual's actions as they relate to the vertical relationship between the individual and God. As a result, social ministries were severely reduced and social reform became non-existent.

But the Church of the Nazarene is now taking steps to return to the city from which it was born. The church has launched a new denominational program, "Thrust to the Cities," which is to locate new churches within the major central cities again. The church has actively cultivated ministries among minority groups. This effort has more than tripled the number of ministries in the last 17 years (see Table 2).

If the major conclusions of this paper are correct, the relocation of churches within central cities may produce a renewal of social ministries and eventually a renewal of social reform within the Church of the Nazarene. The most important factor in determining whether renewal will take place is if these new churches will be targeted for the minority, the poor, the outcast, the "bugs" of society or will be for the affluent sector of the city. Perhaps the social holiness ethic shall live again.

Table I

Congregations Involved in Social Ministries				

	Low		High	
	N	%	N	%
Job Placement	1944	95.7	87	4.3
Housing Renewal	1989	98.3	34	1.7
Housing Placement	1959	96.6	68	3.4
Medical Service	1973	97.5	51	2.5
Day Care or Child Education	1712	84.5	313	15.5
Adult Education	1901	94.3	114	5.7
Clothing & Food Distribution	1752	86.4	275	3.6
Immigrant Counseling	1975	97.5	51	2.5
Alcohol or Drug Rehabilitation	1945	95.8	85	4.2
Legal Counsel	1970	97.2	56	2.8

Low = 0 to 5
High = 6 to 10 (0 = "not at all" and 10 = "very much")

Missing cases excluded from percentages

A total of 621 (31.1% of the responses) churches indicate that they are involved in at least one of these compassionate ministries at a level of six or higher.

Table 2

Nazarene Ethnic Works*
Canada and the United States

Group	1970 Works	1987 Works
American Black	62	103
American Indian	32	57
Arabic	0	3
Armenian	0	5
Cambodian	0	21
Chinese	5	16
Deaf	0	2
East Indian	0	2
Eskimo	1	1
Ethiopian	0	1
Filipino	1	4
Finnish	0	1
French	0	6
Haitian	0	32
Hawaiian	0	1
Indo-Pak	0	1
Japanese	1	3
Jewish	0	1
Korean	0	46
Laotian	0	11
Portuguese	2	5
Samoan	1	6
Spanish	68	202
Vietnamese	0	6
West Indian	9	15
Multiracial	1	13

*A work can be either a "Fully Organized Church," "Church-Type Mission," or "Language Bible Class." These columns include latest data as reported to Church Extension Ministries.

(Source: Office of Church Extension Ministries)

Figure 1

Hunger and Disaster Fund
Total Approved Projects
1976 Through 1986

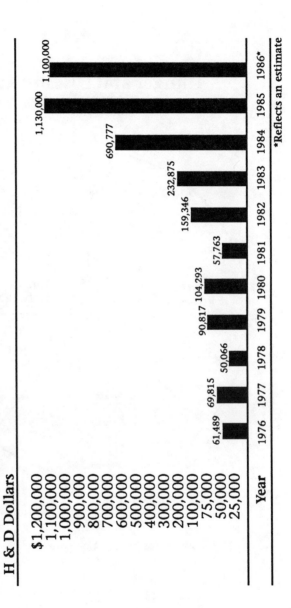

H & D Dollars

Year	Amount
1976	61,489
1977	69,815
1978	50,066
1979	90,817
1980	104,293
1981	57,763
1982	159,346
1983	232,875
1984	690,777
1985	1,130,000
1986*	1,100,000

*Reflects an estimate

Figure 2

Hunger and Disaster Fund
Disbursements by Category
1986

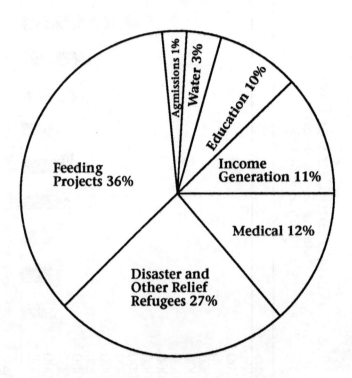

(Source for figures: Cook and Weber, 1987)

References

Abraham, William J., *The Coming Great Revival: Recovering the Full Evangelical Tradition*. San Francisco: Harper and Row, 1984.

Bresee, Phineas F., "The First Nazarene Church Building." *The Nazarene Messenger*. July 3:2, 1899.

Campolo, Anthony Jr., "Assimilation of the Nazarenes." Presented at the Association of Nazarene Sociologists of Religion, Kansas City, MO, 1984.

Cell, George Croft, *The Rediscovery of John Wesley*. New York: Henry Holt and Co., 1938.

Cook, R. Franklin and Steve Weber, *The Crisis: How the Hunger and Disaster Fund is Helping*. Kansas City, MO: Beacon Hill Press, 1987.

Crow, Kenneth, "Nazarene social work: Economic beliefs and compassionate ministry in a holiness denomination." Presented at the Association of Nazarene Sociologists of Religion, Kansas City, MO, 1984.

Dayton, Donald W., "The holiness churches: A significant ethical tradition." *The Christian Century*. February 26:197-201, 1975.

_____, *Discovering an Evangelical Heritage*. New York: Harper and Row, 1976.

Dieter, Melvin E., "The concept of the church in the nineteenth century holiness revival." *The Church*. Edited by E. Dieter and Daniel N. Berg. Anderson, Indiana: Warner Press, Inc., 1972.

Greathouse, William M. and H. Ray Dunning, *An Introduction to Wesleyan Theology*. Kansas City, MO: Beacon Hill Press,1982.

Hunter, James Davison, *American Evangelicalism: Conservative Religion and the Quandary of Modernity*. New Brunswick, N.J.: Rutgers University Press, 1983.

Johnston, Benton, "Do holiness sects socialize in dominant values?" *Social Forces*. 39:309-316, 1961.

Jones, Charles, *Perfection Persuasion: The Holiness Movement and American Methodism*, 1867-1936. Metuchen, N.J.: Scarecrow, 1974.

Manual of the Church of the Nazarene. Kansas City, MO: Nazarene Publishing House, 1980.

Nees, Thomas G., "The holiness social ethic and Nazarene urban ministry." Unpublished doctoral thesis. Wesley Theological Seminary, 1976.

Outler, Albert C., (ed.), *John Wesley.* New York: Oxford University Press, 1964.

Pope, Liston, *Milhands and Preachers.* New Haven: Yale University Press, 1942.

Roberts, Michael K., "Evangelicals' Attitudes Toward Social Ministries: A Study of Nazarenes." Unpublished doctoral dissertation. West Lafayette, Indiana: Purdue University, 1989.

Roberts, Michael K. and James D. Davidson, "An obscure paradox—evangelicals involved in social ministries." Presented at the annual meeting of the Society for the Scientific Study of Religion, 1985.

Schwartz, Karen S, "The role of professional laywomen in the social ministry of the Church of the Nazarene." Unpublished Master thesis. Ohio State University, 1984.

Smith, Timothy, *Revivalism and Social Reform: In Mid-Nineteenth Century America.* New York: Abingdon Press, 1957.

_____,*Called Unto Holiness.* Kansas City, MO: Nazarene Publishing House, 1962.

Warburton, T. Rennie, "Holiness religion: An anomaly of sectarian typologies." *Journal for the Scientific Study of Religion.* 8:130-139, 1969.

Wesley, John, "The almost Christian." *Wesley's Standard Sermons.* Edited by Edward H. Sugden. London: The Epworth Press, 1968.

Wiley, H. Orton, *Christian Theology.* Vol. I. Kansas City, MO: Beacon Hill Press, 1943.

Williams, Colin, *John Wesley's Theology Today.* London: The Epworth Press, 1960.

Wynkoop, Mildred Bangs, *Foundations of Wesleyan-Armenian Theology.* Kansas City, MO: Beacon Hill Press, 1967.

_____, *A Theology of Love.* Kansas City, MO: Beacon Hill Press, 1972.

10

"UNTIL MY CHANGE COMES":
IN THE AFRICAN-AMERICAN BAPTIST TRADITION

Cheryl Townsend Gilkes

African-Americans who are Baptist possess a complex organizational heritage. They are also heirs to a worldview, tradition, and history which inform their approaches to faith and social ministry. If I were a denominational executive, I would perhaps write about the intersection of faith and social ministry in the National Baptist Convention, U.S.A., Inc.(to which my congregation currently belongs), or I would write about faith and social ministry in the National Baptist Convention of America, or I would write about faith and social ministry in the Progressive National Baptist Convention (to which my congregation *formerly* belonged). Since some congregations in each of these conventions are "dually aligned" with the American Baptist Churches (as is my congregation), I could also write about the racial-ethnic minority experience of faith and social ministry in a predominantly white Baptist denomination. Such organizational complexities of African-American Baptist congregations and denominations are rooted in a system of racial dominance and its crises of race and class. Thus the African-American Baptist religious traditions combine African sensibilities, American evangelicalism, and African-American social consciousness in response to biblical mandates and community needs.

This paper will discuss faith and social ministry in the African-American Baptist tradition. That tradition encompasses at least three major denominations and a very vibrant organizational history contributing to their formation. A focus on social ministry highlights the complexities of the African-American religious experience in the United States. It is an experience which is predominantly Baptist in its organizational forms but is a widely shared tradition beyond denominational and congregational boundaries. Definitions of faith are rooted in this larger tradition and appeal to both scripture and personal experience for their authenticity. Both doctrine and folklore appeal to the oft-quoted passage in Hebrews 11: 1, "Now faith is the substance of things hoped for and the evidence of things not seen," as a starting point for a faith which is hope-filled and future oriented. The demand for social ministry antedates the organization of African-American Baptist churches. It is a phenomenon largely actualized in the local church and responds to immediate social crises — a persistent problem for an oppressed population. These responses to local social crises have been constitutive of a larger tradition of social activism, the civil rights movement being the most prominent example.

First, I provide a brief history of African-American Baptists and their tradition in order to clarify the organizational diversity which arises from common historical foundations and the forces which shape the responses which constitute social ministry. I then describe a model of faith that seems to capture the biblical-experiential foundations of the tradition. These are found not only in the minimal amounts of denominational literature focused on doctrine and polity, but they are also found in the stories, songs, testimonies, prayers and sermons—what James Cone has pointed to as the resources for Black theology. After an examination of faith, I then explore its consequences for social ministry in local and national terms. I pay particular attention to the civil rights movement and to the work of Nannie Helen Burroughs. These examples, along with the work of local churches, capture the ways in which needs were defined and addressed. Finally, I point to the primacy of the local church as the setting for social ministry since it is the local examples which become the models for other local churches through denominational and other forms of church interaction.

and other forms of church interaction.

Historically, African-American Baptist churches have addressed a wide range of problems. Congregations learn from one another in formal and informal settings. The current crises of black urban communities (the growth of an underclass, massive economic change, homelessness, the problems of black families, the reorganization of class relations within black communities, and the crisis of A.I.D.S.) all combine to give social ministry an "emergent" or situated character.

The African-American Baptist Tradition of Social Ministry

The earliest African-American Baptists called themselves African Baptists and addressed themselves to abolition and foreign missions. Several historians have pointed to the "radical" and rebellious nature of these early Baptists. They shared, along with other African-American Christians, a line of activities which contributed, according to Paris(1985: 129), to

the emergence of the black church independence movement— a socio-religious event that began to assume institutional expression in the late eighteenth century....The major objective of that movement was the institutionalization of the Christian faith in a nonracist form.

According to Paris's analysis, "that goal alone has constituted the final aim and purpose of the black churches." Because of their aim to live out "their commitment to the parenthood of God and the kinship of all people," Paris (1985: 129-130) argues that black churches share a common "black Christian tradition." Thus the African-American Baptist tradition is, unlike other clearly demarcated denominational faiths, part of an African-American tradition that has provided a persistent ethical and political challenge to the American mainstream.

Ironically, there is disagreement among historians concerning the earliest African Baptist congregations. Suffice it to say that in the late eighteenth century South, Virginia, Georgia, and South Carolina were areas in which enslaved black people organized their "first" churches. The earliest social ministries focused on the problems that enslaved women and men faced in forging an ethical human existence under an inhumane system. Between 1788 and 1834, according to Washington (1986: 23), there was a rapid growth of African Baptist churches that was checked by white reaction to the 1831 Nat Turner rebellion. He writes:

> ...between 1788 and 1834 black Baptists formed their first consciously black Baptist congregations and supported the rise of the major black Baptist leaders who formed regional associations. These leaders argued for the formation of these associations ostensibly for the purpose of engaging in missionary work beyond the local congregation. But more was at stake than the fulfillment of the missionary dream to save the world for Christ. Between 1788 and 1831, black Baptist congregations acquired a peculiar and precarious religious freedom.

The earliest black Baptists were "missionary" Baptists whose ministries emphasized the importance of political freedom, social justice, and religious liberty.

The central problem of African-Americans during this period was slavery and their ministries reflected that fact. One source of conflict between black and white Baptists was the insistence of black Baptists on carrying communion to slaves unable to attend Sunday services. Another area of response was the matter of internal discipline and the ethical underpinnings of family life. African Baptist churches provided the ecclesiastical sanctions which enabled slaves whose spouses were sold away to remarry.

The problems of race and racism were also central to the early organization of these churches. Along with black Methodists and Episcopalians, black Baptists were also the victims of segregation in the slave galleries of northern churches. Protests over such treatment led not only to the formation of the African Methodist Episcopal and African Methodist Episcopal Zion churches, but also to the formation of northern congregations such as the Abyssinian Baptist Church in New York City. Missionary efforts were consistent over racism. Early missions to West Africa in Liberia and Sierra Leone (Fitts, 1985: 111-112) sought to provide a redemptive redefinition to the experience of slavery at the same time these missionaries spread the gospel and laid the groundwork for the local assimilation of Christianity. Other missions in the late nineteenth century, especially those in South Africa, developed land and built roads. The ethic of autonomy and local control led to the establishment of missions which laid the groundwork for church formation by African Christians themselves.

Slavery contributed to the organizational complexity which developed among African-Americans who were Baptist. The fear of slave revolts made it increasingly difficult for slave churches to exist unsupervised, although, as Sobel (1979: 205) points out, a number of white churches hid black Baptist churches on their roll books while collaborating in a religious autonomy where "blacks maintained control over finances, discipline, membership, and prayer." Although African Baptist churches enjoyed the fellowship of "white" or "mixed" associations (and as Sobel also hints, there is a problem in assuming unilateral white dominance in white associations), they also pursued relationships with each other across regional lines. Cooperation with white organizations was problematic because of the conflict over slavery. White Baptists in the South eventually separated from northerners over the issue in 1845. Some abolitionist Baptists withdrew earlier to form the Free Mission Society in 1843 in cooperation with African -Americans and "it appeared that this group might merge with a black convention to become a national 'anti-caste' convention (Washington, 1986: 43)." As Washington (1986: 83) later points out, this organization was the only *national* tie between major white and black Baptist organizations until 1970.

As the history of African-American Baptists developed, the problems of the prevailing political system contributed to the content of their ministries. Such an emphasis in social ministry diverged from the predominant white Baptist approach (i.e., southern) which saw the spiritual and the political as opposites. Washington (1986: 108-8) argues that the post slavery era was one in which:

> Black Baptists discovered that chattel slavery, with its odious advocacy of America as a white Herrenvolk democracy, had spread into nearly every crevice of the body politic....Northern black Baptists, like blacks in other denominations,...dreamed of creating a "Christian America." But their Christian America would most definitely be a multiracial society.

The importance of political ethics as part of the preaching and ministry of Baptist churches was an area of debate and argument which contributed to the foundations of what become the National Baptist Convention, currently "the nation's third largest protestant denomination," (Sernett, 1985: 423).

Overall, the National Baptist Convention was formed in a national context which comprised at least nine national bodies. An impetus for national organization was missions, both home and foreign. In this area, the definitions of social ministry were hammered out.

The most visible area in which social ministry was pursued at the national level was education. The most successful home and foreign mission projects were educational institutions and a substantial proportion of the foreign mission was accomplished by Africans educated at historically black colleges and universities in the United States. These colleges and universities were a focus of home mission activities. One significant line of activity in the formative years of the National Baptist Convention was the formation of a National University. Although unsuccessful, a small group formed a National Baptist Educational Convention because they believed that "education is a 'necessity in the proper development of true Christ-like lives,'" (Washington, 1986: 175).

Over the decades between 1880 and now, two major splits have occurred within the National Baptist Convention, U.S.A., Inc., creating two smaller competing denominations, the National Baptist Convention of America (1915) and the Progressive National Baptist Convention (1961). The most recent of these splits was exacerbated by two competing ideologies of social ministry in the context of the civil rights movement. Public and covert cooperation across denominational lines, since then, has usually involved some form of social ministry.

At the national level, the legacy of slavery and the African-American Christian challenge to racism has created a legacy of social ministry which focuses on education and the advancement of a nonracist Christianity. These emphases are missions and supported by numerous local and regional Baptist associations for schools and colleges. The importance of local congregations in the education of black children throughout the segregated South cannot be detailed here. However, suffice it so say that the provision of primary and secondary education (basic literacy) represents one of the most important dimensions of social ministry. This activity also created "educators," both women and men, who were seen as important leaders within the denomination. Their lives and work became important stories about faith *and* works.

Faith as Trust, Commitment and Works

In addition to its organizational context, the social ministry of African-American Baptists developed in the context of a religious worldview. One historical observer has called this an "Afro-Baptist faith." According to Ninian Smart, religious worldviews comprise six basic dimensions, the experiential, mythic, doctrinal, ethical, ritual, and social. Social ministry usually incorporates some combinations of the social, ethical, and doctrinal dimensions. On the other hand, faith as understood in the western context is often located in the dimensions of ritual, experience, and myth. It is in this area of faith where the sacred texts, community, and the person come together in a coherent whole which actualizes a religious system. This is clearly the case with African-American Christians, especially the majority who are Baptist.

As with other Baptists, the Bible represents the central text for religious discourse and models of faith. For African-American Baptists, the authority of that text is affirmed and established through a tradition of preaching and song which selects a canon within the biblical canon. The actual practices that are sometimes drawn from the recipes contained with Baptist creeds and confessions become linked to the fiduciary faith stressed in selected texts focused on Job, Daniel, Ruth, the "woman at the well," the "least of these," and Jesus. In addition to preaching and song, testimony during Sunday morning devotionals and at weekly prayer services serves to connect biblical and traditional models to the experiential and social dimensions. Trustful faith actually mediates suffering and admonitions such as "take your burdens to the Lord and leave them there" and "tell [God] all about our troubles" serve to actualize this kind of faith.

Doctrines contained in Baptist articles of faith reinforce the importance of the Bible. Such statements are most often taken from the New Hampshire Confession which is reprinted in publications of the three major conventions.[1] The first article deals with the authority of Scripture and is the central pillar upon which subsequent professions of faith, doctrine, and order are constructed. The seventeen articles which follow all begin, "we believe that Scriptures teach that..." Within this confession, "faith" is specifically aligned with the process of repentance and it is depicted as an active orientation required of the believing Baptist: "We believe that Scriptures teach that repentance and faith are sacred duties, and also inseparable graces, wrought in our souls by the regenerating Spirit of God...." The radical consequences of this consciousness of sin are that "... *we turn* to God with unfeigned contrition, confession, and supplication.

Perhaps the most significant faith text is found in the story of Job. African-American ritual, with its pillars of testimony, prayer, song, and preaching, has carefully selected and edited elements of Job's story to create a script that prescribes a trustful adherence to belief in the most outrageous of circumstances. Early in life, African-Americans learn these key passages from the book of Job through the oral traditions of preaching, testimony, and song:

"Though He slay me, yet will I trust in Him (13: 15)."

"I know that my Redeemer liveth and that He shall stand in the latter day upon the earth...yet in my flesh I shall see God (19: 25)."

"All of my appointed time, I will wait until my change comes (14: 14)."

These phrases are prayed, sung, and attested to in a variety of settings— Sunday service, mid-week prayer meeting, funerals, and special services. "All of my appointed time, I will wait until my change comes" is found in the form of a spiritual which is still sung. A very popular gospel song implores, "Lord, help me to hold out... until my change comes." The story of Job is also preached and repreached. Either the text for the sermon itself is taken from Job or Job becomes an example of great faith within the larger context of the sermon, particularly when that sermon addresses the problem of coping with suffering. Job has been extended, within the preaching tradition, to the experiences of both women and men who have endured and overcome the suffering of social injustice, making Job the principal role model for the Afro-Baptist faith tradition.

It is not simply Job's endurance that is important, however. It is Job's expectation and demand for change that is also a critical piece of the story. It is not just Job sitting in the ashes mourning and suffering. It is also Job's demand for an audience with God, his insistence that his situation is unmerited, his ultimate vindication, and his call to prophetic witness which make him a continuing model within the oral tradition of faith. All of these references to faith carry spoken and unspoken scripts which admonish endurance in the face of great suffering and hope-filled anticipation in the most impossible of circumstances.

The tradition of suffering and the socio-political realities of racial oppression in the United States have contributed much to the forging of this "trustful walk with the Lord." The problem of suffering and oppression has been so great that analyses often ignore the other dimensions of social and cultural life that evoke solidarity and identification. The trust model of faith that this oppression and suffering seem to elicit, however, is tied to an optimism that undergirds much of the ritual expression of the Afro-Baptist tradition. The image of Job is tied through a variety of expressions to the articulation of hope that is found in the biblical faith statement of Hebrews 11: 1, "Now faith is the substance of things hoped for, the evidence of things not seen." These are recited quite often in the context of worship and everyday life. Identifying this as part of the core belief system of African Americans, Henry Mitchell (1986) points to the vernacular character of these expressions in his exploration of theology in the clinical and secular settings of African American life.

Stories that emerge from slave folklore point to the importance of this text as an orientation for faith toward hope and action. It also provides an interpretive framework for understanding the traditional relationship between perspectives on the real world and visions of the eschatological future or "the sweet by and by." These visions often shroud this model of faith in stereotypes which affirm the opiate nature of African American religion and ignore the action component of this hope-filled faith. Theologian John Kinney tells a folklore story that highlights the importance of Hebrews 11: 1 as a faith text:

A man and his son were working in the fields. Along about lunch time the young man went into the cabin and found his mother there cooking a large pot of cabbage. He asked her, "Mummy, may I have some of that cabbage?" She replied, "Not now, son, that's for by and by and after while." The young man spotted a loaf of bread and asked if he could have some of it. His mother told him to help himself. He took a big hunk of the bread and carried it over the cabbage pot and held it next to the place where the steam was coming out, until the bread was saturated with the steam smelling of cabbage. He went back to the fields. His father asked him, "What have you got there?" The young man answered, "I've got me some cabbage." His father looked at it and said, "Boy, that's nothing but an old piece of bread." The young man answered, "No, Daddy, this is the substance of cabbage hoped for, the evidence of cabbage unseen."

Such insights from folklore emphasize the connections between faith in an ultimate end and practical action for real world here and now. It is the connection between faith and works. That connection demands strategies to realize the objects of hope. Judging from the content of popular hymns, the idea that "...soon from all life's grief and danger, I shall be free some day" (Tindley, 1905) is inseparable from an image of an everyday journey "through this wilderness below" and, consequently, an inevitable struggle and contest:

> Harder yet may be the fight;
> Right may often yield to might;
> Wickedness a while may reign,
> Satan's cause may seem to gain;
> There is a God who rules above,
> With hand of power and heart of love,
> If I am right, He'll fight my battle,
> I shall have peace some day.

Forged in the midst of social injustice, this faith involves proactive endurance and every day survival along with a simultaneous struggle for social justice and change. Action in the context of faith involves coping with the very real problems which stem from historic racism, class disadvantages, and injustice while at the same time seeking the kind of transformations that make possible the end of suffering. In its historical foundations, this faith was tied to a community that comprised "all God's children" who were making a trustful walk with "the Lord" who has "[never] seen the righteous forsaken" (Psalm 37: 25).

Thus this position of fiduciary faith demands works. Within the Afro-Baptist tradition, these works are shaped in an eschatological context in which Jesus describes the final judgment. Most often quoted is Matthew 25: 31-45 where Jesus emphasizes service to the "least of these" as the ultimate criterion for final reward. In it Jesus tells those being welcomed into the kingdom:

> For I was an hungered, and ye gave me meat: I was thirsty, and ye gave me drink: I was a stranger, and ye took me in: Naked, and ye clothed me: I was sick, and ye visited me: I was in prison and ye came unto me. Then shall the righteous answer him, saying, Lord, when saw we thee an hungered, and fed thee? or thirsty, and gave thee drink? When saw we thee a stranger, and took thee in? or naked, and clothed thee? Or when saw we thee sick, or in prison, and came unto thee? And the King shall answer and say unto them, Verily I say unto you, Inasmuch as ye have done it unto one of the least of these my brethren, ye have done it unto me (Matthew 25: 35-40, King James Version).

Traditional emphasis on this story has served to focus human beings as a pathway to the afterlife. It is this connection with service to God ("the King") and service to humanity, particularly the stranger, which has served to shape social ministry and the ethics of hospitality in African-American communities.

African-Americans' radical stance on this text has been helped but not often not means tested in church practice. When forced to choose between mercy and judgment, church folk will usually err on the side of mercy, an ethic that has gotten African-Americans criticized for their failure to punish sinners such as unwed mothers by refusing to provide for their children, a tension that went all the way back to emancipation (Hill, 1972; Litwack, 1979). The ultimate implications of this text are socialism and the writings and work of George Washington Woodbey, an active socialist and Baptist preacher, represent a significant example of where this text can take one politically. He precipitated an important debate in the journals of the

A.M.E. church which made clear the parallels between socialist ideals (won peacefully) and primitive Christianity. Furthermore, the activities and writings of the Baptist preacher, not the first or only one to advocate socialism (Foner, 1983: 5), underscores the transdenominational character of the African-American religious tradition of social ministry.

Social Ministry as Confrontation with Suffering

Suffering is not the only distinctive component of the Afro-American experience. However, in the construction of social ministry, the needs of a suffering community in the form of the church itself have been a powerful force. Social injustice is an overwhelming external fact with sometimes overwhelming internal consequences. Furthermore, social injustice has been historically persistent and culturally adaptive. The demands for social ministry that flow from this trustful faith and its implications for action are complex and sometimes contradictory. To summarize the complexity and contradiction, it is important to realize that social ministry as confrontation with suffering involves, at many times and under some conditions, social ministry as effort to transform and to challenge existing social arrangements.

The political implications of the free church polity which undergirds Baptist practice also contribute to the entrepreneurial quality of social ministry. The local character of the activities that can be characterized as social ministry means that the efforts of the notable individuals, congregations, and other groups tend to merge with other bodies within and beyond African-American communities who share similar religious and social goals. For instance, the problem of teenage pregnancy in Washington, D.C. prompted sociologist Joyce Ladner to develop a handbook on the problem in association with the local Baptist Ministers Conference, a body which contains approximately 300 African-American Baptist pastors. The cooperative venture is important because it demonstrates the willingness of a religious body to utilize resources within the community which are formally outside of the church in order to address a widespread social problem in a creative and preventive manner.

Other social problems in local communities are addressed through coalitions among the nearby churches. In Boston, Massachusetts, for instance, in addition to the Baptist Ministers Conference of Greater Boston and Vicinity, an organization called the Black Ecumenical Commission (originally funded with a grant from the United Church of Christ) fostered cooperation among African-American congregations across denominational lines.

Peter Paris (1985: xv-xvi), in his seminal study The *Social Teaching of the Black Churches,* discovered a high degree of agreement between National Baptist and African Methodist traditions.   In his "critical ethical analysis of the self-understanding of black denominations in the Baptist and Methodist traditions" Paris observed that:

> Differences of polity and distinctive historic doctrines depict their continuity with their white counterparts, but as black churches their fundamental distinction lies in the principle that we call "the black Christian tradition." In relation to that principle, the black denominations are united.

Paris also discerned a tension between the racial self-development that their autonomous origins suggest and the social transformation necessary to idealism.   As a result, any interpretation of social ministry and its linkage to faith among African-American Baptists must take into account both diversity and unity. It is important to observe individuals engaged in social ministry in non-congregational projects, efforts, and movements in order to acquire a holistic picture. Furthermore, it is important to examine the activities of both women and men, both clergy and laity, in order to account for social ministry.   Finally, it is important to examine the ways in which the symbolic and ethical element of African-American Baptist churches spill over into the larger socio-political culture of the community.

The organizational and institutional approaches to social ministry — especially as expressed in efforts for social change, racial uplift, home missions, and education have been varied and can be characterized by a high degree of conflict and flexible responses to conflict. Two cases in the National Baptist Convention, U.S.A., Inc. illustrate this historical problem and also demonstrate the ways in which different groups develop different organizational settings to respond to community needs and realize the goals of social ministry. The first example comes from the problems that led to the rise of the

Progressive National Baptist Convention in 1961 and the second example is taken from the conflict between Nannie Helen Burroughs, a black feminist nationalist, and the National Baptist Convention. Both reflect the ways in which the politics and problems of the larger community insinuate themselves into the organizational dynamics and political interests of Black Baptist denominationalism and their consequences for the shape of social ministry within and outside Black churches.

Social Ministry and Civil Rights

A local National Baptist pastor named Martin Luther King, Jr. became involved in a ministry aimed at social transformation. After the refusal of Rosa Parks to relinquish her seat in Montgomery, Alabama, King became the head of a local grass roots movement aimed at desegregating the buses in that city. Later King became prominent as the leader of a national movement to establish civil rights — a political movement based in Black churches throughout the South and under the aegis of the Southern Christian Leadership Conference.

To oversimplify the problems leading to the conflict among National Baptist leaders and the eventual split from the National Baptist Convention, a number of progressive clergy had aligned themselves with the growing civil rights movement in the South. They challenged the power of J.H. Jackson, a conservative. The resulting conflict led to a walkout and to the formation of the Progressive National Baptist Convention, a new convention that accommodated these "progressive" pastors. In the meantime, Baptist and other African-American ministers in the South formed an alternative organization called the Southern Christian Leadership Conference (SCLC). While it is normal and accurate to view SCLC as a civil rights organization, Aldon Morris's (1984) recent analysis of the civil rights movement points out that the organization stemmed from its clerical and religious character as opposed to its political character. Calling SCLC "the decentralized political arm of the black church," Morris (1984: 87-91) shows that:

> Ministers who were in the process of leading local movements became leaders of the SCLC....SCLC was a church-

related protest organization...anchored in the church and probably could not have been otherwise.

Other analysts of the movement, failing to see the link between politics and ministry, have described SCLC as "amorphous and symbolic." However, Morris points out that, "what they overlook is that the SCLC functioned as the decentralized arm of the mass-based black church. That mass base was built into the very structure of the SCLC." That mass base was also predominantly Baptist. Later, after Rev. J. H. Jackson was succeeded to the presidency by Rev. T. J. Jemison in 1983, Jesse Jackson, addressing the convention, is reported to have remarked that there would have been no need for the formation of the Southern Christian Leadership Conference if the convention had changed its leadership.

Additional evidence for viewing the civil rights movement as social ministry comes from the character of the movement's popular culture. Much of the success of the direct action movements in the South came from the strength provided by the traditional religious symbols and practices that undergird its philosophies and actions, not an explicit set of ideologies which reflect "militancy." It is interesting to note that when the "time for a change" campaign succeeded in ousting Rev. J. H. Jackson as president of National Baptist Convention, U.S.A., Inc., the convention then elected the Rev. T. J. Jemison to succeed him. Rev. Jemison was the local pastor who lead the 1953 bus boycott in Baton Rouge, Louisiana. Morris (1984) and other observers identify that event as the actual "origin" of the public activist phase of the civil rights movement.

Since succeeding to the presidency of the convention, Rev. Jemison has fostered more denominational emphasis on social ministry within the United States, placing a renewed emphasis on "home" missions to address the problems of inner cities. Urged by South African churches served by the convention, the convention has also become more public about its activities there and the nature of the evil of apartheid. In response to the recent concern in black communities with the problems of the "underclass," Jemison (1987) prepared a statement regarding the social responsibility of churches. He wrote:

The Afro-American churches are still faced with grave

responsibilities today as never before. In spite of the fact that we do have mayors, state senators, congresspersons, and local council members, the church is still the hope of many Black Americans....The Afro-American must minister to those individuals who feel left out and locked out of the mainstream of American life. The AfroAmerican Church has the grave responsibility to reaffirm the humanity of those who are denied personhood because they lack social economic, or physical privilege.

In spite of his own particular denominational leadership, Rev. Dr. Jemison cites a number of outstanding examples of social ministry and that number includes churches that are not Baptist or members of the convention he heads. What they share is the success of local ministries that confront the crises of suffering related to economic and political powerlessness. Jemison wrote, "These churches are characterized not only by their great appeal to the Black masses, but by their great durability. They are characterized by their ability to survive; to survive in spite of the system."

The conflicts surrounding the civil rights movement both highlight and obscure the local and enterprising character of enduring social ministry. On the one hand, disagreements over strategies lead to reorganization and realignment and such changes, for African-American churches, transcend denominational lines. As in the case of SCLC, analysts fail to see the ecclesiastical character of such political organizations. On the other hand, the national visibility of the movement and its leaders deflects our view from the local realities that guide their formation and the every day suffering of people in local communities. This story of conflict and change also indicates that institutional flexibility and individual initiative make possible certain responses in spite of the resistance of conservative elements within the black community and its churches.

Social Ministry and Education

Another important emphasis of all Baptists has been education. The early leadership of the National Baptist Convention consisted of "educators," both women and men who had emerged as the leadership class of "preachers and teachers." The conflicts that have occurred in the organizational history of Afro-Baptists have been related to education and educational philosophies. Again, these conflicts demonstrate the ways in which the creation of organizational alternatives expresses the strength of the linkage between faith and social ministry. Exploring the link between social ministry and education also enables us to examine the role of women in the shaping and execution of social ministries in the black community.

If ever there were a practical linkage between biography, history, and social structure, it is in the story of Nannie Helen Burroughs, the education of African-American women, and the National Baptist Convention, USA, Inc. In her research on Burroughs and on the role of women in the Convention, Evelyn Brooks Barnett (1978) describes Nannie Helen Burroughs, the first corresponding secretary of the National Baptist Convention's Women's Auxiliary, a founder of that organization, and later its president. Burroughs was also a leader in the national African-American community and widely revered by women and men. Her Baptist activism was tied to her model of social ministry which was expressed in a wide variety of energetic ways. She is reputed to be the founder of "Women's Day", a particularly important tradition with black churches that often expresses the connection between faith and social ministry, honoring women's leadership in that area (Dodson and Gilkes, 1986: 80-91, 118-130). Her life was as a noted orator, making speeches throughout the United States that urged race pride, spiritual development, and a Christian witness appropriate for the nurture of change and social justice in the United States. She operated on the strong belief that African-American Christians had the ethical gifts to guide the larger society. In addition to her work with the National Baptist Convention, Burroughs worked with Carter G. Woodson to support his efforts at establishing the Association for the Study of Negro Life and History. She was also a militant feminist and her life was devoted to the empowerment of African-American women as workers as well as Christians, that is, "to raise women." Gerda Lerner (1972) ranks Burroughs with school founders such as Mary McLeod Bethune (Methodist), Lucy Laney (Presbyterian), and Charlotte Hawkins Brown (also Baptist). Lerner highlights the broad sweep of Burroughs's interests citing the importance of her philosophy of education in her writings appealing for funds for her school and of her social and moral philosophies in her writings speculating on the causes of the

Harlem riot, urging a new and more militant black male role model ("Unload Your Uncle Toms"), insisting upon pride in black spirituality ("Glorify Blackness"), and eschewing materialism ("With All Thy Getting, Get Wisdom"). Burroughs was distinctive and outstanding yet stood squarely in the tradition of women leaders associated with the African-American women's club movement and its motto, "Lifting as We Climb."

Burroughs's fusion of faith and social ministry is paradigmatic and illustrative in a number of ways. She identified militance and resistance as Christian duties, and she viewed the empowerment of African-American women wage earners as a component of that resistance. She founded the National (Baptist) Training School for Girls in which, according to Brooks (1978), she conceived of the school "as serving women of all faiths,...attempted to speak concretely to the material conditions surrounding black women,... [and] emphasized the training of spiritual character." Nannie Helen Burroughs connection between faith and social action involved both social transformation and self-sacrifice. This did not stop her from engaging the men of the National Baptist Convention in militant conflict over their attitudes concerning women and social change. Her flexible organizational style illustrates again the ways in which African-American Baptists have worked around the conflicts that have characterized their approaches to organizational power while meeting the demands for and of social ministry. Furthermore, her experience underscores the context of ethnic nationalism and religious idealism in which many social projects are carried out.

Conclusion: Faith and Social Ministry in Dynamic Interaction

These examples of conflict over civil rights among National Baptist pastors and over education between Nannie Helen Burroughs and National Baptist men point to the ways in which the "varieties of religious presence" within the African-American Baptist family express themselves. The life of Burroughs illustrates the way in which the ethic of endurance, shaped largely through the spirituality of African-American women, influences the response of progressive elements within the African-American Baptist tradition to its conservative opposition. The pressure of faith is always toward change, particularly change that empowers the "least of these." These examples also highlight the creative tension inherent in social ministry within black communities between the need to share very limited resources and the need to transform society. Probably the democratic "free church" ethic of Baptist churches serves to make such permanent tension workable and occasionally the foundation for pioneering creativity.

In his discussion of "social responsibility," President Jemison highlighted the importance of the faith emphasis that looks to the "least of these" in the tradition of social ministry. He wrote:

> This goal and objective is related to a fundamental understanding of Christian doctrine and praxis that is expressed with startling clarity in Matthew 25: 34-40. "Then shall the King say unto them on his right hand, come, ye blessed of my father, inherit the kingdom prepared for you from the foundation of the world:...verily I say unto you, Inasmuch as ye have done it unto one of the *least of these* my brethren, ye have done it unto me."

This emphasis reiterates the earlier aspect of faith as a trustful walk with God. Since the only trustful walk is one that engages God, this text serves as a final statement concerning the absolute necessity of social ministry as action where God is. According to Jemison, "This understanding leads to practical interpretation of the message of Christ and His church and demands radical action in order to live out this principle." What follows in Jemison's perspective is an important redefinition of social ministry from the perspective of "the Afro-American churches." Rather than working with the "underprivileged", the task involves what he calls "a re-visioning or redefining of 'privilege.'" Doing social ministry involves "seeing 'underprivileged' as an inoperative term for describing many Blacks who are essentially without the privileges or benefits of the system. We must minister to those who aren't even under-privileged, but unprivileged."

Such a task involves a solidarity with those who face the most serious emergencies of everyday life in local churches and communities. Interestingly, such solidarity involves not only services in the local churches but astute attention to national political issues and public problems. Part of the distinctive importance of the African-

American Baptist tradition, as part of the larger African-American religious experience, is its ability to address the major public issues as part of the consistent political witness of the larger African-American community. Kenneth Wald (1987: 248-252), in his analysis of the interplay between religion and politics in the United States, points to stability of Jews and African-American Protestants as "the most reliable pillars of national support for liberal candidates and causes" and to the "continued presence of members of the black clergy in political leadership roles" in spite of the challenge they face from new secular elites. He writes:

> In social action, too, black ministers have continued to provide the lead. As of 1982, the three top officials in the National Association for the Advancement of Colored People...were Protestant ministers..., as were the founders and leaders of the urban job-training organizations such as the Chicago-based "People United to Save Humanity" (PUSH) and the Opportunities Industrialization Commission (OIC) in Philadelphia. The founder of OIC, Reverend Leon Sullivan, has been instrumental in forging American opposition to the white minority regime in South Africa.

What Wald misses, however, is the fact that all of these ministers are, or were, Baptist pastors, with the exception of Jesse Jackson, who is Baptist but has never pastored. Sullivan was also the prime mover in a major series of boycotts in Philadelphia (Hamilton, 1972). These Baptist ministers are nationally recognized examples of a trend in local leadership which represents an African-American Baptist view of social ministry.

Currently such churches as Allen Temple Baptist Church in Oakland, California provide social ministries to persons with AIDS., community schools, credit unions for the poor, day care services, counseling services, family ministries, food banks and other such programs, adoption services, adolescent parenting programs, drug programs, and elderly clubs and services. These churches also have politically active pastors and church members whose work flows out of their confrontation with social problems in their local parishes. Two outstanding Baptist examples are The Honorable William H. Gray, III (D., Philadelphia), Chair of the House Budget Committee and Pastor, Bright Hope Baptist Church, Philadelphia and Mrs. Marian Wright Edelman, President, Children's Defense Fund and active member of the Shiloh Baptist Church in Washington, D.C., where Rev. Henry Greggory is the pastor. Rev. Gray's church maintains an array of social and community services, including a credit union, in one of the poorest neighborhoods of Philadelphia. Mrs. Edelman's church built and now staffs a large and comprehensive Family Life Center, under the pastorate of Rev. Henry Greggory.[2] The presence of Rev. Gray on one of the most powerful committees in Congress while representing one of the poorer urban districts emphasizes the solidarity demanded by this radical emphasis on the gospel. Congressman Walter Fauntroy is also the pastor of a Washington, D.C., church.

Congregations which represent outstanding national examples of social ministry provide social and community services in a variety of ways. These churches are paradigmatic of the interaction of faith and social ministry in the African-American Baptist tradition. Allen Temple Baptist Church in Oakland, California provides a diverse ministry which many local pastors view as a model. The congregation has job training programs, ministry to persons with AIDS, drug counseling and rehabilitation, as well as the traditional areas of pastoral care. The pastor, J. Alfred Smith, is also known for his constant admonition of affluent members in their relationship with the poor, occasionally coming to service in overalls in order to challenge any bourgeois pretensions in his congregation. Concord Baptist Church of Christ in Brooklyn, New York, has provided a community school and a major fund for supporting projects outside the church. They are credited among the funders for the Public Broadcasting System's series, "Eyes on the Prize, II." Bethany Baptist Church, also of Brooklyn, New York, has begun a restaurant and banquet hall enterprise as a source of employment and job-training. Union Baptist Church of New York City along with Bright Hope Baptist Church of Philadelphia, where Congressman William Gray pastors, have a federal credit union as part of their churches' social ministries. One of the most prominent nationally recognized models of social ministry is Shiloh Baptist Church of Washington, D.C. This church has addressed the problems of poor African-American families comprehensively with its Family Life Center, which employs a full-time social worker along with other professional staff. The center is also capable of providing banquet facilities for the community. Foodbanks represent the most numerous programs; two-thirds of the Baptist churches in my community have such programs and most Baptist churches expect their deacon boards to provide relief for individuals and families in distress. My own congregation recently voted to cease providing loans to people in need and directed the Board of Deacons to provide direct grants which need not be repaid. A former social worker from Oakland, California pointed out that, during the recessions of the 70s, he and his colleagues were able to appeal to African-American churches to fill in the gap that welfare failed to fill. Services to the elderly, like food banks, are quite common in Baptist churches, especially since the elderly are some of the most stalwart members. In addition to formally organized social services, social ministry also takes the form of direct services for poor and indigent members such as food preparation, housekeeping, and financial support. Hartford Memorial Baptist Church and Allen Temple Baptist Church are also nationally visible examples of a growing trend in churches to provide drug counseling and rehabilitative services. Several New York City congregations have also, in partnership with foundations, begun programs focused on parent education, preventive sex education, and drug abuse prevention.

President Jemison's statement closes by emphasizing the wide range of places this kind of solidarity should take the church. He writes:

> The response of the Black Baptist Church...must deal with the homeless and displaced persons...[W]e must make room for the Street People, [t]hose who have no family and no real friends. The church must somehow serve them....Then too, we must as the church, feel the pinch now being placed on the small Black farmers. We must pool our resources and help them reclaim their land. Politically we must become more astute...shar[ing] the real significance of the ballot. The Afro-American Churches must serve as a guidepost in directing our people...[W]e must provide in many instances educational opportunities for those deprived of the opportunity for learning...The Afro-American Church must administer...to "the least of these little ones."

The fundamental ethic in this traditional, scriptural linkage between faith and social ministry speaks to the treatment of the "least of these" in society. The preaching, testimony, song, and prayer traditions of the Afro-Baptist faith are particularly sensitive to these issues. However, much of the action that is linked to this faith, particularly those actions aimed at achieving social change and racial justice, is not exclusive to the church setting. The fluidity with which Jemison and others move among the terms "Black Church," "Afro-American Churches," "Black Baptist Church," "Afro-Christian tradition," "Afro-Baptist faith," and "African-American Baptist" captures the dynamic process of the relations between the majority of African-American Christians (Baptists) and the larger African-American community. In sum, the linkage between faith and social ministry involves the determination to endure and the radical optimism that change, "my change," is coming by means of a faith which lives through works.

Notes

[1]The new hymnbooks published by the National Baptist Convention of America, the second convention formed in 1915 popularly known as "unincorporated" or "the Boyd Convention," have had some interesting unintended consequences. This *New National Baptist Hymnal* contains Baptist articles of faith and is generating a new interest among congregation members in their own doctrine. Ironically, because this hymnbook also publishes the largest collections of gospel songs authored by African Americans it is rapidly becoming popular in congregations of the National Baptist Convention, U.S.A., Inc., the convention from which it split. Additionally, the Progressive National Baptist Convention contracted to have its hymnals printed using the National Baptist Convention of America's publishing house, copyright, etc. In spite of their organizational divisions, the laity's view of Baptist faith is being drawn increasingly from this one source, much to the consternation of National Baptist Convention, Inc.'s executives who find this new "red book" replacing the denominations "green book" in the churches they visit. According to one observer, the president's reminder that the churches should use the convention's hymnbook brought an equally swift reminder of local autonomy.

[2]At a recent conference concerning the church and the underclass, these and a number of other persons addressed the issues of the church and social ministry. Both the presidents of the National Baptist Convention, USA, Inc. (Rev. Dr. Jemison) and of the Progressive National Baptist Convention (Rev. Dr. J. Alfred Smith) were present and made presentations concerning the ministries of their churches as did a number of other ministers and lay people. This meeting served to emphasize the areas of deep agreement regarding social ministry.

References

Barnett, Evelyn Brooks, "Nannie Helen Burroughs and the Education of Black Women," pp. 97-108 in Sharon Harley and Rosalyn Terborg-Penn, *The Afro-American Woman: Struggles and Images*. Port Washington, New York: Kennikat Press, 1978.

Bennett, G. Willis, *Effective Urban Church Ministry: A Case Study of Allen Temple Baptist Church*, Nashville, TN: Broadman Press, 1983.

Dodson, Jualynne and Cheryl Townsend Gilkes, "Something Within: Social Change and Collective Endurance in the Sacred World of Black Christian Women," pp. 80-130 in Rosemary Radford Ruether and Rosemary Skinner, *Women and Religion in America*, Volume 3: 1900-1968. San Francisco: Harper and Row Publishers, 1986.

Fitts, Leroy, *A History of Black Baptists*. Nashville, Tennessee: Broadman Press, 1985.

Foner, Phillip S., Editor, Black Socialist Preacher: *The Teachings of Reverend George Washington Woodbey and His Disciple Reverend George W. Slater, Jr.* San Francisco: Synthesis Publications, 1983.

Hamilton, Charles V., *The Black Preacher in America*. New York: William Morrow and Company, Inc., 1972.

Hill, Robert B., *The Strengths of Black Families*. New York: Emerson Hall Publishers, Inc., 1972.

Lerner, Gerda, *Black Women in White America: A Documentary History*. New York: Random House, 1972.

Lincoln, C. Eric, *Race, Religion, and the Continuing American Dilemma*. New York: Hill and Wang, 1984.

Litwack, Leon F., *Been In the Storm So Long: The Aftermath of Slavery*. New York: Random House, 1979.

Marx, Gary T., *Protest and Prejudice: A Study of Belief in the Black Community*. New York: Harper and Row, Publishers, 1967.

Mitchell, Henry and Nicholas Cooper-Lewter, Soul Theology: *The Heart of American Black Culture*. San Francisco: Harper and

Row Publishers, 1986.

Morris, Aldon D., *The Origins of the Civil Rights Movement: Black Communities Organizing for Change.* New York: The Free Press, 1984.

Paris, Peter J., *The Social Teaching of the Black Churches.* Philadelphia: Fortress Press, 1985.

Raboteau, Albert J., Slave Religion: *The "Invisible Institution" in the Antebellum South.* New York: Oxford University Press, 1978.

Sernett, Milton C., Editor, *Afro-American Religious History: A Documentary Witness.* Durham, North Carolina: Duke University Press, 1985.

Sobel, Mechal, *Trabelin' On: The Slaves' Journey to an Afro-Baptist Faith.* Westport, Connecticut: Greenwood Press, 1979.

Smart, Ninian, *Worldviews: Crosscultural Explorations of Human Belief,* New York: Charles Scribner's Sons, 1983.

Tindley, Charles Albert, "Some Day." p. 10 in *Songs of Zion.* Nashville, Tennessee: Abingdon Press,1905.

Wald, Kenneth D., *Religion and Politics in the United States.* New York: St. Martin's Press, 1987.

Washington, James Melvin, *Frustrated Fellowship: The Black Baptist Quest for Social Power.* Macon, Georgia: Mercer University Press, 1986.

Wilmore, Gayraud S., *Black Religion and Black Radicalism: An Interpretation of the Religious History of Afro American People* (2nd Edition). Maryknoll, New York: Orbis Books, 1983.

_____,*African American Religious Studies: An Interdisciplinary Anthology.* Durham, North Carolina: Duke University Press, 1989.

11

FAITH AND SOCIAL MINISTRY:
A CATHOLIC
PERSPECTIVE

Sister Marie Augusta Neal

Introduction

In the parlance of our times, we can say that history proceeds through
major paradigm shifts, a paradigm being "a fundamental model or
scheme that organizes our view of something" (Babbie, 1989: 47).
The major paradigm shift that characterizes the relationship of faith
and ministry in the Catholic Church in the past forty years is the shift
from a transcendent to an immanent focus on ministry. This has
taken the form of centering preparation for ministry on "a special
option for the poor" as a guide to ministry and expression of faith.
It was raised to consciousness in the Second Vatican Council and was
first conceptualized as an "option for the poor" by the Medellin Conference of the Latin American Church in 1967. It is the intent of this
paper to trace the historical and causal links in that shift as they
influence the direction of emphasis in the Catholic Church's commitment to its perceived mission.

Even though the Catholic Church moved from being an immigrant church in ethnic enclaves, mostly in the inner city in the 1960s,

and took on middle class styles of worship and social interaction in the suburbs (Greeley, 1976); even though many parishes still give low priority to the justice and peace agenda in their weekly cycle of planned activities (Leege et al, 1984-89); still no sociologist studying the Catholic Church today would omit indexes to determine whether or not, and to what extent, the agenda of justice and peace as it relates to the poor is active in parish life, and if not, why not (Gallup, 1988). Even though the right wing resistance to this agenda is strong, and in media perspective, central in news coverage and political analysis, (Lernoux, 1989), still, the evidence is substantial that the dynamic for change operative in the link between faith and ministry over the past forty years is the pressure exerted by the theology of liberation. It is my intent to demonstrate that a causal link exists between "the special option for the poor," formally adopted by the Catholic Church since the Second Vatican Council, and the forms that faith and ministry take in the Catholic Church in America today.

Changing Patterns of Faith

If one chooses to focus on social structure, then the ideographic approach is essential, and every detail of life in the church in society must be described, but if the focus is on social change and the probable main causes, then the nomethetic approach is not only valid but necessary to make sense out of the current reality (Babbie, 1989: 62-63). I choose this second approach because of the striking evidence of a dynamic in the church responding to and helping to shape an emerging global social reality (Beckford and Luckmann, 1989).

In the last century, the Catholic Church's primary emphasis has shifted from an other-worldly orientation to a this-worldly orientation. Right after World War II, Cardinal Suhard, Archbishop of Paris, expressed the growing visibility of this trend in a short monograph entitled *Growth and Decline: The Church Today*, published in 1948, when the immanent emphasis had just begun to be perceptible. In this publication, he examines the mission of the church in the modern world and its current social responsibilities. In the 1950s, Thomas O'Dea, a sociologist, writing about the Catholic Church in the United States, examined some of the causes and issues of this immanent emphasis in *The American Catholic Dilemma*. Published in 1958, it pointed out the new role expectations that a this-worldly emphasis was beginning to place on clergy and laity who were from then on being asked to get involved in social issues that both challenged established authorities and called for more personal responsibility. Yves Congar, writing at that time, (in retrospect seen as remote preparation for the climax of this trend in the Second Vatican Council), redefined the role of work in the world as mission and particularly the part of the laity in social transformation. His book, *Lay People in the Church*, appeared in English in 1957. In *The Act of Social Justice*, published in 1951, William Ferree's 1940 doctoral dissertation from Catholic University demonstrated the problem of structured evil and the necessity of planned action for the reform of the social system. This reform called for a shift in the ethical emphasis in justice education from rights under the existing law systems to an examination of the justice of those very law systems within which nations operate and which the church's moral theology justifies or calls to account. These and many other studies demonstrate the now century-old trend in the church away from an emphasis on salvation outside a world perceived as too evil or secular to reform to a focus on action in the world towards its transformation as the road to salvation. The new emphasis became that of reforming institutions within a redeemed world when they deviate from what we now call protection of basic human rights of all peoples, viewed as God's people. In a study of the priests of the Boston archdiocese, which I completed in 1962, I measured the extent to which priests were aware of and responding to issues of social justice with an intent to reform the community or to resist the new movement directions. I found that 35 percent were open to change for value reasons and 11 percent for interest reasons; 21 percent were resisting change for value reasons and 28 percent for interest reasons. In this study, the stimulus to change focused on taking action against entrenched systems indifferent to human suffering as central to their ministry and rooted in their faith (Neal, 1965).

The evidence in published literature is substantial that the mandate to transform the world in social justice has gradually moved the Catholic Church to its new position on faith and social ministry, now formally defined as "a special option for the poor" (Dorr, 1984). This emphasis is a shift away from the European influence that characterized the Christianity of the United States from its origins. Now the influencing theologies are coming from Latin American to such a degree that it can be safely predicted that liberation theology, despite the current ambivalence to it among significant Catholic role players, will dominate Catholic life in the U.S. and in the world by the mid 1990s (Ellis and Maduro, 1989; Cleary, 1990).

When we study periods of history other than the one in which we live, we investigate religions embedded in the very structure of human life in society. When we examine our own era, we see religions in the context of what we have come to call "the signs of the times." Although this is a biblical phrase, as used today, it is also an analytic concept. It reveals religions involved in the making and changing of the social fabric. It is what we read in the "signs of the times" that sets our perspective on the issues of faith and social ministry. For Catholics, reading the "signs of the times" became a common factor with the pontificate of Pope John XXIII (1959-1963), the Second Vatican Council (1963-1965) and the rise and development of liberation theology from 1970 onward (Gutierrez).[1]

In this perspective then, the modes of faith expressed in the Catholic Church have changed in emphasis through the centuries (Dulles, 1977). Historically, we can see the early saints portrayed as persons engaged in contemplative prayer and directly enlightened by a divine presence. For them, faith appears to have been an illumination wherein God's presence was experienced directly. There were no words, no actions, just the sense of a divine reality. "Faith is a light and it has a point of impact on the human spirit that is more basic and pervasive than assent to particular propositions" (Dulles, 1977: 6). This kind of faith is seldom met today.

In the long influence of scholasticism within the Catholic tradition, faith became a deposit, a collection of beliefs to which one adheres loyally by accepting the formal magisterium definition of what the truths of the faith are. In this mode, the creeds, Apostles' and Nicene, name the basic deposit of faith. But those ordained and consecrated, by reason of the special authority that becomes theirs through sacrament and ritual, can add to this deposit out of the church's living tradition, informed by the Spirit and lived by the faithful. This kind of faith equates faith with beliefs. "Faith is an act of religious submission, an obedience of intellect" (Dulles, 1977: 18). Such faith could be expressed as follows:

We believe the things He has revealed to be true, not because of their intrinsic truth perceived by the natural light of reason but because of the authority of the revealing God himself, who can neither deceive nor be deceived (Dulles, 1977: 18).

This mode of faith is still alive among older and more conservative Catholics trained in the tradition of the Baltimore Catechism. This could be called the "assent mode." It relies on legitimate authority to define what God has revealed. In practice, it leaves the exegesis of the original scriptures to the scholars and the proclamation of the Word to the officials of the Church. This assent mode of faith is still associated with the Catholic practice of formally proclaiming doctrine through decrees issued from the Vatican Congregation for the Doctrine of the Faith. Consider, for example, this recent proclamation of the Vatican Congregation for the Doctrine of the Faith regarding eucharist:

In teaching that the priestly or hierarchical ministry differs essentially and not only in degree from the common priesthood of the faithful, the Second Vatican Council expressed the certainty of faith that only bishops and priest can confect the eucharistic mystery. Although all the faithful indeed share in the one and the same priesthood of Christ and participate in the offering of the eucharist, it is only the ministerial priest who, in virtue of the sacrament of holy orders, can confect the eucharistic sacrifice in the person of Christ and offer it in the name of all Christian people (Ratzinger and Hamer, *Origins*, Vol. 13, No. 14, 1983, p. 230. Paraphrasing *Lumen Gentium*, paragraphs 10, 17, 26, 28, from Vatican II).

To perceive how new doctrine develops from these very formal decrees, however, note how the development is linked to the ongoing life of the Catholic Church, in this later passage in the same proclamation:

Individual faithful or communities who, because of persecution or lack of priests are deprived of the holy eucharist for either a short or a longer period of time, do not thereby lack the grace of the Redeemer. If they are intimately animated by a desire for the sacrament and united in prayer with the whole church, and call upon the Lord and raise their hearts to him, by virtue of the Holy Spirit they live in communion with the whole church, the living body of Christ, and with the Lord himself. Through their desire for the sacrament in union with the church, no matter how distant they may be physically, they are intimately and really united to her and therefore receive the fruits of the sacrament; whereas those who would wrongly attempt to take upon themselves the right to confect the eucharistic mystery end up by having the community closed in on itself. (Ref. is to Pope John Paul II, Council of Trent, etc.) Ibid. p. 232.

This decree was promulgated to condemn a growing new custom within Catholic communities lacking access to ordained priests to assume responsibility for local eucharists by choosing lay leaders to preside over a eucharist. It demonstrates the interactive struggle involved in the formulation of doctrine. The same practice is evident in the papal document on the "Respect for Human Life in Its Origin and on the Dignity of Procreation," published in the spring of 1987 almost simultaneously with a new encyclical *Redemptoris Mater*, describing Mary as model of femininity and dignity.[2] Neither of these documents was preceded by that intense discernment and commitment that is affirmed for lay participation in the church by the Second Vatican Council. Rather they call for the traditional assent mode of faith that, at this time, is not so familiar to Catholics in their education, and even in their experience in many local churches, in the United States certainly. It is lacking in the literature of the pastorals on contemporary social issues in which the laity are called to participate in resolving. So the likelihood of their being taken seriously is lost.

In recent years, since 1960 in fact, charismatic Catholics share with their Protestant counterparts a strong "fiduciary" expression of faith, a faith that approaches God not as revealer of truths, as in the assent mode, but as Savior, relying directly on God's divine intervention, God's promise to save the people. In this mode, the faith emphasis is that, despite all adversity, there remains the power of Jesus to heal, forgive sin and bestow salvation (Dulles, 1977: 23). This faith is really the hope that not only is Jesus coming but that, in prayer, he is already here. While this type of faith finds expression in some local churches today in the United States and elsewhere and is especially familiar today in television evangelism(Hadden and Swan, 1981), still it is not the main faith expression of the whole Catholic Church. The Gallup study of American Catholics places it at 4 percent of their sample (Gallup and Castelli, 1987). My current study of American Catholic sisters also yields a 4 percent identification with charismatic Christianity.[3]

Catholic faith has taken a decidedly different focus since the Second Vatican Council, itself an historically grounded response to the new realities of a global movement of peoples' claiming their human rights, probably the main sign of our times. Catholic faith, in the context of the council, becomes, says Dulles (1977:13) speaking theologically, a "combination of discernment and commitment in which we perceive and dedicate ourselves to the transcendent values disclosed by God in Jesus Christ. The discernment is a process of biblical reflection directed to the historical struggles of people engaged in the process of human liberation. The primary commitment of such faith is to love the neighbor as one loves one's God."[4] The result is a burst of new theological reflection which stems from the local communities in which committed Catholics, now open to ecumenical participation, ponder the meaning of human oppression in the light of the gospel mandate to transform the world in justice toward the peace of Christ (Haughey, 1977). This expression of faith is most alive in Basic Christian Communities, characteristic particularly of parishes in Latin American countries in the 60s and now moving rapidly to those parts of the Third World where struggles for human liberation continue to be deliberated in biblical context (LADOC, 1976; Adriance, 1986; Berryman, 1984). This faith, so alive in Latin America, received encouragement from *Mater et Magistra*, Pope John XXIII's 1961 encyclical, calling attention to the need to revise the unjust division of land in places like Latin America and to sever the unduly close link of the church with the state in those countries wherein needed land and labor reform is now in process. Its influence, however, which spread so rapidly throughout the world in which Third World peoples were organizing against established colonial and imperial control, now generates some resistance within traditional church structures, especially in the United States and Western Europe. The focus of resistance is on a fear of cooptation by its secular counterpart, Marxism (Ratzinger, 1984). It challenges the unequal distribution of resources for life between the societies of declining populations and those that are still growing (Ntwasa and Moore, 1974; Richard, 1983; Sodepax, 1977-78; Tamez, 1982; Peruvian Bishops, 1985; Steidl-Meir, 1984; Schiblin, 1983; Herzog, 1980; and Pope John Paul II's *Sollicitudo Rei Socialis*, 1987).

The Church's Role in Society

Ministry is a newly nuanced word in Catholic vocabulary. It relates to the mission of the church and, in the most abstract formulation, refers to the work of "announcing the kingdom." In specific applications, this ranges from works of religious education and pastoral ministry, which may provide for spiritual experience but at the same time, silently affirm the status quo to that mission most commonly announced now in the church's social documents as "a special option for the poor" (Dorr,1984; Sobrino, 1984; Gutierrez, 1971 and 1983; Synod, 1971; Call to Action,1976; Steidl-Meier, 1984; Haughey, 1977). Today, ministry refers more to the work that people do to realize this newly formulated mission in all kinds of social action activities of community building and transforming that are gospel-related and integrated both into parish life and toward societal transformation. It is most clearly expressed in the synod document of 1971 in which the Catholic bishops of the world declared:

> Action in behalf of justice and participation in the transformation of the world fully appear to us as a constitutive dimension of the preaching of the Gospel or in other words of the Church's mission for the redemption of the human race and its liberation from every oppressive situation. (4, *Justice in the World*, 1971)

In some settings, mission still means participating in ministry work of the local church in religious services, catechetics, and in those institutions of social outreach that alleviate the results of poverty and human misery. In newer forms, it now means especially social action to eliminate causes of poverty and to transform the society in justice and peace (Canadian bishops' statement, 1971; Neal, 1971). This new emphasis divides the local church, as well as national and international administrators. Note, for example, the divisions which this understanding of mission engenders in the church in Nicaragua and in the Philippines at the present time, as well as in the struggle of the Brazilian bishops since 1961 to stand with the poor, despite resistance from those accustomed to a more institutional presence (Adriance, 1986; Lernoux, 1980; O'Gorman, 1987). In the United States, the new action-oriented emphasis has expressed itself in the sanctuary movement, disarmament and world peace projects, new modes of contact within local churches in the United States with local churches in Third World countries (Brown, 1986; Freire, 1985; Endozain, 1981; Cardenal, 1976). This emphasis is expressed through programs for alleviating homelessness and pursuing low cost housing, new pedagogies addressed to peace and justice education at every level from elementary school through university graduate programs, and work in community organization intended ultimately to change unjust social arrangements that belie biblical mandates to love all as neighbor (Johnson, 1986; Evans et al., 1987).

What characterizes the new mission emphasis is the belief that such transforming action is gospel-mandated to make the resources of the world available to its people (SODEPAX, 1977-78). Sociologically, the new mission emphasis is doing for the societal structure of the modern world what Weber saw the Protestant ethic doing in the first stages of the rise of capitalism. Where that consequence is analyzed as unintended, however, this one is intended to effect a more just social order. That, of course does not mean that it will do so (Neal, in Hammond, 1985).

There is little consensus within the Catholic Church at the present time as to the limits or extent of the call to action. But what is unquestionably true is that there have been a hundred years of Vatican teaching about the call to support the struggles of the working class to get its fair share of the profits of industry and of the farmer to get control of the land and now a support of self determination for all peoples. Dorr (1983), writing on this topic, entitled his book: *Option for the Poor: A Hundred Years of Vatican Teaching.* Members of the Center of Concern in Washington D.C., attempting to implement the same mandates, entitled their document: *Our Best Kept Secret: The Social Teachings of the Church,* (Schulteis, 1987).

In both cases, the teachings they refer to begin in 1891 with Pope Leo's encyclical letter *Rerum Novarum,* in which the church affirms its solidarity with the workers' struggle for a just wage. They continue in *Quadragesimo Anno, On the Reconstruction of the Social Order,* published in 1931, wherein Pope Pius XI announces church support of the strike and boycott to assure that organized workers have sufficient power to bargain with management. In 1961, in *Mater et Magistra,* Pope John XXIII continues and develops the theme of human liberation and calls the Catholic Church to account for its compromising with established wealth and power, to the neglect of the poor. This decree introduced two decades of documents, first John XXIII's *Pacem in Terris* in 1963, then *The Pastoral Constitution of the Church in the Modern World.* The latter is a principal document of the Second Vatican Council which, among other teachings, encourages the termination of institutionalized injustice in entrenched culture, thereby also suggesting the desacralization of tradition. In 1967 *Populorum Progressio* was issued. It affirmed the development of peoples as a church ministry. The next anniversary letter, *Octogesima Adveniens,* 1971, called for all Christians to move into political action to transform social, political and economic structures according to principles of justice and peace. This letter was the prelude to the Synod on Justice in the World, quoted earlier regarding action for social justice as being central to church ministry. The American bishops named their 1976 national assembly "A Call To Action", the English translation of *Octogesima Adveniens,* hoping to engender a dynamism that would urge the members to pursue the same social and political agenda. In 1981, Pope John Paul II, pursuing the justice theme further in *Laborem Exercens,* decreed that workers establish ownership rights to the means of production by reason of their work. (For collections of these documents, see Flannery, 1975; Dorr, 1983; O'Brien and Shannon, 1977; Walsh and Davies, 1984; Baum, 1982).

In 1988, Pope John Paul II further articulated the development of social teaching in *Sollicitudo Rei Socialis,* "On Social Concerns," calling the accumulation of wealth and power by both the forces of liberal capitalism and of collectivist Marxism social sin whose expiation is realized only through full sharing of resources for life, health and work with the dispossessed poor of the world. Private property, he claims, has a social mortgage, indicating an obligation to share resources with those in need. Following up on this strong thesis to stand with the poor, in 1989 the Congregation for Religious Education in Rome issued a "Guideline for the Study and Teaching of the Church's Social Doctrine in the Formation of Priests," making it ever clearer that despite the many ambivalences in implementation, the teaching church is expected to participate fully in this new focus on ministry rooted in biblically grounded faith with a new direction of mission. The Catholic Church has formally made its commitment to mission be that of the radical transformation of the world in a model of social justice (O'Brien and Shannon, 1977; Walsh and Davies, 1984; Lernoux, 1989; McGinniss, 1979; Neal, 1977; Medellin, 1970). The ideological struggles of middle class and wealthy Catholics within the American church are manifest in the research on church personnel. (Hoge, 1988; Leege, 1984-89; Neal, 1965; the August 1989 issue of *The New Theology Review*). The ambivalence among Catholics about what emphasis to give the "special option for the poor" is reflected in survey and analyses (Gallup, and Castelli, 1987; Hoge et al., 1988; Leege, 1984-89; Neal, 1965).

It is the thesis of this chapter on the Catholic Church that a mere reporting of what local churches are in fact now doing with various modes of expression of faith, ranging from ignoring the growing trend toward active involvement in societal transformation to accepting it enthusiastically as the expression of faith in our times, does not explain the link of faith and ministry for this church. This dynamic theme of listening to the signs of the times and taking action to change unjust conditions is an accelerating way of ministry invading, intruding, moving, energizing parishes, schools, dioceses, and community development groups to move from whatever pattern is in place to this new one. This is especially true of the Hispanic and Portuguese speaking communities, the fastest growing and least studied segments of the Catholic Church in America (See Gallup and Castelli, 1987: 139-148).

It is the gradual institutionalization of this developmental stance that has brought liberation theology to the fore and promises to make its model of mission the predominant model of Catholic life and practice in the United States, as well as in the Third World in decades to come.

It is true that this agenda parallels policies affirmed by Marxists in the direction of human rights and human services. The fact is, however, that they are the fruits of biblical reflection and provide a strong body of standard Christian sources on theology and faith development. The United States provides the most compelling evidence of these trends. The Call to Action Conference of the American Catholic Church in 1976 and the resultant pastorals on race (1979), Hispanics (1983), peace (1983), the economy (1986), and women (1988), establish the evidence that the teaching role of the hierarchy has been faithful to its continuing commitment to respond to the signs of the times, defined primarily as the response to the just demands of the organizing poor (Neal, 1987). Religious education materials and theology texts are being published now to implement this new direction of church ministry. Some publishing houses, (e.g. Orbis) are almost completely devoted to this ministry.[5]

The most substantial evidence for the claim that this is the dominant trend in the faith and ministry relationship in the Catholic Church is the reform activity of the religious orders and congregations of men and of women in the vowed life, as they have revised their constitutions to bring their life and work into line with the mandated new direction of the church decreed in the Second Vatican Council. Their new statements of mission express the new direction. Although dioceses, national churches and parishes engage in this same action, it is most clearly delineated in the revised constitutions of these religious congregations. This has happened because all women and men in the vowed life doing apostolic work in the church were mandated by one of the decrees of the council, namely, the Decree on Renewal of Religious Life, to revise their constitutions to accord with the decrees of the council and thereby become effectively involved in the implementation of the newly emphasized social justice agenda (Neal, 1984; Daly, 1984). My research of the past twenty-five years, which has focused mainly on the study of these changes in the religious congregations of women, confirms this trend (Neal, 1990).

For a quick summary, it is useful to look at the Jesuits. They are the congregation most closely associated with the development of the church since the division of Christian churches at the time of the Council of Trent. They take a special fourth vow beyond poverty, chastity and obedience, that of loyalty to the Pope. Speaking of their General Chapter of 1975, one Jesuit writes:

> At their recent Thirty-Second General Congregation which closed on the 7th of March, 1975, the members of the

Society of Jesus (Jesuits) solemnly affirmed that Christian faith absolutely requires the pursuit of justice in the world. The Jesuits were not dealing with an intramural matter affecting only their Order; rather, as the largest   Order within the Roman Catholic Church, they were striving to affirm something generally valid about the Roman Catholic understanding of faith which they believe links faith and justice. Their concern, therefore, is shared by all Catholics and Christians concerned with the relationship between Christian faith and justice in the world (Roach, in Haughey, 1977: 181).

Faith and Social Ministry

I think it fair to observe that the evidence from the sequential development of the link of faith and justice in the Catholic Church demonstrates that, for the church, social ministry currently is a mandate of faith in the assent mode and an act of faith in the newer discernment commitment practice of faith in action (Holland and Henriot, 1983; Steidl-Meier; Neal, 1987).

The conditions which have the most influence on the Catholic Church's focus in nurturing faith and promoting social ministry and linking the two seem to me to be these: the global extension of the current struggle for human survival and development (Beckford and Luckmann, 1989); the technological feasibility of a solution to problems of human need (Brown, 1986; George, 1986; Global Possible Conference, 1984; McGinniss, 1979; Murphy, 1983, 1984); the current failure of an armed world to provide this solution; and finally, the similarity and confusion of the Catholic Church's current stated mission of an option for the poor with the Marxist goal of a more just distribution of human resources.

My research leads me to conclude that it is the inequality of access to resources needed for human life, juxtaposed with an abundance of natural resources diverted to destructive uses by a potentially constructive technology, and the leveling off of the size of the world's population at somewhere around 10 billion people that constitute the "signs of the times" that are the content for current church response. These factors, as well as the rising up of the dispossessed to claim their rightful share in resources and planning, put the justice focus of social ministry in the forefront of church action (Neal, 1987). The secular evidence of this saliency is the formation of the Declaration on Human Rights, adopted by the United Nations in its charter in 1948, and the transformation of this declaration to the Covenants on Human Rights by 1967 and their final adoption by the United Nations in 1976.

The institutional church, pressured to adapt its structure to be faithful, experiences both resistance and support from the hierarchy, the religious in vows, and the laity. Each group—the hierarchy, with its challenged authority in the face of a maturing adult humanity; the religious, with the exclusivity of its vowed calling; the laity with the restrictions on the code of sexual ethics—all struggle to respond to the basic reality of a world of people and plenty and a perceived divine call juxtaposed to their own interests. The resultant struggle to define the situation in one's own interests is countered by the faith and ministry that binds beyond those interests in the combining of faith and mission to do justice on the land. The movement of women in the Catholic Church and the formal church response to their struggle highlights this theme (Cf. Ruether, 1974, 1985; Weaver, 1985).

During the Second Vatican Council and since its completion, the groups that gather to implement its decisions usually represent several different parts of the world and often different social classes. When women religious hold their "chapters" every four or six years, delegates may come from twenty or more nation states, representing professionals, peasants, workers, little rural communities and teeming urban centers. As they pray and plan together, they challenge definitions of the situation that advantage some at the expense of others; they learn the needs of other peoples; they have to take each other seriously. Events like eucharistic congresses, pilgrimages to shrines, religious education meetings, synods and congresses bring together the laity and religious with church hierarchy. The new justice agenda challenges out-moded customs and practices; the new solidarity provides new hope. The discernment and commitment mode of faith expression stirs the church at present at every level of encounter.

Catholic theology is now generated more from Latin American, African and Asian countries. Europe and America are no longer the source of most of these reflections. Translations are easily available and religious, as well as secular, publishing companies are eager to distribute them. Recent history shows that Basic Christian Communities associated with Latin American liberation theology have become centers of a lively faith among the poor and dispossessed. People come from First World countries to centers of struggle in Third World areas. They witness a living faith. Stories of their new-found faith and hope get translated into religious education materials in suburb, city and rural areas in several different countries at the same time. This common agenda becomes a source of solidarity in social action and a common ground for new reflection on the message of the gospels. The global dimensions also generate problems. These include: the confusion of the mission of the church with the Marxist revolution and the changing roles of women in all societies of the world. How and why these changes are occurring are part of the current life of the church and the work of its ministers. The analysis of social change provides substantial evidence for linking social ministry and faith in the Catholic Church to the taking of a special option for the poor after the Second Vatican Council, and following the grass roots community-building in Latin America and elsewhere, where local communities are laying claim to their rights to the land in biblical context.

Notes

[1] If one were to content-analyze media reports on the churches over a 10 year span, the number of times the Catholic Church has been featured with respect to liberation theology would be noticeably high. Church officials have carefully defined the meaning of the church's option for the poor when treating assumed error as in the case of Leonardo Boff, the Brazilian Franciscan, but they have, at the same time, clearly affirmed the church's stand with the materially poor in their struggle for liberation from material oppression. See Ratzinger, 1986 and New York Times, p.1, April 6, 1986 "Vatican Backs Struggles of the Poor to End Injustice" and "Guidelines for the Study and Teaching of the Church's Social Doctrine in the Formation of Priests," *Origins*, Vol. 19, No.11, August 3, 1989.

[2] The effect of these two documents is not quite clear yet. The first one is issued by the Congregation for the Doctrine of the faith, March 10, 1987. It is entitled: "Instruction on Respect for Human Life in its Origin and on the Dignity of Procreation"; the second is an encyclical letter written by Pope John Paul II, entitled: "Mother of the Redeemer," and published March 25th, 1987. It reaffirms the traditional doctrines developed about Mary, touching only slightly on her place in the church's social teachings.

[3] The current retest of the Sisters' Survey of 1967 will be completed in 1990.

[4] This analysis of types of faith by Avery Dulles is all the more compelling since his own preference falls short of this final form. See his "The Gospel, the Church and Politics," *Origins*, February 19, 1987, Vol.16, No.36, pp 633-636.

[5] Some have claimed that the Call to Action, a national conference held in 1976 in Detroit with 10 delegates from almost every diocese, the first of its kind in the United States, has not had a significant impact on the church in the United States because so many have either forgotten it or never knew about it in the first place. The fact is that the pastorals issued since then, and referred to in this paragraph, were planned outcomes of that conference. Their content, eventually converted into religious educational materials and used in parochial schools and parish religious eeducation programs, are shaping the church at the grass roots level into a social consciousness of the commitment to the materially poor and to the oppressed to a significant degree. The factors of indifference and planned neglect are there also but the groundings in socialization are real.

References

Adriance, Madeleine Cousineau. *Opting for the Poor: Brazilian Catholicism in Transition.* Sheed and Ward, 1986.

Appalachian Bishops' Pastoral, "This Land is Home to Me." in O'Brien and Shannon, pp. 468-516.

Arroyo, C., S.J. "Justice for Latin America,"LADOC Vol. 11 p.16. Washington D.C.: United States Catholic Conference, 1972.

Babbie, Earl, *The Practice of Social Research,* fifth edition, Belmont CA, Wadsworth, 1989.

Barton, Carol and Barbara Weaver. *The Global Debt Crisis: a Question of Justice.* Interfaith Foundation, 110 Maryland Ave. NE, Suite 509, Washington D.C. 20002.

Baum, Gregory, "The Christian Left at Detroit," *The Ecumenist,* Sept.-Oct., 1975, reprinted in *Theology in the Americas,* ed. by Sergio Torres and John Eagleson, Maryknoll, NY: Orbis Books, 1976.

Baum, Gregory, *Catholics and Canadian Socialism: Political Thought in the Thirties and the Forties.* Toronto: Lorimer, 1980.

Baum, Gregory, *The Priority of Labor: A Commentary on Laborem Exercens, Encyclical Letter of Pope John Paul II.* New York: Paulist Press, 1982.

Beckford, James A, Thomas Luckmann (Ed.),*The Changing Face of Religion.* London: Sage Studies in International Sociology, 37, ISA, 1989.

Berryman, Phillip, *The Religious Roots of Rebellion: Christians in Central American Revolutions.* Maryknoll, New York: Orbis Books, 1984.

Brown, Lester. *State of the World.* World Watch Institute, 1776 Massachusetts Ave., Washington, DC, 1986.

Call to Action, the Justice Conference Resolutions. Origins, NC Documentary Service, Vol. 6, Nos. 20 and 21, Nov. 4 and 11, 1976, pp. 311-340.

Canadian Conference of Bishops, "Towards a Coalition for Development," Strategy Committee Report, 1969.

Cardenal, Ernesto. *The Gospel of Solentiname.* Maryknoll, N.Y.: Orbis Books, 1976.

Chomsky, Noam. *Turning the Tide: U.S. Intervention in Central America and the Struggle for Peace.* Boston: South End Press, 1985.

Clark, Thomas E. "Option for the Poor: a reflection, *America*, January 30, 1988, pp 95-99.

Cleary, Edward, *Born of the Poor: The Latin American Church Since Medellin.* Notre Dame, Indiana, Notre Dame University Press, (to be published in 1990).

Cone, James H., *God of the Oppressed.* New York: Seabury Press, 1975.

Congar, Yves, *Lay People in the Church.* Westminster, Md: Newman 1957.

Cussianovich, Alejandro, S.D.B., *Religious Life and the Poor: Liberation Theology Perspectives.* Maryknoll, New York: Orbis, 1979.

Daly, Robert et al. (Ed.), *Religious Life in the U.S. Church: The New Dialogue.* New York, Paulist Press, 1984.

Dorr, Donal, *Option for the Poor: A Hundred Years of Vatican Social Teaching.* Maryknoll, New York: Orbis Books, 1983.

Dorr, Donal, *Spirituality and Justice.* Maryknoll, New York: Orbis,1984.

Dulles, Avery, S.J. "The Meaning of Faith Considered in Relationship to Justice." In Haughey, 1977, pp. 10-47.

Dulles, Avery, S.J. "The Gospel, The Church and Politics," *Origins*, February 19, 1987, Vol. 16: No. 36. pp. 637-646.

Ellis, Marc H. and Otto Maduro, *The Future of Liberation Theology*, Maryknoll, N.Y., Orbis Books, 1989.

Edozain, Placido. *Archbishop Romero: Martyr of Salvador.* Maryknoll, N.Y., Orbis Books, 1981.

Evans, Alice Frazer, Robert A. Evans & William B. Kennedy. *Pedagogies for the Non-Poor.* Maryknoll, N.Y. Orbis Books, 1987.

Ferree, William, *The Act of Social Justice.* Dayton,Ohio: Marianist Publications, 1951.

Flannery, Austin, ed. *Vatican Council II: The Concilar and Postconcilar Documents.* Northport, New York: Costello Publishing Co., 1975.

Freire, Paulo, *Pedagogy of the Oppressed.* New York: Herder and Herder, 1970.

Freire, Paulo, *The Politics of Education: Culture, Power and Liberation.* Massachusetts: Bergin and Garvey, 1985.

Gallup, George, and Jim Castelli, *The American Catholic People: Their Beliefs, Practices, and Values.* N.Y. Doubleday, 1987.

George, Susan, *Ill Fares the Land: Essays on Food, Hunger and Power.* Washington, D.C. Institute for Policy Studies, 1986

Gottwald, Norman K., ed. *The Bible and Liberation: Political and Social Hermeneutics.* Maryknoll, New York: Orbis, 1983.

Greeley, Andrew M., *The Communal Catholic*. New York: Seabury Press, 1976 .

Global Possible Conference. *The Global Possible World Resources Institute*. 1735 New York Ave. Washington D.C., 20006, l984.

Gutierrez, Gustavo M., A Theology of Liberation. Maryknoll, New York: Orbis, 1971.

Gutierrez, Gustavo M., *The Power of the Poor in History*. Maryknoll, New York: Orbis, 1983.

Hadden, Jeffrey K., and Charles E. Swan. *Prime Time Preachers: The Rising Power of Evangelism*. Reading, Mass.: Addison-Wesley, 1981.

Hammond, Phillip E. *The Sacred in a Post Secular Age*. Berkeley, California: University of California Press, l985.

Haughey, John C. *The Faith that Does Justice: Examining the Christian Sources for Social Change*. New York: Paulist Press, l977.

Herzog, Frederick, Justice Church: *The New Function of the Church in North American Christianity*. Maryknoll, New York: Orbis Books, 1980.

Hoge, Dean R., Joseph J. Shields, Mary Jean Vernieck, "Changing Age Distribution and Theological Attitudes of Catholic Priests: 1970-1985," *Sociological Analysis,* Vol. 69, No. 3. Fall 1988, pp. 264-280.

Holland, Joe, *The American Journey: A Theology in the Americas*. IDOC/North America, in cooperation with the Center for Concern, Washington, D.C., 1976.

Holland, Joe and Peter Henriot, S.J., *Social Analysis: Linking faith and Justice*. Maryknoll, New York: Orbis, rev. ed. 1983.

Houtart, F., "The Church and Development," LADOC: II, 17a. Washington, D.C.: United States Catholic Conference, 1969.

John XXIII, *Mater et Magistra* (Christianity and Social Progress). New York: America Press, 1961.

John XXIII, *Pacem in Terris*. Boston: St. Paul Edition, 1963.

John Paul II, *Laborem Exercens* (On Human Work). Boston: St. Paul Editions, 1981.

Johnson, David M., ed. *Justice and Peace Education: Models for College and University Faculty*. Maryknoll, N.Y.: Orbis Books, l986.

LADOC, Basic Christian Communities. Latin American Documentation, United States Catholic Conference, Washington, D.C. 1976.

Lappe, Frances Moore and Joseph. *World Hunger: Ten Myths Institute for Policy Studies*. 1901 Q St., N.W., Washington, DC.

Leege, David C, et.al., *Notre Dame Study of Catholic Parish Life*. Reports 1-14, Notre Dame University Press, 1984-1989.

Leo XIII, The Condition of Labor (*Rerum Novarum*, 1891), Washington, D.C.: National Catholic Welfare Conference, 1942.

Lernoux, Penny, *Cry of the People*. New York: Simon and Schuster, 1980.

Lernoux, Penny, *People of God*, New York: Viking Press, 1989.

McGinniss, James B., *Bread and Justice: Toward a New International Economic Order*. New York: Paulist Press, 1979.

Medellin Documents. *The Church in the Present Day Transformation of Latin America in the Light of the Council*. Official English Edition. Washington, D.C.: United States Catholic Conference, and Bogota, Columbia: Latin American Episcopal Council, 1970.

Murphy, Elaine, *Food and Population: a Global Concern*(a pamphlet) Population Reference Bureau, 2213 M St. N.W., Washington, D. C. 20037, 1984

Murphy, Elaine. *The Environment to Come: a Global Summary*, (a pamphlet) Washington, D.C.: Population Reference Bureau, 1983.

Neal, Marie Augusta, *Values and Interests in Social Change*. Englewood Cliffs, N.J.: Prentice-Hall, 1965.

Neal, Marie Augusta, *The Sociotheology of Letting Go: A First World Church Facing Third World People*. New York: Paulist Press, 1977.

Neal, Marie Augusta, *Catholic Sisters in Transition from the 1960s to the 1980s*. Wilmington, Delaware: Michael Glazier Inc., 1984.

Neal, Marie Augusta, *The Just Demands of the Poor*. New York: Paulist Press, 1987.

Neal, Marie Augusta, *From Nuns to Sisters*. Mystic, Ct, Twenty-Third Publications, 1990.

Ntwasa, Sabelo and B. Moore. (ed.) *The Challenge of Black Theology in South Africa*. Atlanta, Georgia: John Knox Press, 1974.

O'Gorman, Frances. *Down to Earth: 101 women from rural areas of Brazil tell their struggle to stay in the land*. Sao Paulo, Brazil: CEAR, 1987.

O'Brien, David J. and Thomas A. Shannon. *Renewing the Earth, Catholic Documents on Peace, Justice and Liberation*. New York: Image, 1977.

Paul VI, *Pastoral Constitution on the Church in the Modern World*. Boston: St. Paul Editions, 1965.

Paul VI, *A Call to Action*, Apostolic Letter on the Eightieth Anniversary of *Rerum Novarum*. Washington, D.C.: United States Catholic Conference, 1971.

Paul VI, *Apostolic Exhortation on Religious Life*. Official Vatican Translation of Evangelica Testificatio. Boston: Daughters of St. Paul, 1971.

Paul VI, *The Development of Peoples*. Creative translation by Father R. V. Bogan. Chicago: Claretian Publications, 1968, Also in O'Brien and Shannon, pp.313-345.

Peruvian Bishops, "Liberation Theology and the Gospel," *Origins*, Vol. 14, No. 31, January 17, 1985.

Pius XI, On Reconstructing the Social Order (Quadragesimo Anno) Washington, D.C.: National Catholic Welfare Conference, 1931.

Population Reference Bureau., World Population Data Sheet (a wall chart) published annually. Pop Ref Bur, 2213 M St. N.W., Washington, D.C.

Randall, Margaret, *Christians in the Nicaraguan Revolution*. Maryknoll, New York: Orbis, 1984.

Ratzinger, Joseph, "Instruction on Certain Aspects of the Theology of Liberation," *Origins*. Vol 14: No.13, September 13, 1984.

Richard, Pablo et al., *Idols of Death and the God of Life*. Maryknoll, New York: Orbis, 1983.

Ruether, Rosemary. *New Women, New Earth*. New York: Seabury, 1974.

Ruether, Rosemary. *Womanguides*. Boston: Beacon Press, 1985.

Schiblin, Richard, *The Bible, the Church, and Social Justice*. Liguori, Missouri: Liguori Publications, 1983.

Schillebeeckx, E. "Liberation Theology between Medellin and Puebla," *Theology Digest*, Vol. 28, No. 1, Spring, 1980, pp. 3-9.

Schreiter, Robert J., "The Marks of Being Catholic Today," *New Theology Review*, Vol. II, No. 3, August, 1989.

Schultheis, Michael J, et.al. *Our Best Kept Secret: the Rich Heritage of Catholic Social Teaching*. Washington, D.C., Center of Concern, 1987.

Sivard, Ruth, *World Military and Social Expenditures*, World without War Council, 421 South Wabash Ave, Chicago, Illinois. 60605. 1985.

Sivard, Ruth, *Women, a World Survey*, (Same as above) 1985.

SODEPAX "Rocca di Papa Colloquium on the Social Thinking of the Churches," Parts I, II, III, IV. *Church Alert,* No. 17-20. Geneva, Switzerland: Ecumenical Center, 1977, 1978 .

Sobrino, Jon. *The True Church and the Poor.* Maryknoll, NY: Orbis Books, 1984.

Steidl-Meier, S.J. *Social Justice Ministry: Foundations and Concerns.* New York: Le Jacq Inc., 1984.

Suhard, Emmanuel Cardinal, *Growth or Decline: the Church Today.* South Bend, Indiana: Fides Publishers, 1948.

Synod of Bishops, Synodal Document on Justice in the World, Second General Assembly of Synod of Bishops, Rome, November 30, 1971. Boston: St. Paul Editions, 1971.

Tamez, Elsa, *The Bible of the Oppressed.* Maryknoll, New York: Orbis, 1982.

United Nations, The International Covenants on Human Rights and Optional Protocol. United Nations Information Center, 1976. (This document was later published as the United Nations Bill of Rights, 1978.)

USCC, "Brothers and Sisters to Us" USCC, 1312 Massachusetts Ave., Washington, D.C., 1979.

USCC. "Hispanic Presence, Challenge and Commitment," Washington, D.C. USCC, 1983.

United States Catholic Conference. "The Challenge of Peace: God's Promise and Our Response." *Origins,* May 19, 1983, Vol. 13, No. 1.

United States Catholic Conference. "Economic Justice for all: Catholic Social Teaching and the United States Economy, "Bishops' Pastoral on the economy. *Origins,* Nov. 27, 1986,Vol. 16. No. 24.

Verdeick, Mary Jeanne, Joseph J. Shields, Dean R. Hoge, "Role Commitment Process and Catholic Priests," *JSSR,* Vol. 27, No.4, December, 1988, 524-535.

Walsh, Michael and Brian Davies, eds. *Proclaiming Justice and Peace: Documents from John XXIII-John Paul II.* Mystic, Connecticut, Twenty-Third Publications, 1984.

Welch, Michael R., David C. Leege, "Catholic Parishioners' Social Political Attitudes," *JSSR,* Vol. 27, No. 4, 536-552.

Weaver, Mary Jo. *New Catholic Women: A Contemporary Challenge to Traditional Religious Authority.* San Francisco: Harper and Row, 1985.

12

CONCLUSIONS:
AN ECUMENICAL SYNTHESIS

James D. Davidson,
C. Lincoln Johnson,
Alan K. Mock

In this chapter, we synthesize what the various writers said regarding the issues and concepts presented in the first chapter. We also make note of recurring themes, and ideas which were not necessarily part of our introduction but which represent important insights we had not anticipated. From time to time, we also indicate how the authors' observations relate to our own research on issues related to faith and social ministry.

Preliminary Remarks

We offer two preliminary remarks of a general nature. These comments have to do with the orientations of the authors of chapters 2 through 11, and the way we grouped their religious traditions.

Authors' Orientations
The authors are all people who value the church, have invested a lot of their own time and energy working in their respective

churches, and are sensitive to matters of faith and social ministry. These traits have several implications.

While the authors often criticize particular church policies and practices, they assume the importance of the church, its role in members' lives, and its role in society. They are not as inclined as some other writers (e.g., people with no religious affiliation) are to question the value of religion or to condemn churches in general.

We hoped the authors' personal involvement in their respective churches would yield information, insights, and interpretations which less involved people might not be capable of. We believe our assumption was valid and that the authors' familiarity with their churches has produced unusually rich chapters loaded with information and insights which are helpful to people inside as well as outside of each tradition.

The authors' sensitivity to faith and social ministry issues is evident in the ease with which they dealt with both dimensions of church life. Recall the eloquence with which they described the meaning of faith, and the frequency with which they called attention to the social diversity within their respective traditions.

But, the chapters are written by people who differ in religious status (e.g., some are ordained, others are not), who are involved in different lines of professional work (e.g., some work for the church, others are college professors), and who have their own personal approaches to faith and social ministry (e.g., some are more liberal than others). These personal and professional differences make it difficult to compare their substantive emphases and writing styles. For example, some authors are more candid than others in dealing with the gaps between theological conceptions of faith and social ministry (i.e., how members of their churches *ought* to believe and practice) and social reality (i.e., the ways members *actually* think and act). Some are more willing to discuss differences between national church leaders' approaches to faith and social ministry and the ways local church members' tend to think of them. Some call attention to the tensions between issues (e.g., charity vs. justice), while others prefer to emphasize compatibilities.

The autobiographical uniqueness of each author also makes it foolhardy to assume that they speak for everyone in their respective traditions or that they have a special claim on objective truth. It is not difficult to imagine other people in the same traditions whose experiences and personal commitments might be quite different, who might perceive their churches in very different lights, and who might have quite different interpretations of the issues under discussion.

But, we feel the authors also have taken their assignments very seriously. They were asked to draw upon their expertise and help others gain a better understanding of what faith and social ministry mean in their traditions, what the relationship between these dimensions of church life is supposed to be, and what the relationship actually seems to be. By and large, the authors have achieved admirably high levels of objectivity and, when they have felt compelled toward a particular perspective or minority point of view, they usually have told us how their emphases might be different from others in their churches.

Denominational Groupings

We grouped the ten religious traditions into five categories based on Roof and McKinney's (1987) analysis of *American Mainline Religion*: liberal Protestant, moderate Protestant, conservative Protestant, Black Protestant, and Roman Catholic. After reading the chapters in that order, we feel Roof and McKinney's scheme was useful. On the average, the chapters suggested that liberal Protestant groups have different concepts of faith and social ministry than the moderate Protestant groups, who in turn are quite different from the conservative Protestants in both arenas of church life. The Black Protestant and Roman Catholic traditions appear to be qualitatively different from any of the other groups. We will elaborate these differences later in this chapter.

Yet, as Roof and McKinney (1987) also recognized, there are important variations within some of the categories. Though the liberal Protestant groups share much in the way of social status and theological orientation, they have quite different polities and many different ways of promoting faith and social ministry. Though the moderate Protestant groups also share some middle ground between liberal and conservative Protestants, their conceptions of faith and social concern, and the ways they express them, are not at all the same. Finally, though conservative Protestants tend to emphasize faith over social ministry, they differ among themselves regarding the nature of faith and approaches to social ministry. These theological and social differences make us even more aware, and appreciative, of America's religious pluralism. While some observers see more similarities than differences among Christian groups today, we think the differences outweigh the similarities.

The Meaning of Faith

We asked the authors to address three basic issues: sources of faith, several dimensions of faith, and programs related to faith.

Sources of Faith

We invited the authors to think in terms of four possible bases of faith (scripture, tradition, reason, and experience) and to tell us whether any of them are useful in describing the grounding of faith in their respective traditions. None of the authors indicated that faith has only one basis. Most everyone pointed to some combination of sources, clearly suggesting that their respective churches treat faith as a very complicated, multifaceted phenomenon; that the bases of faith tend to be different for individual Christians; and that one's approach to faith is likely to change from time to time depending on various circumstances in one's life.

Within this context, the authors tended to stress the experiential basis of faith. Most authors said that, according to their churches' teachings, faith involves a very personal experience with God and a willingness to shape one's life according to the Creator's will. Recall, for example, Allen's quotation from Edgar Young Mullins: "First, faith contains an intellectual element...the second element is assent...the third element...is volition. In the last resort, faith is an act of will." The emphasis on the experiential basis of faith was greatest among conservative Protestants, but was found in all the other groups as well, including Roman Catholics who are thought to be most tradition based. There was a consensus that faith is not meaningful unless it is experienced deeply and personally, along with a common recognition that our different autobiographical experiences foster varying degrees of readiness for faith and different approaches to faith.

Tradition and scripture were often presented as important ways of achieving faith. One can grow in faith by reading and understanding scriptures. One also can grow in faith by learning how God's will has been interpreted by church leaders through the ages. In Rodman's words: "...the Episcopal Church can be seen as a bridge between Roman Catholicism and the reform tradition revering in its polity and tradition the office of bishop and the importance of doctrine, while stressing the centrality of scripture and affirming reason and experience as legitimate factors in discerning God's will." While Protestantism has tended to emphasize the scriptural basis of faith, and Catholicism the tradition base, the authors make it very clear that tradition is important for many Protestant bodies (especially confessional and creedal churches) and that scripture is very important in the Catholic Church.

Though some of the authors mentioned the importance of reason (c.f., Rodman), few if any made any vigorous effort to claim that reason is a major cornerstone of faith. Most, especially liberal Protestant groups, tended to see reason as an ingredient in faith, but not the key.

Dimensions of Faith

We also invited the authors to consider four dimensions in their efforts to describe the ways faith tends to be expressed in their traditions: individual-communal, vertical-horizontal, restricting-releasing, and comfort-challenge (see chapter 1 for definitions of these dimensions).

The authors tended to use the individual-communal dimension most often, with most—though not all—saying that, in their groups, faith tends to be more individual than communal. The chapters on the American Baptist Church and the Southern Baptist Convention were particularly emphatic on the importance of individual freedom and volition in faith. Describing the American Baptist approach to faith, Jones said: "...American Baptists stress more heavily scripture and experience, less heavily tradition and reason. We see the community of faith as helping in support of the individual Christian as well as needed correction for interpreting the scriptures." Thus, the "community of faith" is seen as a support system for individuals pursuing personal salvation, not as the repository of faith.

The chapters on Black Protestants and Roman Catholics offered the strongest exceptions to this general pattern, insisting on the communal nature of faith. Listen to Gilkes' analysis of Afro-Baptists' communal conception of faith: "In its historical foundations, this faith was tied to a community that comprised 'all God's children' who were making a trustful walk with 'the Lord' who has [never] seen the righteous forsaken (Psalm 37: 25)."

The authors did not pick up on the vertical-horizontal language quite as much. However, we perceive a tendency for them to say that both dimensions are important, perhaps inseparable. Recall Roberts' assertion that the Nazarene "holiness ethic" is both vertical and horizontal.

Several chapters dealt with the ideas of restricting and releasing faith, whether the authors used those precise terms or not. Scherer's chapter on Lutheranism and the chapter on Presbyterians, by Hargrove and Wilbanks, both called attention to the importance of the "law" and "order." On the other hand, Trost's chapter on the United Church of Christ and Gilkes' concept of "fiduciary faith" gave more emphasis to faith's ability to release the individual to think and do things which otherwise would be unimaginable. The writers seemed inclined to use images of St. Paul restricting and St. James (releasing) to describe these different expressions of faith.

All writers felt that faith is both comforting and challenging. Roberts, more clearly than the rest, said that the Church of the Nazarene has been more comfort oriented, while Neal and Gilkes, more strongly than the others, stressed the challenge dimension in Catholicism and Black Protestantism.

Several authors also claimed that the comforting and challenging effects of faith are experienced differently by people in different levels or positions in the church. The most frequent claim (e.g., by Hargrove and Wilbanks) was that national leaders and local clergy are more inclined to appreciated the challenges of faith, while local laity are more comfort oriented. The minority view (e.g., by Neal and Gilkes) was that faith's challenge dimension is experienced most authentically at the grassroots level among the poor and powerless.

Programs Related to Faith

Churches attempt to nurture faith in a wide variety of ways. Most authors discussed rather traditional methods, usually pointing to the special importance of regular public worship services. For

Catholics, this meant the Mass; for most Protestants, it meant services on Sunday morning, Sunday evening, and usually Wednesday night. The eucharist (or communion) was an especially important sacrament; others included baptism and confirmation. Mechanisms for cultivating faith also included Sunday school classes, vacation Bible schools, a wide variety of adult education classes, and musical groups, as well as various devotional activities such as private prayer and reading the Bible.

A few authors referred to social and religious movements fostering renewal and a revitalization of faith. Neal was especially compelling in her discussion of bottom-up processes of faith renewal within Catholicism since Vatican II:

> The result is a burst of new theological reflection which stems from the local communities in which committed Catholics, now open to ecumenical participation, ponder the meaning of human oppression in light of the gospel mandate to transform the world in justice toward the peace of Christ (Haughey, 1977). This expression of faith is most alive in Basic Christian Communities, characteristic particularly of parishes in Latin American countries in the 60s and now moving rapidly to those parts of the Third World, where struggles for human liberation continue to be deliberated in the biblical context (LADOC, 1976; Adriance, 1986; Berryman, 1984).

The Meaning of Social Ministry

The authors were asked to consider the content of social ministry, the forms it takes, and the ways their respective churches attempt to foster it.

Content

Of the three dimensions we offered the authors (international-domestic, economic/political-personal/familial, service-change), they were most inclined to concentrate on the distinction between service to others (charity) and changing society (justice). Virtually every author felt that their churches placed more emphasis on service than on change and that individual members were more inclined to think in terms of charity than justice. The service-oriented view of social ministry was most pronounced in moderate and conservative Protestant denominations. Liberal Protestant, Black Protestant, and Catholic church teachings put more emphasis on advocacy or social reform, though this emphasis was not always reflected in the priorities of individual clergy and laity.

Most authors also felt that their churches gave higher priority to personal/familial concerns than they did to economic/political problems. The emphasis on personal and family life was most evident in those moderate and conservative Protestant groups which stressed the need to regenerate individual lives (e.g., Southern Baptists). Liberal Protestant groups, Black Baptists, and the Roman Catholic Church were more oriented toward issues of economic justice and ending political oppression (a "radical stance," in Gilkes' words).

Most groups seem to put the greatest emphasis on domestic social concerns, but also allocate significant resources to dealing with needs in other lands. The largest proportions of staff time and annual church income go toward efforts to address social problems in local communities and/or the United States. Smaller, though significant, amounts go to helping people in other nations, especially Third World countries. A couple of authors (e.g., Allen) indicated that some church members would rather see their money go toward service programs anywhere in the world than toward change-oriented programs in the United States.

Form

Most authors stressed churches' tendencies to emphasize individual expressions of social concern over corporate expressions; denominational over ecumenical; and local over national. The prevailing emphasis was on opportunities for individuals to serve others through denominationally-sponsored programs conducted in their local communities.

The emphasis clearly was on the importance of individuals caring for others. Individual believers are to act out their faith in their family lives, in their neighborhoods, and where they work. This emphasis was especially evident in denominations with conservative theologies and congregational-type polities (e.g., American and Southern Baptists). Recall Allen's claim that Southern Baptists "are conservative in theology and with regard to social ministry often say 'changed people change society'."

The authors also discussed institutional church sponsorship of social services and social justice ministries. Corporate expressions of social concern were found in most all denominations, but most often in traditions which have more liberal theologies and/or hierarchical polities. Trost showed how the liberal theology of the United Church of Christ is expressed in that denomination's social programs and priorities. Hargrove and Wilbanks offered a particularly good analysis of how hierarchical polity facilitates institutional forms of social ministry.

While many authors described institutional church achievements in the provision of important social services, several writersthey tended to view issue-oriented social ministry as controversial. Several writers (e.g., Rodman) indicated that church-sponsored advocacy programs related to economic and political matters often surface sharp secular and religious differences among church members.

Most groups tend to devise and support their own forms of social ministry. The emphasis is clearly denominational or parochial. Ecumenical expressions are less common overall, but somewhat more frequent among liberal and moderate Protestant bodies which have a more established record of working together on social concerns. The most common ecumenical efforts are through groups such as the World Council of Churches and the National Council of Churches, but others also take place through local federations or councils of churches and ecumenical urban ministries (Davidson, 1985).

Programs Related to Social Ministry

All of the authors described numerous ways in which their churches seek to give expression to the ethical impulses of faith. In so doing, they made clear distinctions between policies and programs carried out by church functionaries at the national and regional levels, and those which are sponsored by local congregations and administered by local laity and clergy.

Groups with the most hierarchical structures invest the most resources in national social ministry programs. These churches assume that "the church" employs regional, national, and even international leaders to develop social policies and implement social programs. While offices, functionaries, and assemblies beyond the local level have some of the same values and interests as local church leaders, they also have some commitments which are quite different. Thus, national and regional leaders frequently have perspectives which are different from local leaders and are expected to do some things which local leaders cannot do.

They often have responsibility for the analysis of social issues, the formulation of policies related to these issues, and the development of programs which can be implemented at the national and/or local levels. As a result of their value orientations, their job descriptions, and/or their insulation from local constraints, these national and regional leaders tend to address issues which local leaders might not and tend to formulate policies and programs which tend to be more liberal (i.e., economic/political and change oriented) than local leaders are likely to devise. Virtually all of the authors (e.g., Rodman, Hargrove and Wilbanks) spoke of the tendency for national and regional leaders to support causes which tend to create controversy at other levels of church life.

A list of national and regional policy and program areas includes the following (listed alphabetically): abortion, aging, AIDS, arms control/peacemaking, capital punishment, corporate responsibility, criminal justice/prison reform, disaster relief, disinvestment from South Africa, drug and alcohol abuse, economic justice, education/literacy, family violence/spouse abuse, gambling, the handicapped, hospitals/health care, housing/homelessness, hunger, immigration, labor—management relations/unions, pollution, poverty, powerlessness, racial and ethnic equality, refugee resettlement/sanctuary movement, relations with Third World countries, sexual equality, unemployment, and voting rights.

The local congregation or parish is considered by most authors to be the point at which church members are most able to express their concern for others. However, local churches and church leaders are not as actively involved in social concerns. Relatively little church staff time and relatively small percentages of local church budgets are allocated to social ministry. For example, in our recent study of affluent churches, we found that clergy in congregations with affluent members allocated about five percent of their time to their churches' social programs, and only about four percent of the churches' budgets went toward outreach programs (Davidson, Mock, and Johnson, 1988; Mock, Davidson, and Johnson, 1990) .

When local churches and churchgoers are involved in social ministry, they tend to sponsor service-oriented opportunities for individual lay members to assist needy individuals and families. These programs allow relatively liberal and conservative parishioners to work together on assistance programs which people with different social philosophies can agree are clearly needed.

The authors gave us a good feeling for the kinds of programs which are likely to take place at the local level: child/day care, disaster relief, education, food and clothing for the needy, housing/home-lessness, marriage and job counseling.

Finally, it would be a mistake to overemphasize the differences between the national, regional, and local levels. They often work closely together. National and regional leaders have developed many service-oriented programs which have been adopted by local churches and which allow local members to donate money, time, and material goods to help the needy around the world (e.g., CROP). Local church groups also have challenged unjust policies in the economic and political spheres, and these efforts sometimes have had important implications for national and regional church policies (c.f., Gilkes' discussion of black churches' involvement in the civil rights movement).

Linking Faith and Social Ministry

We asked the authors to explain what their traditions say the relationship between faith and social ministry ought to be (i.e., the theological perspective) and to report evidence from research and/or their own experiences concerning the actual relationship between these two dimensions of church life (the sociological perspective).

Theological Perspectives

In the chapters on liberal Protestantism, Black Protestantism, and Roman Catholicism, the authors were most emphatic in saying that faith and social ministry are two sides of the same coin: love—

love of God and love of one's neighbor. Most authors reported that, according to the teachings of their churches, faith and works go hand in hand. They are equally important and inseparable aspects of church life. As Hargrove and Wilbanks put it, "moral activity [is] a necessary accompaniment to faith."

However, within this context, there was considerably more discussion of the ways in which faith can, and should be, expressed in concern for others than there was of ways in which social ministry might enhance faith. If the authors words are any indication of their churches' orientations (we think they are), then even liberal Protestant, Black Protestant, and Roman Catholic churches which say that faith and social ministry are inseparable are more articulate in explaining how faith should foster social compassion than they are in explaining how social concern can enhance faith.

In the chapters on moderate Protestants and conservative Protestants, there was even more emphasis on the importance of faith. In the chapters on Lutherans and Southern Baptists, for example, Scherer and Allen stressed the concept of "faith alone;" the belief that faith is a gift from God; it cannot be earned through good works. According to this perspective, faith is the key to salvation, not the way we treat others. Concern for others is an expression—or by product—of faith, not a way to salvation.

Sociological Perspectives

What do studies and the authors' experiences tell us about the actual relationship between faith and social ministry? By and large, they suggest that the integration of faith and social ministry which most all churches espouse theologically is hard to maintain sociologically. Sometimes the two goals seem to reinforce each other (love of God fosters, and is enhanced by, love of neighbor). But, other times, there seems to be considerable tension between them (as when churches emphasize love of God to the exclusion of loving one's neighbor, or when they stress the social gospel to the neglect of personal salvation). More often than not, faith and social concern seem to be separate domains of church life. What churches and churchgoers do in one sphere seems to have little or no impact on the other.

Several authors pointed to the uneven ways their churches allocate resources for faith and social ministry, with faith usually receiving more than social ministry. For example, relatively few local congregations in the faith-oriented American Baptist and Nazarene traditions are actively involved in social ministry (c.f., Jones, Roberts). United Methodist and Lutheran church members attach higher priority to faith programs than social ministry programs (c.f., Amerson and Brewer, Scherer). Others used language that clearly suggested the difficulty members of their traditions have linking the two. Rodman, for example, said that "many Episcopalians are self conscious about publicly expressing the relationship between their faith and involvement in a given social ministry."

This overall finding is consistent with several studies the editors have done in recent years (c.f., D'Antonio, Davidson, and Schlangen, 1966; Davidson, 1972; Davidson, 1977; Davidson and Knudsen, 1977; Roberts and Davidson, 1984; Myers and Davidson, 1984; Davidson, 1985; Mock, Davidson, and Johnson, 1988; Davidson, Mock, and Johnson, 1988; Mock, Davidson, and Johnson, 1990). Over and over again, we have found little or no correlation between various measures of faith (e.g., belief in God, Christ, and life after death; frequency of religious experience; devotional activity; participation in worship; the personal benefits church members derive from faith) and various measures of social concern (e.g., belief in the need to love one's neighbor and do good for others; egalitarian attitudes about minorities and the poor; the importance of social ministry in church members' lives; involvement in church sponsored social ministry programs; and participation in civic groups and activities trying to help the poor).

This finding challenges the theological assumption found in most chapters—especially those dealing with moderate and conservative Protestants—that, once people commit themselves to Christ (are "born-again", or—using Allen's phrase—are "regenerated"), they will become more compassionate in their dealings with others. While theologians and church leaders say that religious commitment *should* lead to more concern for others, they sometimes overlook societal conditions which prevent this relationship from developing. For example, Americans tend to believe that people toward the top of our society are the most talented and ambitious and that people toward the bottom lack these attributes; they say, if the poor aren't willing to help themselves, we don't really have much obligation to help them. While religious scholars and clergy may *hope* that believers will be more inclined than others to care about the poor and powerless, they sometimes underestimate the way such countervailing social influences and personal constraints stifle the relationship between faith and social concern. Simply acting out the social implications of faith may involve heavy social, economic, and political costs which church members are sometimes unwilling to pay.

The conclusion that faith and social ministry tend to be separate spheres of church life is a challenge for religious leaders at all levels of church life. Conservative theologians may need to rethink claims that love of God will necessarily lead to love of neighbor. Liberal theologians also may need to rethink their view that caring for others will necessarily result in greater love of God.

While the overall pattern may be one of separation between faith and social ministry, the relationship between the two varies a great deal. As most authors suggested, the two can and do go hand in hand for some churches and churchgoers. The authors were less inclined than the editors are to also point out that faith and social ministry are often in conflict. Let's explore what the authors said about the conditions under which these different outcomes seem to occur.

The connections between faith and social ministry are stronger in some types of denominations than others. One denominational factor which seems especially helpful in accounting for these variations has to do with conceptions of faith. Faith and social ministry seem more highly integrated in those groups which foster the most communal, horizontal, releasing, and challenging conceptions of faith. Churches and churchgoers who have such "social justice" theologies (Mock, Davidson, and Johnson, 1988; Davidson, Mock, and Johnson, 1988; Mock, Davidson, and Johnson, 1990) seem most inclined to help others and support reforms which might bring about a more just and equal society. On the other hand, when churches and church members stress more individualistic, vertical, restricting, and comforting patterns of faith, there may be considerable conflict between faith and social concern. Groups and individuals with such "good fortune" theologies (Mock, Davidson, and Johnson, 1988; Davidson, Mock, and Johnson, 1988; Mock, Davidson, and Johnson, 1990) are rather suspicious of, or negative toward, minorities and the poor and not inclined to support changes which might foster a more equal distribution of society's resources.

Another denominational factor concerns polity. Groups with the most hierarchical patterns of organizational life and decision making tend to nurture both faith and social concern. When national and regional offices are able to influence the quality of faith and social ministry which takes place in local churches, we are most likely to find faith linked with social service and advocacy (especially the economic and political arenas). The connection between faith and social ministry tends to break down in groups which have the most congregational structures. When there is little or no accountability to regional or national offices, faith might flourish but churches tend to be relatively uninvolved in social concerns. When decisions tend to be made at the local level, churches tend to focus on personal-familial service and avoid the more reform or justice-oriented types of social ministry.

The authors also suggest that faith and social ministry are more integrated at some levels of church life than others. In particular, the linkage between the two seems stronger at the national and regional levels than at the local level. Trost says we can use church budgets and programs to assess church commitments to faith and social ministry. When he does so for the United Church of Christ, he finds that about 32 percent of the UCC national budget goes toward faith-related activities (e.g., church development and evangelism, theological education), 29 percent goes toward social ministry (e.g., health and welfare services, emergency aid for disaster victims), and the remainder (39 percent) goes toward administrative costs (e.g., pensions, fundraising). Our own studies (cited earlier) indicate that, in most local churches, a far larger share of the budget goes to faith and a much smaller share goes to social concerns.

Several authors (e.g., Hargrove and Wilbanks, Rodman) also argued that faith and social ministry are more highly integrated for church leaders (e.g., clergy and fulltime church functionaries) than for the average lay person. This claim was based on the fact that leaders usually are more deeply immersed in scripture and church teachings; the evidence from other studies suggesting that scriptures and church teachings (i.e., religious values) are more likely to guide their behaviors than they are to guide the laity's (Wood, 1981); and data showing that the laity's orientations to faith and social ministry are not as well grounded in scripture and Church teachings and, consequently, are more likely to be influenced by secular values (especially individualism) and interests (economic and political investments in maintaining the status quo).

The authors also suggested that faith and social ministry are more closely linked in some places than others. Writers such as Hargrove and Wilbanks, Rodman, and Roberts suggest that, when churches and churchgoers are in affluent contexts, they struggle to maintain the connection between faith and social ministry. Roberts, Gilkes, and Neal tell us that faith and concern for the poor are tied most closely when the church is grounded in the experiences of the poor and powerlessness.

Several authors also noted that larger churches are more able than smaller ones to maintain the connection between faith and social ministry. According to Amerson and Brewer, and Allen, larger churches, with bigger budgets, and more staff tend to develop more specialized ministries, including efforts to link the faith life of congregations to the social concerns of their communities.

Most authors also felt that the connections between faith and social ministry are greater at some times than others. Roberts talked about the possibility that we may be witnessing a reversal of "the great reversal" within the Church of the Nazarene, with some Nazarenes wanting their church to return to the social consciousness it had in the nineteenth century. Amerson and Brewer, Rodman, and Scherer pointed to sharp differences between the 1960s (when churches and church members were more concerned about the poor and the powerless) and the 1980s (when denominational and congregational commitments in these areas seem to have waned, or least appear to be more "uncertain"). Neal claims that the winds of change in the Roman Catholic Church are blowing away from otherworldliness to thisworldliness, from a European worldview to a Latin American perspective, from transcendence to immanence, from an "assent mode" to an emphasis on "discernment and commitment," from God as Revealer to God as Savior, from the Baltimore catechism to liberation theology. Apparently, we are in a very volatile period during which most religious groups are struggling to realign the relationship between faith and social ministry.

Final Comments

When we initiated this project, we thought the issues of faith, social ministry, and the connections between them were timely and important. When we asked the scholars and church leaders from the ten different traditions to join us, they responded with enthusiasm and indicated that these were "hot issues" in each of their respective groups. We think the papers they presented in 1986 and the chapters they have prepared for this volume are excellent overviews of their traditions and sophisticated efforts to grapple with the issues. Together, we have been able to clarify some of the issues, but we also leave many issues unresolved.

The overviews and evidence presented in these chapters should be a challenge to religious leaders and religious scholars alike. We hope church leaders will be able to address the relationship of faith to social ministry with even more understanding of their own traditions. We also hope they will have a greater appreciation of, and openness to learning from, the others. Clearly, a great deal more can be done in each tradition to bring about a more authentic bond between Christians' love of God and their love of neighbor. We also hope religious scholars will examine the issues of faith and social ministry even more carefully from both the theological and social scientific points of view. We need to learn more about the conditions under which the two tend to reinforce each other, the conditions which tend to separate them, and the conditions under which the cultivation of one tends to stifle the other.

References

D'Antonio, William V., James D. Davidson, and Joseph A. Schlangen," 1966. Protestants and Catholics in Two Oklahoma Communities," Department of Sociology and Anthropology, University of Notre Dame, 1966

Davidson, James D., 1985. *Mobilizing Social Movement Organizations*, Storrs, Ct.: Society for the Scientific Study of Religion, 1985

Davidson, James D., 1977. "Socio-economic Status and Ten Dimensions of Religious Commitment,"*Sociology and Social Research*, 16 (Winter): 83-93

————, 1972. "Religious Belief as an Independent Variable," *Journal for the Scientific Study of Religion.* 11 (March): 65-75

Davidson, James D. and Dean D. Knudsen, "A New Approach to Religious Commitment, *Sociological Focus*, 10(April): 51-273

Davidson, James D., Alan K. Mock, and C. Lincoln Johnson, 1988. "Affluent Churches: Nurturing Faith and Pursuing Justice," report to Lilly Endowment, Inc.

Mock, Alan K., James D. Davidson, and C. Lincoln Johnson, 1988. "Social Differentiation and Individual Beliefs: Affluent Christians' Beliefs about Inequality," report to Lilly Endowment, Inc.

————, Davidson, and Johnson, 1990. "Threading the Needle: Faith and Works in Affluent Churches," in Carl S. Dudley, James Wind, and Jackson Carroll (eds.), *Carriers of Faith: Lessons from Congregational Studies*, John Knox-Westminster Press.

Myers, Phyllis Goudy and James D. Davidson, 1984. "Who Participates in Ecumenical Activity?" *Review of Religious Research.* 25 (March): 185-2003

Roberts, Michael R. and James D. Davidson, 1984. "The Nature and Sources of Religious Involvement," *Review of Religious Research*, 25 (June): 334-350

Roof, Wade Clark and William McKinney, 1987. *American Mainline Religion*, New Brunswick, N.J.: Rutgers University Press.

Contributors

William Jere Allen

William Jere Allen is an employee of the Home Mission Board of the Southern Baptist Convention in Atlanta, Georgia, and Director of the Metropolitan Missions Department. He also has been a pastor of local congregations in Kentucky and Virginia. He is the co-author with George W. Bullard of *Shaping a Future for the Church in the Changing Community* (1981) and co-author with Kirk Hadaway of "Moving the Church off the Plateau" in *Shooting the Rapids: Effective Ministry in a Changing World* (1990).

Philip A. Amerson

Philip Amerson is pastor of Broadway United Methodist Church in Indianapolis, Indiana. He received his Ph.D. from Emory University in 1976, and his Master of Divinity degree from Asbury Theological Seminary in 1971. He has been actively involved in urban ministry through Patchwork Central (a covenant community in Evansville) and the Seminary Consortium for Urban Pastoral Education in Chicago. An active consultant with churches, Phil also has authored many articles in journals such as *The Other Side, Sojourners,* and the *Review of Religious Research.*

Earl D.C. Brewer

Earl Brewer is the Charles Howard Candler Professor of Sociology of Religion "Emeritus" at the Candler School of Theology of Emory University. He received Ph.D. degree from the University of North Carolina in 1951 and the Bachelor of Divinity from Candler School of Theology in 1941. An active teacher and researcher, Earl has been the chief investigator in over sixty research projects and the author or co-author of several works, including *The Church at the Crossroads* (1948), *Life and Religion in Appalachia* (1962), *Protestant Parish* (1967), *Continuation or Transformation: the Social Involvement of United Methodism in Social Movements and Issues* (1982), *Gerontology in Theological Education* (1989), *World Methodism and World Issues* (1990), and many journal articles. He has been active in the Religious Research Association and was invited to give RRA's prestigious H. Paul Douglass Lecture in 1972.

James D. Davidson

James Davidson is Professor of Sociology at Purdue University. He received his Ph.D. at the University of Notre Dame in 1969. He is author of *Mobilizing Social Movement Organizations* (1985) and co-author with William D'Antonio, Dean Hoge, and Ruth Wallace of *American Catholic Laity in a Changing Church* (1989). He is Executive Officer of the Society for the Scientific Study of Religion, president of the Religion Research Association and past president of the North Central Sociological Association, and former editor of the *Review of Religious Research.* Jim is working with Lincoln Johnson and Alan Mock on a study of affluent congregations.

Cheryl Townsend Gilkes

Cheryl Townsend Gilkes is Associate Professor of Sociology at Colby College in Maine, where she teaches courses on intergroup relations, the sociology of religion, and Afro-American women. She is actively involved in several professional associations and is widely published in journals such as the *Journal of Religious Thought* and the

Journal of Feminist Studies in Religion. Her Ph.D. is from Northwestern University in 1979.

Barbara Hargrove

When this project began, Barbara was Professor of Sociology of Religion at Iliff School of Theology in Denver. She died quite suddenly in 1988. Barbara received her Ph.D. at Colorado State University in 1968. She was the author of numerous books (including *The Emerging New Class* (1986), *Women of the Cloth* (1984), *Religion and the Sociology of Knowledge* (1987), and *Sociology of Religion* (1989); editor of *Sociological Analysis*; and chair of the Committee on the Statistical Needs of the Church in the Presbyterian Church.

C. Lincoln Johnson

Lincoln Johnson is Associate Professor of Sociology at Notre Dame and Director of Notre Dame's Social Science Research and Training Laboratory. He received his Ph.D. from the University of Kansas in 1974, and his Bachelor of Divinity degree from Southern Methodist University in 1966. He is an ordained minister in the Kansas East Conference of the United Methodist Church. Along with James Davidson and Alan Mock, Lincoln is involved in a study of affluent congregations.

Richard M. Jones

Richard Jones is the Deputy Executive Director of the National Ministries of the American Baptist Churches, USA. He also is manager of the Program Support Unit which has the responsibility for research, evaluation, planning, theological reflections, staff and board development, personnel management, mission interpretation and public relations. He received his divinity degree from the Berkeley Baptist Divinity School in 1953. He also is author of *Personal Decision and Corporate Action.*

Alan K. Mock

Alan Mock is Visiting Assistant Professor of Sociology of Religion at Iliff School of Theology. He received his Ph.D. from Purdue University in 1988. While at Purdue, he worked with Jim Davidson and Lincoln Johnson on the affluent church project. His dissertation dealt with the social bases of affluent church members' beliefs about inequality. Alan also is a member of the research team working on the Church and Community Project with Carl S. Dudley.

Sister Marie Augusta Neal

Sister Marie Augusta Neal is Professor of Sociology at Emmanuel College in Boston. Her Ph.D. is from Harvard University (1963). Her publications include *Values and Interests in Social Change* (1965), *A Socio-Theology of Letting Go—A First World Church Facing a Third World People* (1977), *Just Demands of the Poor* (1986), *From Nuns to Sisters* (1990), and many articles in professional journals. She has conducted several studies of religious orders of women. Sister Marie is past president of the Society for the Scientific Study of Religion and of the Association for the Sociology of Religion. She gave the Religious Research Association's H. Paul Douglass Lecture in 1970.

Michael K. Roberts

Michael Roberts is Associate Professor of Sociology at Eastern Nazarene College in Quincy, Massachusetts. He received his Ph.D. from Purdue University in 1987 and his Master of Divinity degree from Nazarene Theological Seminary in 1974. He has been actively involved in faith and social ministry issues within the Nazarene church, as a pastor, researcher, and consultant.

Edward W. Rodman

Edward Rodman has been Canon Missioner to the Minority Community for the Episcopal Diocese of Massachusetts since 1971. He received his Doctor of Humane Letters from St. Augustine's College in Releigh, North Carolina (1990) and his Bachelor of Divinity from Episcopal Theological School, Cambridge, Massachusetts (1967). His research interests include the contemporary history of the Union of Black Episcopalians and other religious and ethnic caucuses. He is very active as a consultant to churches at the local and national levels.

Ross P. Scherer

Ross Scherer is Professor of Sociology at Loyola University of Chicago. He received his Ph.D. at the University of Chicago in 1963. His areas of interest include religious organizations, community, and occupations. He is a member of the Ministerium of the Evangelical Lutheran Church of America. He also is the editor of *American Denominational Organization* (1980), was editor of the *Review of Religious Research,* and is past president of the Religious Research Association.

Fredrick R. Trost

Frederick Trost is Conference Minister and President of the Wisconsin Conference of the United Church of Christ. A graduate of the Yale Divinity School, he also is on the board of trustees at United Theological Seminary. Throughout his ministry, a main theme has been the rooting of peace and justice ministries of the church in the biblical faith and in the traditions that have come together to form the United Church of Christ.

Dana W. Wilbanks

Dana Wilbanks is Professor of Christian Ethics at the Iliff School of Theology. He received his Ph.D. at Duke University (1968) and his Master of Divinity degree at Union Theological Seminary (1965). He is coauthor with H. Edward Everding of *Decision Making and the Bible* (1975), coauthor with Mary Wilcox of *Evaluating Christian Education Curriculum Materials* (1976), and coeditor with Ronald H. Stone of *The Peacemaking Struggle* (1985), and author of numerous articles. An ordained clergyman in the United Presbyterian Church of USA, he is very active in church task forces and advisory councils.

Index

church government in, 110
church politics in, 98-99
clergy in, 113, 114
Denominational Ministry Strategy (DMS), 111, 112
laity in, 114
leadership of, 98
merger with Lutheran Church in America, 98
social ministry in, 105, 106, 107, 113
stands of, on public issues, 106, 114-17
Western Pennsylvania Synod, 111
American Mainline Religion (Roof and McKinney), 229
Amerson, Philip A., 79-93, 242, 245
Ammerman, Nancy Tatum, 149
Anglicanism.
See Episcopal Church
Apartheid, Episcopal Church on, 30, 31
Apostles Creed, 208
Armstrong, James, 85-86
Association for the Study of Negro Life and History, 195
Association of Evangelical Lutheran Churches (AELC), 98, 107.
See also Lutheran Church

B

Baltimore Catechism, 209
Baptism, in Southern Baptist Convention, 138
Baptist Faith and Message (Hobbs), 141
Baptist Ministers Conference, 190, 191
Baptists.
See African-American Baptist Tradition; American Baptist Church; Southern Baptist Convention
Barnett, Evelyn Brooks, 195-96
Basic Christian Communities, 211
Benne, Robert, 98

Bethany Baptist Church, 199
Bethune, Mary McLeod, 195
Bible.
See Scripture
Black Ecumenical Commission, 191
Bloomquist, Karen, 104
Bohr, Nils, 147
Bondivalli, Bonnie J., 115
Bonhoeffer, Dietrich, 35, 45, 102
Bork, Robert, 31
Boyce, James P., 135
Bradford, William, 39
Brauer, Jerald, 116-17
Brekke, Milo L., 114
Bresee, Phineas, 158, 166
Brewer, Earl D.C., 79-93, 242, 246
Bright Hope Baptist Church (Philadelphia), 199
Broadman Press, 136
Brown, Charlotte Hawkins, 195
Browning, Edmond L., 15-33
Bullard, George W., Jr., 151-52
Burroughs, Nannie Helen, 180, 192, 195-96
Burt (Bishop), 24
Bush, George, 16

C

Call to Action Conference of the American Catholic Church, 216
Calvin, John, 40, 54
Campolo, Anthony, 169
Candler School of Theology, 149
Canterbury, Archbishop of, 15
Capital Region Conference of Churches (Conecticut), 125
Carter, Jimmy, 148
Catholic Church, 205-6
Basic Christian Communities in, 211
and Call to Action Conference of American, 216
and Center of Concern, 213-14
changing patterns of faith in, 206-12
clergy in, 207
charismatics in, 210-11

and Urban Bishops Coalition,
24, 27-28
and Volunteer for Mission programs, 23
women in, 19-20, 24
Episcopal Church Persons for
Free South Africa, 24
Episcopal Peace Fellowship, 24
Episcopal Urban Caucus, 16, 28
Eucharist, in Catholic Church,
209-10
Evangelical Church of the Union
(EKU) (Germany), 48
Evangelical Lutheran Church in
America (ELCA).
See also American Lutheran
Church; Lutheran Church;
Lutheran Church in America
Churchwide Assembly (CWA),
106-7
Commissions
for Church in Society, 104,
105
for Multicultural Ministries,
104
for New Lutheran Church,
108
for Women, 104
comparison of, with Missouri
Synod, 100
formation of, 97, 98, 99
government of, 110
purposes of, 109
women in, 100
Evangelical United Brethren, 84
Evangelism and Social Involvement
(Miles), 147
"Eyes on the Prize, II" (PBS series),
199

F

Faith
in African-American Baptist Tradition, 185-90
in American Baptist Church,
124-25

in Catholic Church, 206-12
in Church of the Nazarene,
159-65
dimensions of, 4, 6-7
comfort and challenge, 5
individualistic and communal, 5
restricting and releasing, 5
vertical and horizontal, 5
and ecumenical synthesis of
social ministry
dimensions of, 231-32
programs related to, 232-33
sources of, 230-31
sociological perspectives,
238-42
theological perspectives,
237-38
in Episcopal Church, 17-20
in Lutheran Church, 99-102
in Presbyterian Church (USA),
54-57
programs related to, 7
relationship between, and social
ministry, 88-89
in African-American Baptist
Tradition, 196-201
in American Baptist Church,
127-31
in Catholic Church, 217-19
in Episcopal Church, 26-33
in Lutheran Church (American), 103-9
in Presbyterian Church(USA),
62-68
sociological perspectives,
12-13
in Southern Baptist Convention, 146-53
theological perspectives,
11-12
in United Church of Christ,
46-49
in United Methodist Church,
88-89
sources of, 2-4, 6-7
ecumenical synthesis, 230-31

Neal, Marie Augusta, 205-19, 232,
233, 242, 248
New Hampshire Confession (1833),
124-25, 185
New Religious Political Right
(NRPR), 144
Nicene Creed, 208
Niebuhr, H. Richard, 81-82, 102
Niemoeller, Martin, 49

O

Octogesima Adveniens (encyclical),
214
O'Dea, Thomas, 206-7
O'Kelly, James, 38
Opportunities Industrialization
Commission (OIC), 198
*Option for the Poor: A Hundred Years
of Vatican Teaching* (Dorr), 213
*Our Best Kept Secret: The Social
Teachings of the Church*, 214
Outler, Albert, 80

P

Pacem in Terris (encyclical), 214
Paris, Peter J., 181, 191
Parks, Rosa, 192
Pelagianism, 83
Pendleton, J. M., 135, 136
People United to Save Humanity
(PUSH),198
Phillipines, Catholic Church in,
213
Pius XI, Pope, 214
Politics
link between religion and
in African-American Baptist
Tradition, 192-93, 198
religious and political leaders
on, 148
Populorum Progressio (encyclical),
214
Prayer
Lutheran Church on, 106
United Church of Christ on, 50
Presbyterian Church (USA), 53

and Advisory Council on
Church and Society, 60
Book of Order in, 59
clergy in, 58-59, 62, 67, 69-73
and Committee on Social
Witness Policy, 60, 66, 67
and Confession of 1967, 57
faith in, 54-57
General Assembly in, 58, 60,
63, 66
hunger program in, 61
individual conscience in, 64-65
laity in, 58-59, 62, 67, 69-73
peacemaking program in, 61
reconciliation in, 56-57
and Reformed tradition, 54
relationship between faith and
social ministry in, 62-68
responsibility to society in, 55
reunification of branches in, 60
scripture in, 56-57, 69-70, 73-74
on separation of church and
state, 55-56
social ministry in, 57-62
experience of church in,
68-74
institutionalization of, 59-61
on sovereignty of God, 54-55
structure of, 58-59, 60-61
women in, 61, 67
worship in, 57
Presbyterian Layman, 74
"Presbyterians and Peacemaking:
Are We Now Called to Resistance?," 66
Progressive National Baptist
Convention (1961), 179,
184, 192

Q

Quadragesimo Anno (encyclical),
214

R

Rauschenbusch, Walter, 123, 125,
127, 131-32

Catholic Church on, 213, 216
Church of the Nazarene on, 165
Lutheran Church on, 104, 105,
111-12, 114-17
Presbyterian Church (USA) on,
60, 61, 65-73
Southern Baptist Convention
on, 140-42, 142, 143
United Church of Christ on,
42-44
United Methodist Church on,
86-87, 88, 90-93
Social ministry, 7.
See also Social issues in African-
American Baptist Tradition,
181-85, 190-92
and civil rights, 192-94
and education, 194-96
in American Baptist Church,
125, 126
in Church of the Nazarene,
165-76
content, 8-9
ecumenical synthesis of
content, 233-34
and faith, 238-42
form, 234-35
programs related to, 235-37
in Episcopal Church, 20-26
form, 9-11
in Lutheran Church, 102-3
in Presbyterian Church (USA),
57-62
experience of church in,
68-74
institutionalization of, 59-61
understanding of, 57-62
programs related to, 11
relationship between faith and,
88-89
in African-American Baptist
Tradition, 196-201
in American Baptist Church,
127-31
in Catholic Church, 217-19
in Episcopal Church, 26-33
in Lutheran Church (American), 103-9

in Presbyterian Church(USA),
62-68
sociological perspectives,
12-13
in Southern Baptist Convention, 146-53
theological perspectives of,
11-12
in United Church of Christ,
46-49
in Southern Baptist Convention,
140-46
in United Church of Christ,
40-45
in United Methodist Church,
85-88
Social Teaching of the Black Churches
(Paris), 191
Social Teachings, 64-65
Sola fide, Protestant slogan of, 160
Sola scriptura, Protestant slogan of,
160
Sollicitudo Rei Socialis (encyclical),
214
Songer, Harold, 150-51
Southeastern Baptist Theological
Seminary, 147
Southern Baptist Convention, 84
on abortion, 142, 143
American Coalition for Traditional Values (ACTV), connection to, 144
baptism in, 138
Baptist Faith and Message (1963)
in, 136-41
and Baptist Joint Committee on
Public Affairs (BJCPA), 144,
146
and Brotherhood Commission,
145
and Calvinistic Philadelphia
Confession (1742), 136
and Charleston Tradition, 134
and Christian Life Commission,
143, 144, 145
comparison with other denominations,150-51
and Elliot Controversy, 136

DATE DUE

OCT 2 2 2002			